Dr. Agnes Y. Doody
Rm - Independence 145

Please return if
it strays

Speed - 1"

1 July - 2 speed typings due
5 July - p. 28, 13A, "Do the work..."
6 July - p. 29 14A, Fluency
7 July - p. 30 15A Fluency
8 July p. 32 - 16A Fluency

13 July - owe - 01 one minute timings, 60 spaces
          owe 1 2 minute timing, p. 41

          A p. 45

14 July p. 55 30A - 1 min.
14 July p. 60 - 3 min timing

       p. 62 letter

practice p. 41
self-improvement
66 lines = 8½ X 11

p. 52, 26D - 2nd A 3 min.
          No more than 4 errors!

          3 + minutes

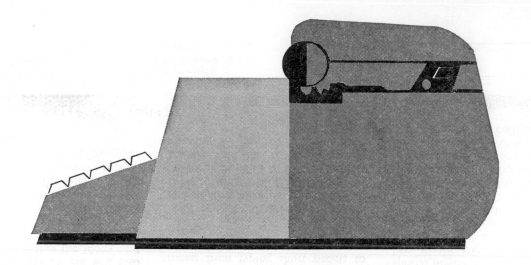

College Typewriting

BASIC COURSE • SEVENTH EDITION

T15—H265   Printed in U. S. A.

D. D. LESSENBERRY *Professor of Education, Emeritus University of Pittsburgh*

S. J. WANOUS *Associate Dean, School of Education, UCLA (Los Angeles)*

C. H. DUNCAN *Professor, Business Courses State College, Indiana (Pa.)*

SOUTH-WESTERN PUBLISHING COMPANY

*Cincinnati • Chicago • Dallas
Burlingame, Calif. • New Rochelle, N. Y.*

Special Features

Four-to-One Ratio of New Learning and Review in the keyboard introduction lessons to insure quick coverage of the letter keys and to assure reach-stroke mastery

Graduated-Difficulty Copy to assure smooth skill development and to provide realistic measurement of skill growth

Interesting and Informative Copy to motivate learning and to impart knowledge

Precalculated Rates for timed writings and *Word-Counted Copy* for problems to reduce time required to determine rates

Meaningful Labeling of drills to give purpose to practice and of problem models to give quick orientation

"Telegraphed" Directions and *Easy-to-Follow Procedures* to reduce reading and hesitation time and increase the time available for typing to build skill

Marginal Technique Reminders to guarantee emphasis on the important elements of the <u>process</u> of learning to type

Preapplication Manipulative Drills to orient the student to the new elements of the problem being introduced

Problem-and-Production Cycles (of learning, skill building, and measurement) to assure proficiency in <u>using</u> the skill

Special Projects at the end of the book to enrich the course for the one-semester student

Preface

● TO THE INSTRUCTOR

A noted philosopher said, ''What we should aim to produce is men who possess both culture and expert knowledge in some specific field. Their expert knowledge will give them the ground to start from and their culture will lead them as deep as philosophy and as high as art.'' It is to help build expert skill in typewriting to give ''the ground to start from'' that this Seventh Edition of COLLEGE TYPEWRITING has been written.

The typewriter is a tool of communication. The purpose of learning to use this tool is to speed up the communication process. The function of both the instructor and the textbook is to speed and facilitate this learning.

The best way for the instructor to assist the learner is to: (1) give him direction (and fewer directions); (2) lead him to see the purpose of specific practice materials and guide him in the selection of appropriate practice procedures; (3) appraise the effectiveness of the method of practice as much as the output of practice; and (4) provide the stimulus that will keep him working hopefully and confidently to achieve the goals he accepts as those he can reasonably expect to attain. This is teaching.

Just as hammering hardens steel and crumbles putty, so the high pressure that will cause some to reach effectively for high goals will overwhelm others disastrously. The understanding instructor will know when to hammer with force so that those who can achieve excellence will practice to do so. He will also know when to soften the blows and lower the high expectations so the less able will achieve the most of which they are capable. This is teaching at its best, with the instructor knowing the proper limits of his role and the students accepting the appropriate responsibility for their learning.

● ABOUT THIS TEXTBOOK

The 75 carefully planned lessons and special projects provide structured practice materials and practice procedures that have been classroom tested and proved effective. The materials are graduated in difficulty, technique centered, and goal directed. Line identification and marginal notations tell the student the kind of copy to be typed so he will know how to practice for maximum gains in typing skill.

''Telegraphed'' directions in color are easily read and easily followed. Suggested procedures for practice are given in sequence so the student always knows what he is to do next. Multiple-use, word-counted copy reduces rate calculation time and provides for students of different levels of ability.

Right techniques of typing are given initially greater importance than the attainment of a certain number of words a minute, but appropriate emphasis is given at appropriate times to both accuracy and speed to the end that maximum typing power may be developed in minimum time.

The early application of straight-copy skill to typing simple problems (Lesson 22 on) is in keeping with sound psychological principles of learning. The problems move from line-by-line typing to copy that calls for knowing how to divide words; from the simple memorandum to personal and business letters; from simple centering to short tabulations of two, three, and four columns; from simple themes of quality writing to pages of manuscript with footnotes; from typing short poems to composing creatively at the typewriter.

Of special interest to instructors and students alike are the lessons on inventorying basic and problem-typing skills. This is a do-it-yourself activity with the focus on understanding the process.

● TO THE STUDENT

COLLEGE TYPEWRITING is written for you. Used intelligently, it will aid in building good typing skill. Each of the lessons is timed for 45 minutes of fast-paced practice. Self-Improvement Practice material provides for your extra-practice needs.

You will learn to compose at the typewriter so you can bypass the laborious method of composing in longhand. You will type first from arranged models to get an eye picture of well-placed typing on the page. Then, much of your typing will be from unarranged copy to give practice in organizing the material as well as in typing it. You will type a wide variety of material of both a personal and a business nature, with greatest emphasis on the most frequently used kinds of communications. All this is provided, plus continued emphasis on building basic skill, too.

How you practice *what* you practice will determine the level of skill you will develop more than how much you practice. Make all your practice purposeful, and it will be resultful.

You can learn to type if you want to learn and will work to learn to type. Work intelligently and confidently, and you will learn to type with good speed and accuracy.

● ACKNOWLEDGMENTS

We express our grateful thanks to the teachers, students, and others who have contributed so generously of their ideas for the content and organization of this book. Our very special thanks are given to the members of the editorial department of the publishing company for their critical appraisal of the learning materials and for their distinctive styling of the lessons. All these have helped us to make this book an effective aid to those who wish to learn to type with maximum skill in minimum time and to those who teach typewriting at the college level.

Lessenberry • Wanous • Duncan

Division I | Basic Typewritten Communication

Get Ready to Type; Correct Typing Position; Carriage Return and Spacing; Stroking Technique Practice; Continuity Practice; Self-Improvement Practice; Remove the Paper; Center the Carriage; Typewriter Spacing; Paper Size; Hand Alignment with Keyboard; Typing from Dictation; Sentence Guided Writing; Paragraph Typing

Building Typewriting Facility

Technique Practice; Typing from Dictation; Paragraph Guided Writing; Typing for Control; Levels of Practice; Growth Index; Self-Improvement Practice

Syllable Intensity; Stroking Technique Practice; Technique Practice; Building Speed and Control; Paragraph Guided Writing; Stroking Technique Review; Growth Index; Self-Improvement Practice

Stroking Technique Practice; Typing from Dictation; Memorandum on the Block Style; Sentence Guided Writings; Memorandum with Subject Line; Stroking Technique Review; Response Patterns; Growth Index

Building Basic Skill

Technique Practice; Typing from Dictation; Building Speed and Control; Paragraph Guided Writing; Sentence Guided Writing; Building Control; Growth Index; Memorandums

Centering, Personal Notes, and Postal Cards

Building Speed and Control; Horizontal Centering; Sentence Guided Writing; Proofreader's Marks; Typing Outside Margins; Listening for the Bell; Personal Note; Technique Practice; Centering Lines on Odd-Size Paper; Postal Cards; Vertical Centering; Growth Index; Self-Improvement Practice

Personal Letters, Themes, and Composing

Building Speed and Control; Growth Index; Personal Letter in Block Style with Open Punctuation; Addressing a Small Envelope; Typing Outside Margins; Typing from Printed Copy; Listening for the Bell; Themes; Composing at the Typewriter; Postal Cards; Growth Index; Self-Improvement Practice

Business Letters

Paragraph Guided Writing; Centering from Rough Draft; Business Letter in Modified Block Style with Blocked Paragraphs and Mixed Punctuation; Sentence Writings for Control; Building Control; Composing and Typing; Folding a Letter for a Small Envelope; Guides for Erasing; Guided Writing; Growth Index; Self-Improvement Practice

Tabulation and Word Division

Horizontal Placement of Columns; Tabulations; Building Speed and Control; Aligning and Typing Over a Word; Horizontal and Vertical Pencil Lines; Sentence Guided Writing; Typing on Ruled Lines; Building Control; Word Division; Assembling and Inserting a Carbon Pack; Erasing Original and File Copies; Letters with Tabulated Items; Growth Index; Action Typing

Outlines, Manuscripts, and Composing

Typing from Script; Poems; Composing at the Typewriter; Aligning Roman Numerals; Spacing Between Related and Unrelated Columns; Numerals in Outlines; Outline of Unbound Manuscripts; Ratchet Release; Building Speed and Control; Unbound Manuscript Pages; Page-End Indicator; Sentence Guided Writing from Corrected Script; Footnotes; Typing a Superior Figure; Growth Index; Leftbound Manuscript Page; Ellipsis; "X-ing Out" Words; "Squeezing" Letters; Form Letters with Enclosures; Multiple Carbon Pack; Columnar Headings; Headings Between Vertical Lines; Rough-Draft Tabulation; Composing a Letter; Check; Composing a Manuscript; Self-Improvement Practice

Inventorying Basic and Problem-Typing Skill

Selected Techniques; Discovering Speed Range with Maximum Accuracy; Basic Skills; Manipulative Skills; Special Symbols; Parts of a Business Letter; Parts of a Manuscript with Footnotes

Measurement of Basic Skill and Problem Typing

Growth Index; Manuscript; Letter; Announcement on a Postal Card; Footnoting; Letter with Tabulated Items; Personal Letter; Tabulations; Rough Drafts; Tabulation with Columnar Headings; Rough Draft of Enumerated Items; Typing for Control

Projects 1–4 are provided for those students who want additional applications or for those students for whom this course is the final formal instruction in typewriting.

● TYPEWRITER OPERATIVE PARTS

Typewriters have similar operative parts, the names of which vary somewhat from typewriter to typewriter even when the function is the same. These similar operative parts are identified in the four typewriter segments illustrated below. Each segment is a composite and not an exact segment of any one typewriter.

For this reason, the exact location of a part identified in the segment may be slightly different from that on your typewriter; but the differences are— for the most part—few and slight.

ADDITIONAL TYPEWRITER OPERATIVE PARTS

Extra parts that are peculiar to the typewriter you operate and not common to most typewriters can be identified by reference to the instructional booklet distributed by the manufacturer of the typewriter. This booklet can be very helpful to you because all its content is directed to the operation of one specific make of machine.

USING THE ILLUSTRATIONS

Follow the line from the number to the part location. Know the function of each part, as explained in the textbook, and learn to operate it with maximum efficiency.

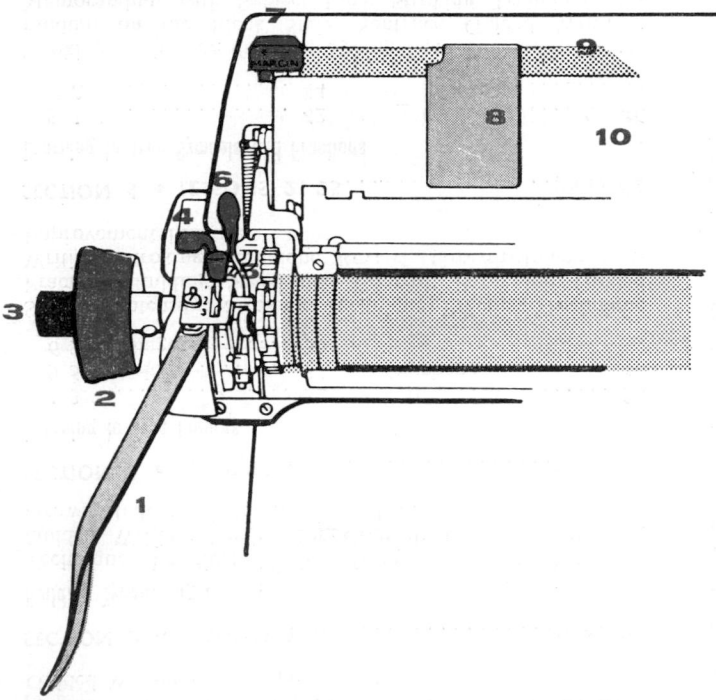

TOP LEFT SEGMENT OF A TYPEWRITER

Carriage-Release Lever, Left 4	Line-Space Regulator .. 5
Carriage Return and Line-Space Lever 1	Margin Set, Left 7
Cylinder Knob, Left 2	Paper Guide 8
Line Finder (Ratchet Release) 6	Paper-Guide Scale 9
Line-Space Lever (Carriage Return) ... 1	Paper Table 10
	Ratchet Release (Line Finder) 6
	Variable Line Spacer .. 3

NOTE The Underwood margin sets are located at the front of the machine with a corresponding margin scale.

TOP RIGHT SEGMENT OF A TYPEWRITER

Aligning Scale 33	Cylinder Scale 20
Card and Envelope Holders 12	Margin Set, Right ... 15
Carriage-Release Lever, Right 18	Paper Bail and Scale. 11
	Paper-Bail Rolls 13
Cylinder (Platen) 14	Paper-Release Lever . 16
Cylinder Knob, Right. 19	Platen (Cylinder) 14
	Ribbon Carrier 21

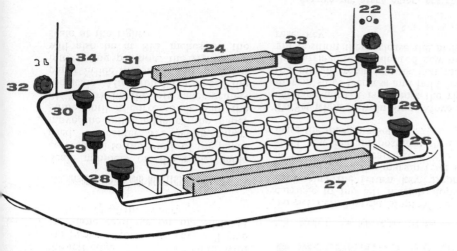

LOWER SEGMENT OF A NONELECTRIC TYPEWRITER

Backspace key ..	**30**	Shift Key, Right .	**26**
Margin Release Key	**25**	Shift Lock, Left and Right	**29**
Ribbon Control and Stencil Lock	**22**	Space Bar	**27**
		Tab Clear Key ..	**31**
Ribbon Reverse .	**32**	Tab Set Key	**23**
Shift Key, Left ..	**28**	Tabulator Bar ...	**24**
		Touch Regulator .	**34**

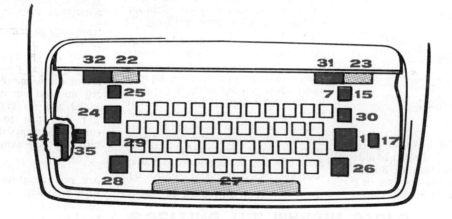

LOWER SEGMENT OF AN ELECTRIC TYPEWRITER

Backspace Key	**30**	Ribbon Reverse	**32**
Carriage Return (Line-Space Key)	**1**	Shift Key, Left	**28**
Electric Switch	**17**	Shift Key, Right	**26**
Impression Control	**35**	Shift Lock	**29**
Line-Space Key (Carriage Return)	**1**	Space Bar	**27**
Margin Release Key	**25**	Tab Clear Key	**31**
Margin Reset Key **7, 15**		Tab Set Key	**23**
Ribbon Control and Stencil Lock	**22**	Tabulator Key	**24**
		Touch Regulator (Shown in X-Ray View)	**34**

• *Check your typewriter to see if:*

1 The position is different for:
   ¢ @ _ (underline)

2 These keys have "repeat" action:
   Backspace
   Space bar
   Carriage return
   Hyphen-underline

3 Extra keys are used:
   + = ! 1

● SETTING THE PAPER GUIDE; CENTERING THE PAPER

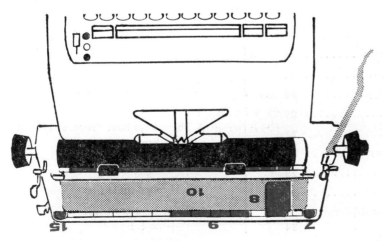

IBM; OLYMPIA, R. C. ALLEN; ROYAL; SMITH-CORONA

Set the paper guide 8 so the indicator at the left will point to 0 on the paper-guide scale 9, which is on or near the paper table 10.

NOTE On the IBM the paper-guide scale is located on the "copy guide," which is near the cylinder for the "Model C" and on the front of the machine for the "Selectric."

When paper of standard size (8½" by 11") is inserted with the guide at 0, the centering point will be:

42 for pica machines

51 for elite machines

Note the difference between pica and elite type illustrated in the two lines above. Compare this type with the type on the machine you are using.

Smith-Corona "Deluxe 400" Electric. This typewriter provides for "automatic centering" of 8½" by 11" paper. Two pointers on the paper table scale indicate the position for setting the paper guide when paper of this size is used. For 8½" wide paper, set the guide at the inside pointer. The pointer on the paper bail indicates the center of the sheet.

NOTE The R. C. Allen nonelectric also has indicator lines on its paper table for the "automatic centering" of 8½" by 11" paper.

REMINGTON ELECTRIC AND NONELECTRIC

The fixed centering point is 0 for both pica- and elite-type machines. Before inserting the paper, line up the left edge of the paper guide with the paper edge mark. This will give the same readings on the scale at both edges of the paper.

UNDERWOOD ELECTRIC AND NONELECTRIC

Scale numbers on the paper table correspond to the width of the paper used. To center 8½"-width paper, move the outer edge of the paper guide until it corresponds with the 8½" mark on the left paper centering scale. After you have placed the paper inside the guide and moved it into typing position, the right edge will also be at 8½ inches on the scale at the right.

● SETTING THE MARGIN STOPS

PLANNING THE MARGIN STOPS (7, 15)

To center typed material horizontally, set stops for the left and right margins. Typewriters differ in their mechanical adjustments and the bell rings at different points on different typewriters; but the carriage locks at the point where the right margin stop is set. After the bell rings, there will be from 8 to 11 or more spaces before the carriage locks, some machines allowing more but none fewer than 8 spaces.

Test out your typewriter and determine the number of spaces the bell rings before the carriage locks. Take this into consideration when setting the right margin stop. Since the ringing of the bell is a cue to

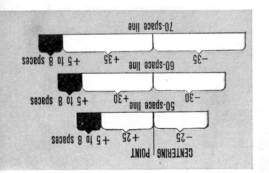

the point at which you want the line to end.

Approximately 3 spaces before the desired line ending so the ringing will come at 5 to 8 spaces beyond the desired line ending, set the right stop

● MECHANICS OF SETTING MARGIN STOPS

IBM "MODEL C" AND UNDERWOOD ELECTRIC

To Set Left Margin Stop: Move the carriage to the left margin stop by depressing the return key. Depress and hold down the margin reset key as you move the carriage to the desired new margin position; then release the margin reset key.

To Set Right Margin Stop: Move the carriage until it is against the right margin stop. Depress and hold down the margin reset key as you move the carriage to the desired new margin position then release the margin reset key.

IBM "SELECTRIC"

To Set Left and Right Margin Stops: Press in on either the left or right margin stop and glide it to the correct reading on the margin scale. Occasionally the typing position indicator (connected to the carrier) may have to be moved first since the stops will not slide past it. As there is no movable carriage as on other typewriters, stops can be moved left or right as the line length requires. The typing position indicator may be moved by tapping the space bar.

● Continued on page vii.

● SETTING MARGIN STOPS (Continued)

OLYMPIA AND UNDERWOOD NONELECTRIC

To Set Left and Right Margin Stops:
Move the left and right margin stops to the desired position on the front scale for the Underwood typewriter and on the scale in back of the cylinder for the Olympia.

The Underwood typewriter has margin indicators (solid geometric shapes) on the front scale to indicate balanced margin set positions. The Olympia has an easy-to-see red line, on the upright plastic guide, to indicate exact position of setting.

R. C. ALLEN NONELECTRIC

Tilt the paper table to find the margin stops. Move the left or right margin stop to the desired position, set, and release.

REMINGTON ELECTRIC AND NONELECTRIC

To Set Left and Right Margin Stops:
Move the left margin stop to the desired position to begin the line of writing. Move the stop for the right margin to the desired position to set the right margin stop.

ROYAL ELECTRIC AND NONELECTRIC

To Set Left Margin Stop: Place your left index finger behind the left "Magic" margin control and move it forward; move the carriage to the desired position and release the margin control.

To Set Right Margin Stop: Move the right "Magic" margin control forward; move the carriage to the desired position and release the margin control.

SMITH-CORONA ELECTRIC

To Set Left and Right Margin Stops:
Depress the left carriage-release button and the left margin button and move the carriage to the desired location for the left margin stop; release the two buttons simultaneously.

Use a similar operation to set the stop for the right margin.

SMITH-CORONA NONELECTRIC

To Set Left Margin Stop: Press the left margin set button to the left in

SMITH-CORONA NONELECTRIC (Continued)

the direction of the arrow as you move the carriage to the desired position; then release the margin set button.

To Set Right Margin Stop: Press the right margin set button to the right in the direction of the arrow as you move the carriage to the desired position; then release the margin set button.

● Know your typewriter
Your machine may have time-saving features not included in this discussion of operating parts. Learn these features from a study of the manufacturer's pamphlet which describes and illustrates the operating parts of the typewriter you are using. You can get this pamphlet without cost from the manufacturer of your typewriter. The pamphlet will have many ideas for your operative improvement.

● TABLE OF QUARTER-MINUTE CHECK POINTS

GOAL	QUARTER	HALF	THREE-QUARTERS	ONE
16	4	8	12	16
20	5	10	15	20
24	6	12	18	24
28	7	14	21	28
32	8	16	24	32
36	9	18	27	36
40	10	20	30	40
44	11	22	33	44
48	12	24	36	48
52	13	26	39	52
56	14	28	42	56
60	15	30	45	60
64	16	32	48	64
68	17	34	51	68
72	18	36	54	72
76	19	38	57	76
80	20	40	60	80
84	21	42	63	84
88	22	44	66	88
92	23	46	69	92
96	24	48	72	96
100	25	50	75	100

USING THE TABLE FOR PARAGRAPH GUIDED WRITING

Use the table at the left to identify the quarter-minute goals for guided writing. First, decide the goal rate at which you want to type for the minute; then get from the scale the quarter-, half-, three-quarter-, and one-minute goals and check the copy at these points.

The paragraphs are marked with the 4-word count shown in figures and with an in-between count shown by a . (dot). To check the goals, place a small mark above each quarter-minute goal. If your goal is not shown in the copy by a figure or a dot, spot the approximate midpoint between the dot and the figure and check this point. Do not take time to count the exact strokes; rather, estimate the correct placement of the goal check when there is no figure or dot to show the exact count.

● INDEX

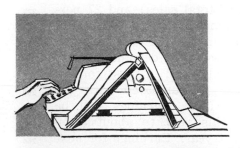

LESSON 1 | 1A ● GET READY TO TYPE

1. ARRANGE YOUR WORK AREA

a. Place this book in good reading position, to the right of the typewriter on a bookholder, or put something under the top of the book to raise it slightly for improved readability.

b. Have the front of the frame of the typewriter even with the edge of the desk or table.

2. INSERT THE PAPER

a. Adjust the paper guide **8** as directed on page vi.

b. Place a full-size sheet of paper on the desk to the left of the typewriter and turned so the long side of the paper is close to you.

c. Pull the paper bail **11** forward—toward you.

d. Grasp the paper with the left hand, the thumb under the sheet, as shown at the left.

e. Bring the paper to the cylinder or platen **14** and drop it between the platen and the paper table **10**, against the paper guide **8**; *at the same time*, bring the right hand to the right cylinder knob **19** and twirl the knob with a quick movement of the fingers and the thumb.

f. Replace the paper bail **11** to hold the paper firmly against the platen. Place the paper bail rolls **13** about 1½ inches from the side edges of the paper.

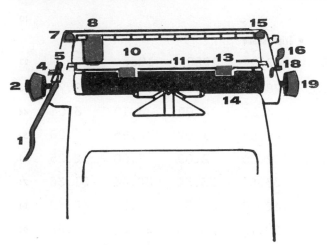

The numbers shown in boldface in the text above are those assigned to the machine parts shown at the left and on the illustrations presented on pages iv and v.

1 Carriage Return and Line-Space Lever

2 Left Cylinder Knob

4 Left Carriage-Release Lever

5 Line-Space Regulator

7 Left Margin Set

8 Paper Guide

10 Paper Table

11 Paper Bail and Scale

13 Paper-Bail Rolls

14 Cylinder (Platen)

15 Right Margin Set

16 Paper-Release Lever

18 Right Carriage-Release Lever

19 Right Cylinder Knob

Problem 4–4: Investment Research Report

Full sheet	65-space line
2″ top margin •	Blocked ¶s
Single spacing	Current date

Words

DARCEY, NEILSON & COMPANY, INC. 6

• Triple-space

Research Department   (Date) 13

• Triple-space

Lawson Oil Well Cementing Company 27

• Triple-space

(¶ 1) The company provides services for 34
the drilling and operation of oil and gas 42
wells. This includes pumping equipment 50
for cementing and hydraulic fracturing; 58
jet perforating and electric well services; 67
packers and tools for formation testing. 75
(¶ 2) This year's sales and earnings have 82
been adversely affected by a sharp decline 91
in domestic and foreign drilling activity 99
as well as a lower level of remedial work 108
on producing wells. With a resumption 116
of the growth in U. S. oil consumption 123
next year coupled with an improved inven- 132
tory position, domestic crude production 140
should show a good gain over last year's 148
level. Under these circumstances, a recov- 157

ery in drilling activity from an estimated 165
49,000 wells to at least 52,000 wells is pre- 174
dicted. (¶ 3) Lawson's growth in foreign 181
sales since 1955 has outpaced the domestic 190
market by a wide margin with sales in- 198
creasing from 17.5 million (10.8 percent 206
of total sales) in 1955 to $31.0 million 214
(16.5 percent of total sales) and 27 per- 222
cent of net income last year. This trend 231
should continue in view of the projected 239
increase in free world oil demand and the 247
lower cost of finding oil in most foreign 256
producing areas as compared with the 263
United States. (¶ 4) Earnings will be 270
down sharply this year to about $3.50 277
versus $4.80 last year. Earnings for next 286
year should show a recovery to the $4.50 294
level. In view of the lower level of capital 303
expenditures over the next year or two 311
and the good cash position, a more liberal 320
payout of earnings is expected in the 327
future. Capitalization consists of only 335
$4 million in debt and about 4 million 343
shares of common stock, so the financial 351
position is strong. (¶ 5) This quality 358
stock is considered a good long-term 366
investment. 368

Problem 4–5: Wide Tabulation Typed Lengthwise

Full sheet inserted	Center the problem
lengthwise •	vertically
Double spacing	4 spaces between columns

TABLES TYPED LENGTHWISE

In typing a table that is to be typed lengthwise on an 8½″ by 11″ sheet of paper, follow the vetrical and horizontal placement directions on pages 59 and 64. Keep in mind, however, that there are only *51 vertical spaces* on a sheet inserted in this manner.

Words

A SEVEN-YEAR FINANCIAL COMPARISON 7

Per Common Share 10

• Triple-space

	1963	1962	1961	1960	1959	1958	1957	
Net Sales	$94.58	$98.14	$98.56	$78.65	$91.16	$92.44	$89.78	36
Net Income	2.64	3.16	3.55	3.10	3.09	3.10	3.04	44
Depreciation	2.54	2.20	1.25	.97	1.02	.95	.86	52
Dividends Declared	2.00	2.00	2.00	2.00	2.00	2.00	2.25	61
Shareholders' Equity	37.99	37.35	36.19	33.54	33.54	32.44	31.36	71
Price of Shares, High	38.75	37.50	41.12	42.50	42.50	38.12	42.62	81
Price of Shares, Low	28.00	29.50	34.50	28.75	28.75	27.88	32.88	91

(1963 ... 1957 header row: 23)

● CORRECT TYPING POSITION

eyes on copy

book at right of machine elevated for easy reading

fingers curved

elbows close to body, forearms parallel to keyboard

wrists down

table free of unneeded books

sit back in chair; body erect

feet flat on floor, one slightly in advance of the other

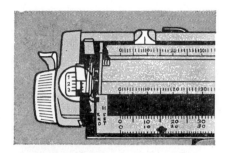

3. ADJUST THE LINE-SPACE REGULATOR

Set the line-space regulator **5** on "1" for single spacing the lines you are to type in this lesson.

(Set the regulator on "2" for double spacing and on "3" for triple spacing when such spacing is needed.)

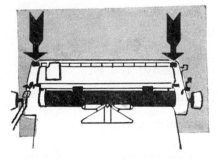

4. SET THE MARGIN STOPS

Move the left margin stop **7** to approximately 25 spaces to the left of the center of the paper. Move the right stop **15** to the end of the scale. You will type the copy line for line and, thus, do not need the right margin stop to indicate the line ending.

1B ● FINGER POSITION, KEY STROKING, CARRIAGE RETURN, AND SPACING

1. FINGER POSITION

Look at the keyboard chart at the right and locate **f d s a** (the home keys for the left hand).

Look at your typewriter keyboard and place your left hand in typing position. The first (index) finger rests lightly on the **f** key, the second finger on **d**, the third finger on **s**, and the fourth (little) finger on **a**.

Look again at the keyboard chart at the right and locate **j k l ;** (the home keys for the right hand).

Look at your typewriter keyboard and place your right hand in typing position, the first (index) finger lightly on **j**, the second on **k**, the third finger on **l**, and the fourth (little) finger on **;** (semicolon).

Full sheet	•	65-space line	•	2" top margin	•	5-space indention	•	Correct errors, unless otherwise directed

Words

DATA SHEET
2

• Triple-space

Underline
italicized
words ➤ *Personal Information*
10

• Double-space

Name	:	Margaret L. Creighton	16
Age	:	21 on August 28, 19––	22
Address	:	7951 Fordham Street, South Bend, Indiana 46605	33
Telephone	:	621–8138	38

• Double-space

Education
41

High School	:	South Bend High School; academic major	52
College	:	Two years, Ohio University, economics major	63
Business School	:	Two years, Indiana School of Business; major in	76
		management	78

Work Experience
84

Typist-clerk for Ardmore Construction Company, South Bend, Indiana, — 98
during one summer — 102
Stenographer for First National Bank, New York, New York, during — 115
three summers — 117

Skill
120

Typing: 65 to 70 words a minute on 5-minute writings — 130
Shorthand Speed: 110 words a minute dictation speed on unfamiliar — 144
material; 35 words a minute transcription speed — 153
Machines: Electric typewriter, calculators, and Mimeograph — 165

References (by Permission)
176

Mr. G. H. Weston, Treasurer; Ardmore Construction Company; 108 N. — 189
Main Street; South Bend, Indiana 46602; 721–4987 — 199
Mr. Alvin T. Riley, Vice-President; First National Bank; 500 Fifth — 213
Avenue; New York, New York 10015 — 219
Miss Gladys A. Harris, Head; Secretarial Department; Indiana School — 233
of Business; South Bend, Indiana 46604; 581–4000 — 243

Problem 4–3: Application Follow-Up Letter
(errors corrected)

Full sheet	FOR RETURN ADDRESS: Use
60-space line	data-sheet address given
Modified block, indented ¶s, •	in Problem 4-2
mixed punctuation	Current date
5-space ¶ indention	1 large envelope

• 6 blank line spaces after the date

Words

(*Return address; date*) Mr. B. L. Leslie, — 16
Personnel Manager Palmer-Lowe Manu- — 23
facturing Company 2045 E. La Salle — 30
Boulevard South Bend, Indiana 46603 — 37
Dear Mr. Leslie (¶1) I appreciated the — 45
opportunity of talking with you this morn- — 53
ing about a position as a secretary in your — 62
company. The data sheet you requested, — 70
giving in detail my qualifications for this — 79
position, is enclosed. (¶2) At the end of — 86
this month I am to be graduated from the — 94
Indiana School of Business of this city. — 103
Upon graduation, I shall want a business — 111
position; but even more, I desire employ- — 119
ment in a progressive company where I — 127
will be assigned to new responsibilities as — 136
soon as I prove my capability. (¶3) I — 142
can arrange to take at your convenience — 150
the tests given for this position. Sincerely — 160
yours Miss Margaret L. Creighton En- — 167
closure — 169/208

2. STROKING

Type **f** with the *left first finger*; then type **j** with the *right first finger*. Strike and release each key quickly. Type **fj** four or five times as shown below.

fjfjfjfjfj

Type the home keys for the left hand (**fdsa**) and the home keys for the right hand (**jkl;**) three times as shown at the right.

STROKING TECHNIQUE EMPHASIS Strike the key with a firm, quick stroke and release the key quickly. Keep the stroking action in the fingers, with the hands and arms held as quiet as possible.

➡fdsajkl;fdsajkl;fdsajkl;

---

3. USING THE CARRIAGE RETURN 1

Locate the carriage return **1**. It is a lever on a non-electric typewriter, a key on an electric typewriter. Return the carriage as directed below and at the right.

Nonelectric Typewriter. Move the left hand, with the fingers bracing one another, to the carriage-return lever and move the lever forward to take up the slack; then return the carriage with a quick wrist and hand motion. Drop the hand to typing position without letting it follow the carriage across the line.

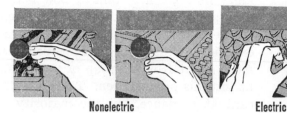

Nonelectric   Electric

Electric Typewriter. Reach the little finger to the return key, flick the key lightly, release it quickly, and return the finger to its typing position.

---

4. USING THE SPACE BAR 27

To space between words or groups of letters, strike the space bar **27** with a quick down-and-in motion of the *right thumb*. Hold the thumb close to the space bar.

---

5. TRYOUT PRACTICE (STROKING AND SPACING)

● Type the lines as shown below with a space between the two-letter groups.

NOTE Space with the right thumb, using a quick down-and-in motion. At the end of the line, return the carriage without spacing after the final stroke in the line. Start the new line without a pause.

Operate carriage return lever or key again to leave a blank line space →

```
ff jj ff jj dd kk dd kk ss ll ss ll aa ;; aa ;;   Return the carriage

ff jj fj fj dd kk dk dk ss ll sl sl aa ;; a; a;

fj dk sl a; fj dk sl a; fj dk sl a; fj dk sl a;
```

1C ● NEW KEYS: h and e

You are now to learn the location and control of two new keys: the **h** and the **e**. As each new key is introduced in this lesson and in those that follow, use the four-step procedure given below:

1 Find the new key on the keyboard chart.
2 Locate the new key on the typewriter keyboard.
3 Study the reach-stroke illustration for the key.

4 Watch your finger make the reach to the new key and move back to home position.

● Operate the return lever or key three times to have extra space between the Tryout Practice lines and the lines to be typed from the next page.

Turn to page 4 for the location of the new keys **h** and **e**.

PROJECT 4 ● TAKING AN EMPLOYMENT TEST

Problem 4–1: Timed Writing

2 full sheets, 70-space line,
double spacing,
5-space ¶ indention

PROCEDURE Type at a controlled rate. Let your goal be to type as slow as you must and as fast as you can to demonstrate your typing skill.

● All letters are used in the paragraphs.

	GWAM 1'	5'	10'

¶ 1
1.40 si
138 words

Applying for work is something of an ordeal. The job seeker does not know what to do with his hat, his hands, or his feet. He does not know how much to talk or how long to stay. It is just about as hard on the employer as on the prospective employee, too. In a few moments and frequently with very meager information about the training, business experience, interests, and personal ambitions of the applicant, a man must select from a group of young men and women the one who will best fit into his organization. There may be some men who can judge an applicant at a glance, but the majority of employers who are looking for a new worker want more than a glance at a would-be employee.

13	3	1
27	5	3
42	8	4
56	11	6
70	14	7
84	17	8
98	20	10
113	23	11
127	25	13
138	28	14

¶ 2
1.40 si
152 words

Why is one applicant rejected in the first few minutes of an interview while another is hired for the position when both seem to have equal ability? The men who do the hiring for a number of firms were asked to explain the basis on which they employ workers. They said there are three types of persons who apply for work. There is the obvious misfit in personal qualities, though not always in training. Skill is just one of the qualifications demanded by employers, although young workers do not always know this to be true. In this misfit group are the boys who are too often sloppy in dress and lacking in poise. In this same group are the girls who do not recognize the fact that manners either stagey or coyly familiar are out of place in an office.

13	30	15
28	33	17
43	36	18
56	39	20
71	42	21
85	45	22
100	48	24
114	50	25
128	53	27
143	56	28
152	58	29

¶ 3
1.40 si
123 words

The second type of applicant gives the employment manager the most trouble. In this group are those greatly in need of work, eager to do their best, but untrained. Experience may be the best teacher, but the employer frequently finds it too costly to take over the task of giving the training that should have been taken in school. Out of this second group of applicants, however, some fine workers are sometimes found. It takes time and patient quizzing to select from the great number who belong to this group those who show promise of being able to do the work and make adjustments that the position demands.

13	61	30
28	64	32
42	66	33
56	69	35
71	72	36
85	75	38
99	78	39
114	81	40
123	83	42

¶ 4
1.40 si
118 words

The third group of workers seeking employment includes those who are well trained and who are blessed with a pleasing manner, natural or acquired. They do not work just for the income that comes as a result. They realize that work gives them many opportunities to learn, to grow, and to advance toward that full life and social security that all expect to achieve. Employers prefer well-trained workers, of course; but they will often take a chance on those with less specific training if they have the personal qualities that make for quick adjustment to those with whom they must work.

13	85	43
27	88	44
42	91	46
56	94	47
71	97	48
85	100	50
99	103	51
114	105	53
118	106	53

1' | 1 | 2 | 3 | 4 | 5 | 6 | 7 | 8 | 9 | 10 | 11 | 12 | 13 | 14 |
5' | 1 | 2 | 3 |
10' | 1 | 2 |

1C ● NEW KEYS: h and e (Continued)

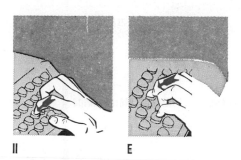

H   E

1. REACH TECHNIQUE FOR H

Reach the *right first finger* to the left to type **h** without moving the other fingers from their home keys. Watch your finger type **hj** a few times; then type the following Try-out Practice.

Tryout Practice. Type the drill twice on the same line; then return the carriage.

hh hj has had had has had

2. REACH TECHNIQUE FOR E

As you move the *left second finger* up to type **e**, lift the *left first finger* slightly to free the controlling finger. Watch your finger type **ed** a few times; then type the following Try-out Practice.

Tryout Practice. Type the drill twice on the same line; then return the carriage.

dd ed ed ee eel feel feel

STROKING TECHNIQUE

Type the key with a firm stroke and a quick release; then type the next key without pausing. After striking the key, snap the finger slightly toward the palm of the hand as the key is released. The finger should not follow the key all the way down. Keep most of the stroking action in the fingers. Keep the hands and arms quiet, almost motionless.

1D ● STROKING TECHNIQUE PRACTICE

PROCEDURE Operate the return lever or key three times; then type the lines as shown below. Do not type the numbers at the beginning of the lines.

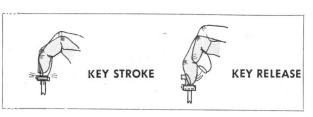

KEY STROKE   KEY RELEASE

1 Curve the	ff jj dd kk fd jk fd jk ss ll aa ;; as fj as fj ad	Return carriage
2 fingers	ff jj dd kk fd jk fd jk ss ll aa ;; as fj as fj ad	quickly
		← Double-space
3 Space with	as ask ask all all ask all fall fall all fall fall	(operate the
4 right thumb	as ask ask all all ask all fall fall all fall fall	return lever or
		← key again) to
5 Keep carriage	hh hj has has hj had had hj hall hall hj hall hall	leave 1 blank
6 moving steadily	hh hj has has hj had had hj hall hall hj hall hall	line space
		← between pairs
7	as ash as ash lash hash flash as ask ash flash ash	of lines
8	as ash as ash lash hash flash as ask ash flash ash	
		←
9	ee ed eel eel feel keel ed ell fell fell sell dell	
10	ee ed eel eel feel keel ed ell fell fell sell dell	
		←
11 Space quickly	he she she shed shed head heal ell fell sell shell	
12 after words	he she she shed shed head heal ell fell sell shell	

Problem 3–3: Statement of Account

PROCEDURE Type one copy of the statement of account illustrated; use single spacing for items in columns.

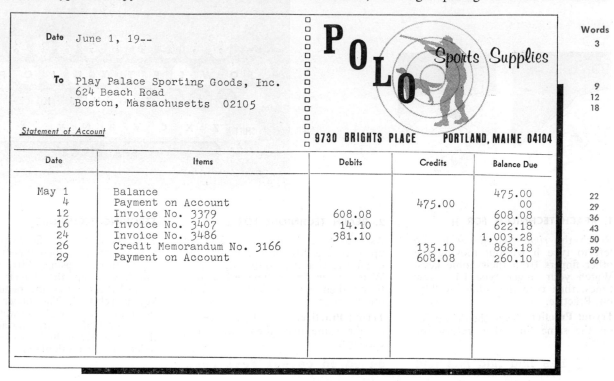

					Words
Date June 1, 19--					3
To Play Palace Sporting Goods, Inc. 624 Beach Road Boston, Massachusetts 02105					9 12 18

POLO Sports Supplies

9730 BRIGHTS PLACE   PORTLAND, MAINE 04104

Statement of Account

Date	Items	Debits	Credits	Balance Due	Words
May 1	Balance			475.00	22
4	Payment on Account		475.00	00	29
12	Invoice No. 3379	608.08		608.08	36
16	Invoice No. 3407	14.10		622.18	43
24	Invoice No. 3486	381.10		1,003.28	50
26	Credit Memorandum No. 3166		135.10	868.18	59
29	Payment on Account		608.08	260.10	66

Problem 3–4: Voucher Check

PROCEDURE Type one copy of the voucher copy illustrated. Align the copy on the ruled lines.

McMAHON BUILDERS, INC.
400 ADAMS STREET
ALBANY, INDIANA 47320

71-631
712

	Words
April 1, 19 -- No. 103	3

Pay to the
order of Kentucky Suppliers, Inc. $405.65   10

Four hundred five and 65/100--   33

ALBANY NATIONAL BANK
ALBANY, INDIANA 47320

James C. Wood
Treasurer, McMAHON BUILDERS, INC.

- -

DETACH THIS STUB BEFORE
CASHING THIS CHECK

TO Kentucky Suppliers, Inc.
965 E. Dixie Highway
Louisville, Kentucky 40203

IN PAYMENT OF THE FOLLOWING INVOICES:

McMAHON BUILDERS, INC.
400 ADAMS STREET
ALBANY, INDIANA 47320

	Words
	38
	42
	48

Date	Invoice	Amount	
3/17	B-38465	⁻ 405.65	52

1E ● CONTINUITY PRACTICE

PROCEDURE Insert a clean sheet of paper. Type the copy as shown with a double space after the second typing of the line. Do not type the numbers at the beginning of the lines. *Keep the carriage moving steadily throughout each line.*

SPACING TECHNIQUE Strike the space bar with a quick down-and-in motion of the right thumb immediately after you have typed the final letter of the word, except that you will not space after the last stroke in the line.

● Only 1-syllable words are used in the practice materials of this section.

1	Curve the	he she she shed shed ale hale kale lake half shelf
2	fingers	he she she shed shed ale hale kale lake half shelf

Double-space
← as you return the carriage

3	Space once	ask dad; he has a desk; he had a sale; a lad fell;
4	after ;	ask dad; he has a desk; he had a sale; a lad fell;

5	Down-and-in	she led all; she led all fall; she has had a fall;
6	space-bar action	she led all; she led all fall; she has had a fall;

Return carriage without spacing after final stroke in line

7	Keep carriage	he has a desk; he has a desk flash; she leads all;
8	moving steadily	he has a desk; he has a desk flash; she leads all;

1F ● SELF-IMPROVEMENT PRACTICE

● *Self-Improvement Practice is provided for those who have extra time for typing or who need additional practice before going to the next lesson.*

PROCEDURE Type the copy as shown with a double space after the second typing of the line.

1	Space once	she leads; he held a lead all fall; he has a deal;
2	after ;	she leads; he held a lead all fall; he has a deal;

Double-space as
← you return the carriage

3	Strike space bar	he had a sled; he has fled; he fled as a lad fell;
4	with right thumb	he had a sled; he has fled; he fled as a lad fell;

5	Keep carriage	she sells jade; dad feels she has had a fall sale;
6	moving steadily	she sells jade; dad feels she has had a fall sale;

Return carriage quickly

1G ● REMOVE THE PAPER AND CENTER THE CARRIAGE

1. LOCATE THE PAPER-RELEASE LEVER 16

To remove the paper, operate the paper-release lever **16** and remove the paper with your free hand. Return the lever to its original position.

2. LOCATE THE RIGHT CARRIAGE-RELEASE LEVER 18

To center the carriage, depress the right carriage-release lever **18** with your *right first finger* as your thumb and other fingers hold the carriage; move the carriage so it is approximately centered.

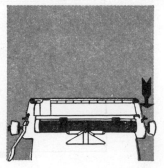

Problem 3–1: Purchase Order with Ruled Columns

Purchase order form 1 carbon copy on a plain half sheet	•	Type from the model Use single spacing for items in columns	•	Set left margin stop for 1st column 3-5 spaces from left edge Set tabulator stops for other columns as illustrated in the model

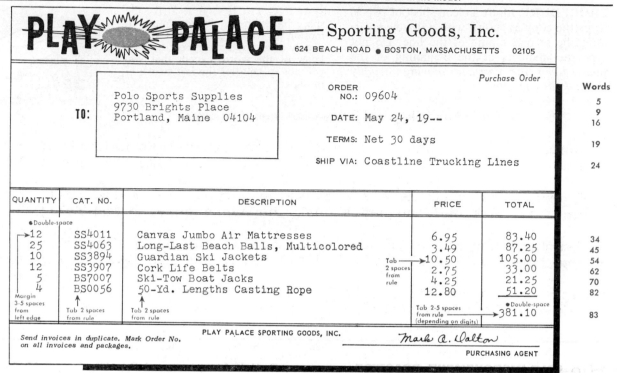

PLAY PALACE — Sporting Goods, Inc.
624 BEACH ROAD ● BOSTON, MASSACHUSETTS   02105

Purchase Order

	Words
TO: Polo Sports Supplies	
9730 Brights Place	
Portland, Maine 04104	
ORDER NO.: 09604	5
	9
	16
DATE: May 24, 19--	
TERMS: Net 30 days	19
SHIP VIA: Coastline Trucking Lines	24

QUANTITY	CAT. NO.	DESCRIPTION	PRICE	TOTAL	Words
● Double-space					
12	SS4011	Canvas Jumbo Air Mattresses	6.95	83.40	34
25	SS4063	Long-Last Beach Balls, Multicolored	3.49	87.25	45
10	SS3894	Guardian Ski Jackets	10.50	105.00	54
12	SS3907	Cork Life Belts	2.75	33.00	62
5	BS7007	Ski-Tow Boat Jacks	4.25	21.25	70
4	BS0056	50-Yd. Lengths Casting Rope	12.80	51.20	82
			● Double-space	381.10	83

Margin 3-5 spaces from left edge
Tab 2 spaces from rule
Tab 2 spaces from rule
Tab 2 spaces from rule
Tab 2-5 spaces from rule (depending on digits)

Send invoices in duplicate. Mark Order No. on all invoices and packages.

PLAY PALACE SPORTING GOODS, INC.

Mark A. Walton
PURCHASING AGENT

Problem 3–2: Invoice Without Ruled Columns

Invoice form	•	1 carbon copy on a plain half sheet	•	Single-space column items	•	Set tab stops	•	Circle errors

Kentucky Suppliers, Inc.
965 E. Dixie Highway / Louisville, Kentucky 40203 / 502-941-7716

invoice

	Words
Sold To McMahon Builders, Inc.	
400 Adams Street	
Albany, Indiana 47320	
Date March 17, 19--	3
Our No. B-38465	9
Cust. Order No. CN-2098	13
	19
Shipped Via National Transport	23
Terms 2/10, n/30	
Salesman Bixler	26

Quantity	Description	Unit Price	Amount	Words
12 ea.	825-NW Pneumatic Door Closers	2.55 ea.	30.60	37
5 sets	620-X Cylindrical Lock, Brass	8.60 ea.	43.00	48
3 ea.	CO-453 24" 6-Light Cluster Fixtures	68.75 ea.	206.25	60
8 pr.	3/8" Copper Offset H-Hinge	.85 pr.	6.80	70
2 ea.	B-616 Magnesium Extension Ladders	59.50 ea.	119.00	83
			405.65	84

LESSON 2 | 2A ● GET READY TO TYPE

(for each lesson in this section)

1 Clear the desk of unneeded books and papers; then place this book at the right of the typewriter with the top elevated slightly for easier, more accurate reading.

2 Have the front of the typewriter frame even with the edge of the desk or table.

3 Adjust the paper guide and paper-bail rolls as directed on pages vi and 1.

4 Have a full-size sheet of paper on the desk at the left of the typewriter, turned so the long side of the paper is close to you.

5 Insert the paper. (Review the steps on page 1.)

6 Set the line-space regulator on "1" for single spacing.

7 Set the left margin stop 25 spaces to the left of the center of the paper so that your work will be centered horizontally. Move the right margin stop to the end of the scale (see page 2); you will be taught its use later.

*Note the numbers on the margin scale **11** at which the stops are set and use the same settings for the remaining lessons of this section.*

8 Take correct position at the typewriter—body erect; feet on the floor;

fingers curved; wrists low; elbows near the body.

9 Review the typing techniques: quick, sharp stroking; quick, smooth carriage return; down-and-in space-bar motion.

10 Begin to type at a slow, even pace. Increase your rate of stroking gradually. Type steadily—keep the carriage moving without pauses. Striking and releasing a key should be thought of as one motion with the release motion started almost at the same instant as the downward motion of the finger.

2B ● KNOW YOUR TYPEWRITER

TYPEWRITER SPACING

If your typewriter has elite type, you can type 12 spaces to a horizontal inch; if it has pica type, 10 spaces. Note the difference between elite and pica type in the illustration at the right.

PAPER SIZE

Paper used for typing is usually 8½ inches wide. Thus, there are 102 elite spaces or 85 pica spaces in a full line 8½ inches long. The center of the paper, therefore, is 51 for elite type or 42 for pica type.

Elite type has 12 type spaces to an inch.

Pica type has 10 type spaces to an inch.

Tryout Practice. Type the words **she has a sled** and compare the type with that shown above to determine whether your typewriter has elite or pica type. You will need this information later when setting stops for exact margins.

● Operate the carriage return lever or key three times to provide extra space between drills; then type the following Preparatory Practice.

2C ● PREPARATORY PRACTICE

PROCEDURE Type the copy as shown. Double-space after the second typing of the line. Begin the new line immediately. *To double-space when the line-space regulator is set for single spacing,* operate the carriage return lever or key twice as you return the carriage after the second typing of the line.

Curve the fingers	ff jj dd kk ss ll aa ;; hh hj ee ed he he ed hj he ff jj dd kk ss ll aa ;; hh hj ee ed he he ed hj he	Return carriage without spacing after final stroke in line
	● Double-space (to leave 1 blank line space)	
Space quickly with right thumb	he she she led elf self she shelf shelf lake shake he she she led elf self she shelf shelf lake shake	
Space once after ;	he fled; she leads; she sells jade; he has a sled; he fled; she leads; she sells jade; he has a sled;	

PROJECT 3 ● SIMPLE BUSINESS FORMS

Problem Typing Information

PREPARING BUSINESS FORMS

Use printed forms if they are available, or half sheets of paper with the typewritten material arranged as it would be on printed forms. Do not type the headings that would ordinarily be printed on the forms.

Number of Copies. At least two copies (an original and a carbon) are made of invoices, credit memorandums, and similar forms. As a rule, single copies are made of statements of account.

Tabulator Mechanism. Make full use of the tabulator mechanism to insure proper alignment of figures in the columns and to speed up your work. For a column of numbers, set a tabulator stop for the indention that occurs most often. Space forward for short amounts; backspace for long amounts.

Abbreviations. Periods may be omitted after abbreviations, and they may be omitted in columnar tabulations of figures where the ruling separates the dollars from the cents. It is customary to use abbreviations such as *gal.*, *ft.*, *ea.*,% for *percent*, @ for *at*, C for *hundreds*, M for *thousands*, # for *No.*, and other similar special abbreviations. Names of months may be abbreviated when limited space on the form makes this desirable.

Spacing. Single-space invoices, statements, and similar forms (such as credit memorandums, purchase requisitions, purchase orders, etc.) unless you have three or fewer lines, in which case use double spacing. Many companies require business forms to be typed with double spacing.

For single-spaced business forms having items that require more than one line for the description, type the description on successive lines (indenting the second line 3 spaces); then double-space between items.

Items in Columns. Items in the first column ("Quantity" or "Date," as a rule) are either centered in the column or started at the left margin of the column. Allow a margin of 3–5 spaces from the left edge of the paper unless one or more of the items in the first column is unduly long. Begin items in the other columns 2 spaces to the right of the ruled line. These items are usually not centered under the heading.

WINDOW ENVELOPES

Window envelopes are provided with transparent or cut-out openings in the lower center through which the address typed on a business form may be seen. Window envelopes are rarely used for letters; but when they are used, keep in mind that the complete address must show through the "window" space in the envelope.

FOLDING A HALF-SIZE SHEET FOR A WINDOW ENVELOPE

Many business forms specify the position for the address so that when the forms are folded, the address will be in proper position for the "window" of the envelope. Follow these steps:

Step 1 Place the sheet face down, top toward you.

Step 2 Fold back the top far enough for the address to show through the "window."

Step 3 Insert the form into the envelope with the crease at the bottom.

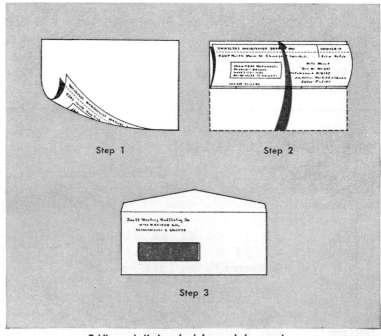

Folding a half-size sheet for a window envelope

2D ● NEW KEYS: i, t, and . (period)

PROCEDURE Use the four-step procedure for learning the new keys, page 3.

I

T

(Period)

1. REACH TECHNIQUE FOR I

As you move the *right second finger* up to type **i**, lift the *right first finger* to give freedom of movement to the controlling finger. Type **ik** a few times; then type the following Tryout Practice.

Tryout Practice. Type the following drill twice on one line.

```
ik if ik is if is did did
```

2. REACH TECHNIQUE FOR T

Relax the curvature in the *left first finger* and move the finger up to **t** without arching the wrist or moving the hand forward. Type **tf** a few times; then type the following Tryout Practice.

Tryout Practice. Type the following drill twice on one line.

```
tf the tf the tf the that
```

3. REACH TECHNIQUE FOR . (Period)

As you reach the *right third finger* down to type **.** (period), extend the finger without moving the hand downward. Type **.l** a few times; then type the following Tryout Practice.

Tryout Practice. Type the following drill twice on one line.

```
ll .l .l ll .l .l 1.1 1.1
```

2E ● STROKING TECHNIQUE PRACTICE

PROCEDURE Operate the carriage return lever or key three times to have two blank line spaces before typing the following drill. Then type the drill lines as shown.

TECHNIQUE CONDITIONER: Quiet Hands and Arms When striking a key, use finger action with as little arm motion as possible. Hold the hands and arms quiet, almost motionless.

1	Reach to	`if if is did did aid laid is his did did laid laid`	Return carriage
2	i and t;	`if if is did did aid laid is his did did laid laid`	quickly without
	do not move	● Double-space (to leave 1 blank line space)	spacing after
3	hand forward	`tf the tf that that flat that flat the these these`	final stroke
4		`tf the tf that that flat that flat the these these`	in line
5	Curve the	`it is a fit; this is a hit; he said this is a hit;`	Feet on floor
6	fingers	`it is a fit; this is a hit; he said this is a hit;`	
7		`she said this is the jade she likes as it is less;`	Use finger
8	Hold elbow	`she said this is the jade she likes as it is less;`	action when
	in position		striking key
9	as you reach	`ll .l it .l fit .l this .l list .l fist .l lift .l`	
10	to.	`ll .l it .l fit .l this .l list .l fist .l lift .l`	

FORM LETTER FILL-INS

1 Place a letter in the typewriter. Set the left margin stop so that it is even with the left margin of the letter.

2 Type the date about 12 spaces from the top of the page in a position consistent with the style of letter you have used.

3 Turn the platen forward until you have the first mimeographed line even with the aligning scale. Turn the platen back two lines and insert the salutation.

4 When you have completed typing the salutation, turn the platen back the required four (sometimes more) lines and insert the address. The mimeographed letter now has the date, address, and salutation typed on it.

5 Turn the platen back to the date and count the number of lines from the date to the address. This is the number of lines you will allow on the remainder of the letters.

6 After filling in a letter, place it under the flap of its envelope and turn it face down; then precrease the letters by folding them all together as if they were to be inserted in one envelope. This will give each letter a preliminary crease that will make the final folding easier and quicker. Be careful to place each letter in the proper envelope. Make certain, also, that the letter is inserted in the correct manner (as illustrated on page 139).

NOTE Study your hand motions and try to eliminate all wasteful motions in folding and inserting the letters in the envelopes. You are to assume that the letters will be sealed by a machine.

Problem 2–12: Form Letter Fill-Ins

PROCEDURE For each envelope addressed as Problem 2–11, page 145, fill in the date, address, and salutation on one of the letters duplicated as Problem 2–9, page 144. After you type the fill-in, place the letter under the flap of the envelope, address side up. Glance at the letter and envelope address to check for accuracy; then turn the letter face down on the desk. (*Total words for fill-ins: 298*)

Problem 2–13: Resolution

Full sheet	Type in the form of a
1 carbon copy	leftbound manuscript
10-space ¶ indention	(2″ top margin; 1½″
Double spacing	left margin; 1″ right margin)

	Words
Type heading on two lines: RESOLUTION	2
AUTHORIZING INSURANCE ON LIFE OF | DON	10
N. HAMMOND, CHAIRMAN OF THE BOARD	16
(¶ 1) RESOLVED, That in order to compen-	23
sate this Corporation for financial losses	32
which it may suffer in the event of the	40
death of Don N. Hammond, Chairman of	47
the Board of Directors of this Corpora-	55
tion, the Secretary-Treasurer be author-	63

	Words
ized and requested to apply to the National	72
Insurance Company for a straight life	79
insurance policy upon his life, in the prin-	88
cipal sum of One Hundred and Fifty	95
Thousand Dollars ($150,000), irrevocably	103
naming this Corporation as beneficiary of	112
said policy. (¶ 2) RESOLVED FURTHER, That	119
all premiums on the said policy shall be	127
paid by this Corporation as they become	135
due and payable, and that all dividends,	144
accumulations, and other benefits and	151
rights accruing from the said policy shall	160
belong and be payable to this Corporation,	168
including the right, when so authorized	176
by resolution of the Board of Directors, to	185
surrender the said policy and receive the	194
cash surrender or other value thereof.	202

● 2 double spaces; type the following
two lines to end at the right margin.

	Words
To be presented at the May 15, 19––,	209
meeting of the Board of Directors.	216

2F ● SHIFTING FOR CAPITALS: Left Shift Key

To type a capital letter controlled by a finger of the right hand, as H, depress left shift key **28** with the *left fourth (little) finger* without moving the other fingers from typing position. Hold shift key down until the key for the capital has been *struck and released*; then release shift key and return the finger to typing position quickly.

Tryout Practice. Study the illustration; then watch your left hand to see that it does not move out of position as you type **Hal** three times: **Hal Hal Hal** Now type the following sentence.

```
Hal Hall said Kit filed the list.
```

2G ● CONTINUITY PRACTICE

PROCEDURE Operate the carriage return lever or key three times to have two blank line spaces before typing the drill given below. Type the lines as shown.

TECHNIQUE CONDITIONER: Curved Fingers
Keep each finger curved and in its home-key position except when it makes a reach-stroke; then extend the controlling finger (relaxing the curvature only as much as you must to reach to the center of the key). Do not move the hand up or down.

SPACING RULE Space twice after a period at the end of a sentence, except when the period comes at the end of the line of writing; then do not space, but return the carriage immediately and begin the new line without a pause.

● All keyboard characters taught are used in this practice.

1	Space twice	`Hal did this list.  Kit has the last list Hal did.`	Return without spacing after . at line end
2	after .	`Hal did this list.  Kit has the last list Hal did.`	
3	Space once	`Lee said that Jed is still at the lake; he is ill.`	
4	after ;	`Lee said that Jed is still at the lake; he is ill.`	
5	Shift firmly	`I said that I had failed the last test that I had.`	Use finger action—keep hands and arms quiet
6	with the little finger	`I said that I had failed the last test that I had.`	
7		`Jake said that this is the last list Hal Hale did.`	
8		`Jake said that this is the last list Hal Hale did.`	

2H ● SELF-IMPROVEMENT PRACTICE *(each line twice, as shown)*

● All letters taught are used in this practice.

1	Curve your	`Jeff likes this file desk.  He had it at the lake.`	Reach—don't leap—to i and t
2	fingers	`Jeff likes this file desk.  He had it at the lake.`	
3	Space twice	`Keith Hall is still at the lake.  He has the file.`	
4	after .	`Keith Hall is still at the lake.  He has the file.`	
5	Space quickly	`Kit said that this is the last list that Jeff did.`	
6	with the right thumb	`Kit said that this is the last list that Jeff did.`	

Problem 2–10: Index Cards

15 index cards (or paper slips cut to the proper size)
Type in a form similar to the model

PROCEDURE Number each card consecutively beginning with *215* for Mr. Allison. Type the notation *LIBRARY FUND SOLICITATION: 10/12/--* on each card.

When the cards have been typed, identify them by typing another index card and place it on the card stack. Center the following information vertically on this identifying card, using double spacing and centering each line horizontally:

```
MAILING LIST
(Your Name)
GATEWAY COLLEGE
Newark, New Jersey   07102
```

```
3d line from top edge
-½"→  Allison, Bernard C.  (Mr.)          Name arranged        215
                                          in index order

          • 3 blank line spaces                               Card
                                                              index
      Mr. Bernard C. Allison              Complete            number
      4115 Longmire Street                mailing
      Newark, New Jersey   07107          address

          • 5 blank line spaces

      LIBRARY FUND SOLICITATION:   10/12/--    Reference
                                               notation
```

Index card with mailing information

		Words
		14
1	Mr. Bernard C. Allison | 4115 Longmire Street | Newark, New Jersey 07107	41
2	Mr. Edwin I. Anderson | American Foundry Company | Aliquippa, Pennsylvania 15001	70
3	Mrs. Beulah C. Baker | P. O. Box 865 | Fond du Lac, Wisconsin 54935	96
4	Mr. Alfred E. Donaldson | 647 Ranier Avenue | Spokane, Washington 99206	124
5	Miss Elsie A. Fitzroy | 292 W. 10th Street, North | Bountiful, Utah 84010	151
6	Dr. Stephen P. Gordon | Medical Arts Building | Camden, New Jersey 07103	172
7	Miss Amelia J. Peterson | 2946 Lexington Road | Newark, New Jersey 07102	200
8	Mr. Francis P. Thompson | 567 Mannington Place | Lakehurst, New Jersey 08733	228
9	Mrs. C. Norton Uphoff | 670 N. Barton Boulevard | Newark, New Jersey 07108	256
10	Mr. Albert O. Worthington | 908 W. 27th Street | New York, New York 10023	284
11	Dr. Mary Alice Young | 906 Garden Parkway | Trenton, New Jersey 08609	310
12	Mr. Robert K. Ziegler | Box 96, R. 2 | Exeter, New Hampshire 03833	336
13	Mrs. Boris M. Zinc | 29 Las Cruces Road | Clovis, New Mexico 88101	362
14	Mr. Albert O. Zuggmeister | 619 W. Broadway Street | Newark, New Jersey 07109	390

Problem 2–11: Chain Feeding Envelopes

PROCEDURE Study the interoffice memorandum given as Problem 2–7, page 143, on the chain feeding of envelopes, and the information on the addressing of a large envelope, page 139.

For the names on the index cards typed as Problem 2–10, above, chain feed and address 14 large envelopes. Keep the cards in alphabetic order with a rubber band around them and keep the envelopes in alphabetical order for use when typing Problem 2–12, page 146. (*Total words for envelopes: 196*)

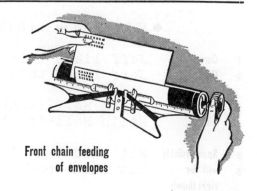

Front chain feeding of envelopes

LESSON 3 | 3A ● GET READY TO TYPE *6 minutes**

Full sheet, single spacing,
50-space line

PROCEDURE Review *Steps for Inserting Paper*, page 1, and *Getting Ready to Type*, page 6. Set the left margin stop 25 spaces to the left of the center of the paper for the beginning of a 50-space line. Move the right margin stop to the end of the scale.

A time schedule for the parts of this lesson and the following ones is given as a guide for your minimum practice. If the time schedule permits, retype selected lines from the various drills.

3B ● PREPARATORY PRACTICE *7 minutes (each line twice)*

PROCEDURE Up to this point each drill line has been shown twice in the book, just as you were asked to type it. In the copy given below, however, notice that each drill line is shown only once. Even though the copy is shown in this different manner, you are to type each line twice (as before) with a double space after the second typing of the line.

TECHNIQUE EMPHASIS Begin to type with easy, rhythmic stroking. Strike and release each key quickly. Move from one letter to the next without pausing between strokes. Space quickly between words.

● All letters and punctuation marks taught are used in this practice.

Think the letter   `tf hj ed ik is .l as ;l it he it if he as it is it`   Return carriage quickly without

Space once after ;   `Hal said Kit has the file; she has it at the lake.`   spacing after final stroke

Shift firmly   `Jeff said that Keith has laid all the tile he has.`   in line

3C ● NEW KEYS: o, r, and n *10 minutes*

O   R   N

1. REACH TECHNIQUE FOR O

As you reach the *right third finger* up to type **o**, lift the first two fingers slightly to free the movement of the controlling finger. Watch your finger type **ol** a few times.

Tryout Practice. Type the following drill twice on one line.

`ol of ol old to told told`

2. REACH TECHNIQUE FOR R

Reach the *left first finger* up to type **r** without moving the hand forward and without moving the other fingers from their typing position. Watch your finger as you type **rf** a few times.

Tryout Practice. Type the following drill twice on one line.

`rf sir rf fir rf air hair`

3. REACH TECHNIQUE FOR N

Move the *right first finger* down to type **n** without moving the other fingers from typing position and without moving the elbow in or out. Watch your finger as you type **nj** a few times.

Tryout Practice. Type the following drill twice on one line.

`nj an and an and hand and`

Problem Typing Information

STENCILING

Several hundred copies of a typed page can be made through the use of the stencil duplicating process. Follow these steps:

1 Type a model copy of the material to be stenciled. Check it for accuracy of form and typing.

2 Clean the typewriter type thoroughly.

3 Adjust the ribbon-control lever for stenciling.

4 Insert the cushion sheet between the stencil sheet and the stencil backing sheet.

5 Place the top edge of the model copy at the corner marks of the stencil to see where to type the first line of the copy.

6 Insert the stencil and type it with even stroking.

7 Correct errors by applying correction fluid as directed on the container.

8 Study the instructions on the operation of the duplicating machine you are to use. Run a few trial copies slowly to distribute the ink evenly. Look at both sides of the sheet to make certain it is free from ink smudges.

9 Clean the stencil if it is to be filed for future use.

Problem 2–8: Typing a Model Copy of a Letter for a Stencil

PROCEDURE Use a full sheet; determine the line length and the letter and punctuation style you consider appropriate. Leave space for the date, inside address, and salutation, which will be filled in later after the stencil (to be typed as Problem 2–9) has been run.

Begin the typing of the opening paragraph of the letter about 4 inches (24 line spaces) from the top of the sheet to allow for 5 or 6 blank line spaces after the date.

Center the college name and address as a letterhead, beginning on Line 8. "Spread" the name of the college, but do not "spread" the address.

	Words
GATEWAY COLLEGE	6
• Double-space	
Newark, New Jersey 07102	11

(¶ 1) Next year Gateway College will take 18
another great stride forward when the new 27
south wing of Heiner Memorial Library 34
will be officially opened to students. The 43
new wing can house 10,000 books--books 51
that are greatly needed by our students. 59
If we rely on the general library fund for 68
these books, it will take several years to 76
get them. (¶ 2) We hope to raise the money 84
needed to buy the 10,000 books by the 92
time the library opens. This hope is backed 101

by confidence that you and other loyal 108
alumni will help to make our dream come 116
true. (¶ 3) The average cost of a book 123
on the shelves of the library ready for 131
student use is about $10. This includes 139
the price of the book and its cataloging. 148
If each alumnus will contribute just two 156
books, our immediate needs will be met. 164
Your loyal support in the past indicates 172
that you will help us to acquire the books 181
our library needs now. A pledge card is 189
enclosed. I hope you will sign and return 198
it to me soon. (¶ 4) The student body 204
and the faculty join me in thanking you 212
for your loyal support, now and always. 221
sincerely yours lincoln r andrews presi- 229
dent enclosure 233

Problem 2–9: Typing a Stencil from a Model Copy

PROCEDURE Check the model copy for accuracy in form. Make needed adjustments, if any are needed. Then study Steps 2–7, above, and type a stencil from the model copy typed as Problem 2–8.

Study Step 8, above, and run 15 acceptable copies to be used for Problem 2–12, page 146. President Andrews has given you permission to sign his name with a signature stylus. Do this before running the stencil.

3D ● STROKING TECHNIQUE PRACTICE *12 minutes*

TECHNIQUE EMPHASIS: Shifting for Capitals
Reach with the little finger of the left hand to the shift key without moving the elbow in or out or without changing the arm position.

Depress the shift key and hold it down until the capital letter has been typed and the key released. Shorten the time taken for typing capitals by using quick, smooth movements.

PROCEDURE Type each line twice; double-space after the second typing of the line.

● All letters and punctuation marks taught are used in this practice.

1	Strike and release the	`ol old fold so sold to told do dot do dote so sole`	Return carriage quickly without
2	keys quickly	`rf rid fir rf rife ride rise hard lard frill drill`	spacing after the final letter
3		`nj an and hand ail jail hail end lend send an lane`	
	Space once		
4	after ;	`Jane Kane has done this drill; it is a fine drill.`	Return and start new line quickly
5		`Ned said I had to lend a hand to Jen and Len Kean.`	

3E ● CONTINUITY PRACTICE *10 minutes*

TECHNIQUE EMPHASIS: Spacing Hold the right thumb close to the space bar. Strike the bar in the center with a quick down-and-in motion of the right

thumb; release the bar instantly. Make spacing a quick, short stroke in rhythm with your stroking of the keys.

PROCEDURE Type each line twice; double-space after the second typing of the line.

1	Space twice after .	`Ken and Hal had a fine ride.  Joe took a ride too.`	Return without looking up
2		`Ned said he thinks Jean has sold her land to Jake.`	
3		`Karl and Neal had to stand drill in the hard rain.`	Return without spacing
	Keep carriage		
4	moving steadily	`Kit thinks that Joe or Lon has the file she needs.`	

● *Self-Improvement Practice*
is provided for those who have extra
time for typing or who need additional
practice before going to the next lesson

eyes on copy
elbows close to body, forearms parallel to keyboard
fingers curved
book at right of machine elevated for easy reading
wrists down
table free of unneeded books
sit back in chair; body erect
feet flat on floor, one slightly in advance of the other

3F ● SELF-IMPROVEMENT PRACTICE *(each line twice)*

1	Curve the fingers	`Joe rode the horse.  Len sold the horse for a lot.`	Return quickly
2	Space quickly	`Karl is a fine friend and has done a lot for Hank.`	Type with finger action
3	Shift firmly	`Hank thinks he has to learn to do this drill soon.`	

Problem Typing Information

INTEROFFICE CORRESPONDENCE

An interoffice letterhead form is used for correspondence between offices or departments of a company. Printed headings on the form enable the typist to set up information quickly. If an interoffice form is not available, type the direction headings (*TO:*, *FROM:*, etc.) in positions similar to those illustrated in Problem 2–7 below.

Omissions in Interoffice Correspondence. Personal titles (*Mr.*, *Mrs.*, *Dr.*, *Miss*, etc.), the salutation, the complimentary close, and the signature are usually omitted.

Writing Line; Spacing. The length of writing line to be used will depend on the length of the message to be typed, but generally a 6-inch line is used. Short messages may be double-spaced; longer ones are single-spaced with a double space between paragraphs. Triple-space between last line of heading and first line of the body of the message.

Reference Initials; Notations. Include reference initials, and type them a double space below the last line of the message at the left margin. All other notations (enclosure, carbon copy, etc.) are typed in the same position they occupy in regular correspondence.

Envelopes for Interoffice Correspondence. Envelopes of a special color may be used for interoffice correspondence. When such envelopes are not used, type the words *COMPANY MAIL* in the space normally used for the postage stamp.

Use a personal title with the name when addressing the envelope. Type the address on two lines, unless the envelope is to go to a company office in some other city, in which case the complete address must be typed. Note the way to type an envelope used for interoffice correspondence.

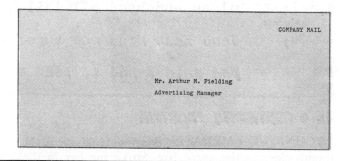

Problem 2–7: Interoffice Memorandum on Chain Feeding Envelopes

PROCEDURE Type from the model. If an interoffice form is not available, use plain paper and type headings for the special sections as shown in the illustration.

Interoffice memorandum form • 6-inch writing line

Interoffice Correspondence

Georgia Steel Products, Inc.

7154 SOUTHERN HIGHWAY ATLANTA, GEORGIA 30319

	Words
TO: Beginning Office Typists	5
FROM: Rose A. McRay, Office Manager	11
DATE: June 15, 19--	14
SUBJECT: Chain Feeding Envelopes	19

● Triple-space

Stack the envelopes <u>face down</u>, flap up and toward you, on the — 33
left side of the typewriter, for FRONT chain feeding. — 44

Insert and address the first envelope; then roll it back — 55
(toward you) until about a half inch shows above the alignment — 68
scale. Insert the next envelope from the front, placing it — 80
between the first envelope and the cylinder. Turn the cylin- — 92
der back (toward you) to position the second envelope to be — 104
addressed. (The first envelope will stack against the paper — 116
table, as will the next envelopes addressed.) After eight or — 129
more envelopes are addressed, remove them with the right hand — 141
and place them <u>face down</u> on the right of the desk. — 153

lns — 154

- Printed headings
- Personal titles omitted
- Salutation omitted
- 6-inch writing line
- Single-space long messages
- Complimentary close and signature omitted

Full sheet, single spacing,
50-space line

PROCEDURE Follow the steps in Get Ready to Type, page 6. With the paper centered and the left margin stop set 25 spaces to the left of the center of the paper, you will have the correct machine adjustments for the beginning of the 50-space line.

* Beginning with this lesson and for all following lessons, getting ready to type will be timed as a part of the Preparatory Practice and will not be given a special identification.

TECHNIQUE EMPHASIS Type with easy, rhythmic stroking. Move from letter to letter without pausing between strokes. Operate the space bar with a short, quick down-and-in thumb stroke in rhythm with the typing.

● All reach-strokes taught are used in the first line of the practice.

Space once after ; and twice after .

Jean has the drill; she thinks it is fine for Ken.

Return without spacing after . at end of line

Keith is fine. Len is fair. Joe has a lot to do.

Keep on!

Ned has done one line of the drill for his friend.

Space quickly

4B ● **NEW KEYS: w, u, and c** *10 minutes*

W

U

C

1. REACH TECHNIQUE FOR W

As you move the *left third finger* up to type **w**, lift the first two fingers slightly to free the movement of the controlling finger. Watch your finger type **ws** a few times.

Tryout Practice. Type the following drill twice on one line.

ws wit ws with show shows

2. REACH TECHNIQUE FOR U

Reach the right first finger up to type **u** without moving the other fingers from typing position. Type **u** and pull the finger quickly to home position. Watch your finger type **uj** a few times.

Tryout Practice. Type the following drill twice on one line.

uj us just hush shun shut

3. REACH TECHNIQUE FOR C

As you reach the *left second finger* down to type **c**, lift the first finger slightly and make a direct reach without twisting the elbow in or out. Watch your finger type **cd** a few times.

Tryout Practice. Type the following drill twice on one line.

cd can clad cod code coal

Problem Typing Information

PREPARING TELEGRAMS

Services Available. Two services are used: (1) *domestic* (for a message communicated within the continental United States) and (2) *international* (for an overseas message).

Classes of Domestic Service. Classes of domestic service available are: (1) the *fast telegram* (taking precedence over all other classes), (2) the *night letter* (an overnight service and the least expensive), and (3) the *day letter* (subordinated in transmission time to the fast telegram and used at any time of the day or night). Indicate the service desired by typing "X" in the appropriate box at the top of the form.

Method of Sending. Show the method of sending the message—*paid, collect, or charged*—in the appropriate headings provided on the blank. If the message is to be charged, type the name of the account in the space headed "Charge to the Account of."

Sender's Address; Date. Type the sender's city, state, and ZIP code with the date on the same line a double space below the last line of the printed heading.

Addressee's Name and Address. Double-space from the date to type the addressee's name and address in block and single-spaced form; include all information that will facilitate delivery of the telegram. The title *Mr.* before the addressee's name will not be transmitted, but *Miss* and *Mrs.* will be transmitted and should be used. Western Union does not charge for the necessary address and signature.

Body of the Message. Begin the message a double space below the address. A telegram is preferably double-spaced, but use single spacing for long messages. Use long lines for long messages; short lines for short messages. The message may be typed in all-capital letters; use punctuation marks as there is no charge for them.

Sender's Name; Address. Type the sender's name a double space below the message. If the sender's address is to be transmitted, it will be charged for; type it with the sender's telephone number on the line directly below his name. If this information is not to be transmitted, type it at the left margin a double space below the reference initials.

Carbon Copies. Usually a minimum of three copies are prepared—the *original copy* (for transmittal), the *file copy*, and the *billing* or *accounting copy*. Sometimes a fourth copy, the *confirmation copy*, is prepared and mailed to the addressee with a covering letter to make certain that the message was transmitted correctly.

Problem 2–6: Telegram (*errors corrected*)

1 telegram form (or half sheet)
1 carbon copy on a half sheet

● Type from the model

NOTE To type the account charged, set a tabulator stop 2 spaces inside the appropriate box; use this same stop to begin the sender's address and date; then, use it again to begin the sender's name and title.

4C ● STROKING TECHNIQUE PRACTICE *12 minutes*

PROCEDURE Type each line twice with a double space after the second typing of the line.

1	Curve your fingers	ws wit with sow sown show shown law laws who whose	Return carriage without looking up
2	Strike and release keys quickly	us use sue due hue us just rust dust just hue hunt	
3		cd cod code coal code dock check checked cite sick	Keep feet on floor
4	Space twice after .	Jack works well. He can work with us for an hour.	
5	Shift firmly	I know June wants to show the house to us at four.	Return without spacing

4D ● SHIFTING FOR CAPITALS: Right Shift Key *5 minutes*

To type a capital controlled by a finger of the left hand, as A, depress the right shift key **28** with the right *fourth (little) finger*. Hold the shift key down until the key for the capital has been *struck and released*; then release the shift key and return the finger to typing position without pausing in the typing.

Tryout Practice. Study the illustration. Watch your right hand to see that it does not move out of position as you type **Alf** three times: **Alf Alf Alf**

Now type the following line.

Alf can work well with Sue. Cal cashed our check.

4E ● CONTINUITY PRACTICE *10 minutes*

TECHNIQUE EMPHASIS: Shifting for Capitals
Reach with the little finger to the *shift key* without moving the elbow or changing the arm position. Depress the shift key and hold it down until the capital has been typed and the key released. Reduce the time taken for typing capitals by going from one movement to the next quickly and smoothly.

PROCEDURE Type each line twice with a double space after the second typing of the line.

1	Use a sharp, quick stroke	Ruth said it is true that she will work with Dick.	Hold wrists low
2		Charles and Claire would like to sell their house.	
3	Shift firmly	Sue Wicke liked the show as well as Ruth liked it.	Hands quiet— don't be a "Leaping Lena"
4		Carl Duff will ride with us in the hunt if he can.	

4F ● SELF-IMPROVEMENT PRACTICE *(each line twice; double-space between pairs)*

● All letters taught are used in this practice.

Relax—but don't slouch	Dick said Cliff was hurt when he rode in the hunt.	Hold shift key down firmly
	It is just as well that we cashed our four checks.	
	We want to do all our work just as well as we can.	

Problem 2–5: Personal Two-Page Letter *(errors corrected)*

| 2 full sheets
1 carbon sheet
2 file copy sheets | • | 65-space line
Block style
Open punctuation | • | Address a large envelope
5 blank line spaces after current date
Block form of second-page heading | • | Refer to page 138 for
discussion on "TYPING
LETTERS OF TWO OR MORE PAGES" |

NOTE The bottom margins in letters of two or more pages should approximate the width in the left margin. Bottom margins may be narrower, however, to avoid carrying a single line or two to the following page.

Words

Return address: 257 sunset drive seattle, washington 98106 *Date | Address:*   12
miss dorothy l norris school for secretaries 1825 w lincolnway street cheyenne,   28
wyoming 82001 dear miss norris (¶ 1) The very limited time for discussion   42
that followed my talk at the conference last week did not permit me to answer   58
the question you asked about the curriculum in sufficient detail to make my   73
position clear. Perhaps the following comments will more adequately do so.   88
(¶ 2) The business education curriculum of many schools is broad enough, demand-   103
ing enough, and interest-compelling enough to challenge even the best students.   119
These schools have been notably successful in developing the skills needed for   135
initial office jobs. Many of them, however, have often overlooked the big   150
cavities in the education of their graduates—the humanities and the sciences.   166
(¶ 3) I believe in the worth of what we teach and in the worth of those we   180
teach, but I see the humanities and the sciences as necessary and desirable   195
partners in education if our graduates are to have their skilled hands guided   211
by reflective heads. It seems to me to be a waste of time to argue about the   226
relative merits of "learning to earn a living" and "learning to live a life."   242
The two are inseparable. It is also a waste of time to argue about the "areas   258
of the disciplines." All areas of education can accurately be considered   273
areas of discipline. (¶ 4) The worth of a subject is in the experience it pro-   287
vides for leading from immaturity toward maturity. The end product of educa-   303
tion must not be an immature mind housed in a mature body, for this can be   318
disastrous because of the opportunities to put the immaturities into effect.   333
(¶ 5) The task of leading from immaturity toward maturity is big enough, impor-   348
tant enough, and difficult enough to challenge all teachers. When we share   363
the task with those in other areas of learning, we halve the difficulties and   379
enrich the experience for our students and ourselves. It was this concept of   394
shared responsibility that I tried to emphasize in my talk, a concept that does   410

Determine
when to
begin the
next page ➤ not accept sole responsibility for the whole education of our students but   425
insists that we are but partners with teachers in all other areas of education—   441
partners in education, which we truly are. sincerely yours edward hill warder   457/489

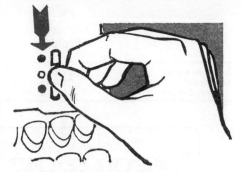

LESSON 5 | 5A ● PREPARATORY PRACTICE *8 minutes*

KNOW YOUR TYPEWRITER

The ribbon-control lever **22** can be set to type on the upper, middle, or lower part of the ribbon if there are four adjustments on your typewriter for this control. If there are just three adjustments, the typing will be on the upper or lower part of the ribbon. Set the *ribbon-control lever to type on the upper part of the ribbon.* Make this a part of your daily Get Ready to Type.

Full sheet, single spacing,
50-space line

PROCEDURE Type each line twice.
Double-space after the second typing of the line.

● All letters taught are used in the first line of this practice.

Type smoothly	Frank said Jack will work with us for three hours.
Drill on w	We do not need luck to win if we will work to win.
Type quickly	The cut of this suit is just fine for Ruth or Sue.

No need to look up as you return the carriage

5B ● STROKING TECHNIQUE REVIEW *10 minutes*

TECHNIQUE CONDITIONER

Hand Alignment with the Keyboard Hold the elbow steady and the hand as quiet as possible as you make the reach-stroke. As you make the down reach to **c** or the up reach to **o**, for example, let the finger make a short, low, direct movement to the key without twisting the hand or the elbow. Make direct finger reach-strokes with as little hand motion as possible.

● All letters taught are used in these lines.

1   fd jk ds kl sa l; rf ol tf ik cd uj ed hj ws nj cd

2   it wit with with so sow sown sown do down cur curl

3   Jeff is ill and will not write the check just now.

4   Frank will use just such a drill as Lew Howe used.

5   This is the work Sue likes to do and does so well.

● Sit erect
● Curve the fingers
● Space quickly
● Strike the keys with quick, sharp strokes and release them quickly
● Return carriage smoothly

5C ● TYPING FROM DICTATION *7 minutes*

PROCEDURE Follow these steps to effective dictation typing:

1 Type each line once from dictation with the book open so you can readily understand the words as they are dictated. *Think the word.*

2 Type each line twice from dictation with the book closed or with the page covered so that you will get the impulse to type from the dictation and not from the printed page. Listen to the *word* and type the *word.*

Think the word

us to us he or he or to is it is it do it is to us

he he the the or for or for or for he the the then

if it with with or work or work he will drill well

Release the key quickly

Problem 2–4: Letter with Special Parts *(errors corrected)*

2 carbon copies Letterhead (or full sheet)	•	2 carbon sheets 2 file copy sheets 50-space line	•	Modified block, blocked ¶s Mixed punctuation	•	5 blank line spaces after the date Address a large envelope See pages 137-138 for letter-parts discussion

Bangor National Bank
1376 UNION STREET   BANGOR, MAINE 04408

	Words
November 20, 19--	4
Maine Paper Company	8
3896 Eaton Boulevard	12
Bangor, Maine 04405	16

• Attention line   Attention Mr. R. N. Briggs, Manager   23

Gentlemen: 26

• Subject line   SUBJECT: Certifying Trade Name   32

Your trade name "Verastrong" is sometimes used on   42
checks made payable to you and presented at this   52
bank for payment. For us to accept your endorse-   62
ment on these checks, it will be necessary for you   72
to complete an affidavit of ownership, as provided   82
for on the enclosed card.   87

You can protect yourself by filing a certificate of   98
fictitious firm name. To do this, use the enclosed   108
form.   110

Please give this matter your prompt attention so we   120
can give you the kind of service we try to give all   130
our good customers.   135

                    Sincerely yours,   138

• Company name in closing lines   BANGOR NATIONAL BANK   142

Earle M. Craighead

• Dictator's name and title   Earle M. Craighead   146
                    Vice-President   149

• Reference initials   dif   150

• Enclosure notation   Enclosures 2   152

• Carbon copy notation   cc Mr. Paulson, Cashier   157/176

5D ● SENTENCE GUIDED WRITING *20 minutes*

PROCEDURE

1 Type each sentence three times with goals as stated below:

a First, type at an easy pace and with even, continuous stroking.

b Second, type with faster finger motions and improved space-bar action; return the carriage quickly.

c Third, speed up the stroking. Keep on typing—avoid pausing between strokes, between words, and between lines.

2 Type each sentence for a half minute, trying to type to the end of the sentence just as time is called. Pace your typing to hit your goal "right on the nose" as time is called. The goals are indicated as *gwam* (gross words a minute) in the second column at the right.

3 Type each sentence for 1 minute without the call of the line ending. Type the sentence as many times as you can during the minute.

Summary of Techniques and Conditioners Curve the fingers and hold them lightly in home-key position. *Reach* with the fingers. Hold the hands and arms quiet (almost motionless). Return the carriage without looking up from the copy; begin the next line without pausing. *Reach* the little finger to the shift key and hold it down until the capital letter has been struck and released. Strike the space bar with a quick down-and-in-motion. Work for easy, rhythmic stroking.

● All reach-strokes taught are used in these sentences.

				Words in Line *	GWAM 30" Guide
1	Curve the fingers	Dick can aid us with the work.	Return carriage quickly without looking up.	6	12
2	Sit erect	Hold the wrists low for this drill.	Do not space at end of the line.	7	14
3	Shift firmly	He who knows he can do well can do well.		8	16
4	Space quickly	Jack or Joe will show us how to do this work.		9	18
5	Keep on typing	He knows how to do what he is to do; then does it.		10	20

. . . . 1 . . . . 2 . . . . 3 . . . . 4 . . . . 5 . . . . 6 . . . . 7 . . . . 8 . . . . 9 10

＊HOW TYPEWRITTEN WORDS ARE COUNTED

Five strokes are counted as one standard typewritten word. The figures in the first column at the right of the copy show the number of 5-stroke words in each of the lines. The scale beneath the copy shows the word-by-word count (5 strokes at a time) for each of the lines.

TO DETERMINE TOTAL WORDS TYPED

(1) List the figure at the end of each complete line typed during a writing. (2) Note in the scale the figure directly below the point at which you stopped typing. (3) Add these figures to determine the total gross words typed. (Gross words are the same as *gwam* for a 1-minute writing.)

5E ● SELF-IMPROVEMENT PRACTICE *(each line three times)*

1   The drill we do counts for less than how we do it.

2   Ken or Jack can do the work just as well as I can.

3   I should not check the word I write as I write it.

4   It will take us an hour or so to do all the lines.

. . . . 1 . . . . 2 . . . . 3 . . . . 4 . . . . 5 . . . . 6 . . . . 7 . . . . 8 . . . . 9 10

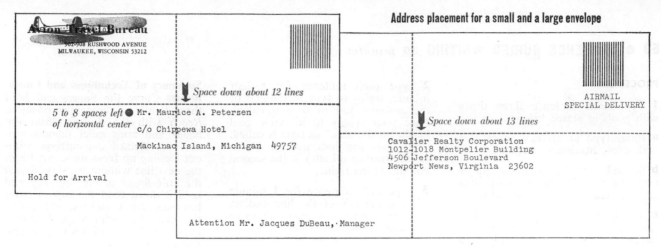

Address placement for a small and a large envelope

Avion Travel Bureau
902-908 RUSHWOOD AVENUE
MILWAUKEE, WISCONSIN 53212

Space down about 12 lines

5 to 8 spaces left ● Mr. Maurice A. Petersen
of horizontal center
c/o Chippewa Hotel

Mackinac Island, Michigan 49757

Hold for Arrival

Attention Mr. Jacques DuBeau, Manager

AIRMAIL
SPECIAL DELIVERY

Space down about 13 lines

Cavalier Realty Corporation
1012-1018 Montpelier Building
4506 Jefferson Boulevard
Newport News, Virginia 23602

ADDRESSING ENVELOPES BY "EYE MEASUREMENT"

Information on envelopes should be typed *approximately* in the positions illustrated above. Note the address position and the placement of special notations. Learn to use "eye measurement" so that you can twirl envelopes into the typewriter and type them without hesitation.

Small Envelope Use a small envelope (*No. 6¾—3⅝ by 6½* inches) for one-page letters without enclosures.

Large Envelope A large envelope (*No. 10—4⅛ by 9½* inches) is used for a letter of more than one page and for letters with enclosures.

Folding Procedures Procedures for folding and inserting letters into envelopes are shown below. A letter should be placed inside the envelope so that the addressee can easily withdraw it and open it for reading.

GUIDES FOR ADDRESSING ENVELOPES

1 *Spacing.* Double-space a three-line envelope address. Single-space an address of four or more lines.

2 *Style.* Most envelope addresses are typed in the block style without end-of-line punctuation, except for the period when an abbreviation is used. Spell out state names.

3 *Notations.* Postal directions (such as AIRMAIL, SPECIAL DELIVERY, etc.) are typed in capitals immediately below the space required for the stamp. Addressee instructions (*Hold for Arrival, Please Forward, Personal*, etc.) are typed in the lower left corner of the envelope; capitalize the first letter of each principal word.

4 *Personal Titles.* Always use an appropriate personal title on a letter, envelope, or card addressed to an individual. When a woman's marital status is not known, use *Miss* as the personal title. (*Ms.* may also be used.)

FOLDING A LETTER FOR A SMALL ENVELOPE

Step 1 With the letter face up on the desk, fold from the bottom up to ½ inch of the top.

Step 2 Fold right third to left.

Step 3 Folding from left to right, fold left third to ½″ of last crease.

Step 4 Insert last creased edge first.

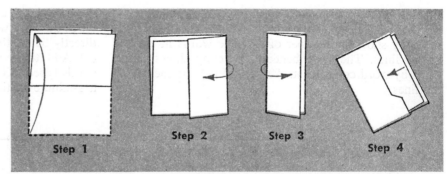

Step 1 Step 2 Step 3 Step 4

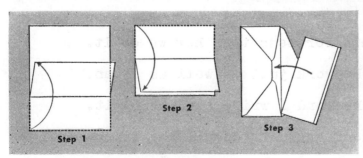

Step 1 Step 2 Step 3

FOLDING A LETTER FOR A LARGE ENVELOPE

Step 1 With the letter face up on the desk, fold slightly less than one third of the letterhead up toward the top.

Step 2 Fold down the top of the letterhead to within ½″ of the bottom fold.

Step 3 Insert the letter into the envelope with the last crease toward the bottom of the envelope and with the last fold up.

LESSON 6 | 6A ● PREPARATORY PRACTICE *8 minutes*
(each line twice)

eyes on copy
fingers curved
book at right of machine elevated for easy reading
elbows close to body, forearms parallel to keyboard
table free of unneeded books
wrists down
sit back in chair; body erect
feet flat on floor, one slightly in advance of the other

Full sheet, single spacing,
50-space line

PROCEDURE

1 As you type each sentence the first time, pace yourself at a rate slow enough for you to type without breaks or pauses but fast enough to keep the carriage moving steadily.

2 As you type each sentence the second time, speed up the stroking slightly and pass from one word to the next smoothly and quickly. Use a quick down-and-in space-bar motion with the right thumb.

● All letters taught are used in the first line of this practice.

Jack checked the work for us when it was all done.

Double letters   Nell will soon tell all of us how to do the drill.

Cliff has less faith in his luck than in his work.
. . . . 1 . . . . 2 . . . . 3 . . . . 4 . . . . 5 . . . . 6 . . . . 7 . . . . 8 . . . . 9 10

6B ● NEW KEYS: p, g, and m *8 minutes*

P   G   M

1. REACH TECHNIQUE FOR LETTER P

Straighten *right fourth finger* slightly and move it up to type the letter **p**. Hold the elbow and the other fingers in position. Watch your finger type **p**; a few times.

Tryout Practice. Type the following drill twice on one line.

p; cup lap p; put nap cup

2. REACH TECHNIQUE FOR G

Relax the curvature of *left first finger* and move the finger to the right to type **g** without moving the other fingers from typing position. Watch your finger type **gf** a few times.

Tryout Practice. Type the following drill twice on one line.

gf gun gf got dug rug tug

3. REACH TECHNIQUE FOR M

As you move the *right first finger* down to type **m**, hold the elbow in its position and the hand in alignment with the keyboard. Watch your finger as it types **mj** a few times.

Tryout Practice. Type the following drill twice on one line.

mj mat mj man sum jam hum

Problem Typing Information

COMPANY NAME IN THE CLOSING LINES

When the company name is included in the closing lines, it is usually typed in all capitals a double space below the complimentary close. The dictator's name and title are typed 3 blank line spaces below the company name. The name and title may be typed on the same line or on two lines, whichever will give the best balanced lines.

> **NOTE** When a long company name appears in the closing lines, begin the closing lines 5 or more spaces to the left of the center point.

Sincerely yours,

BANGOR NATIONAL BANK   ←   Company name in closing lines

• 3 blank line spaces

Earle M. Craighead   ←   Dictator's name and
Vice-President   title on two lines

REFERENCE INITIALS

As a rule, reference initials consist of the dictator's initials followed by the typist's initials or, infrequently, a number. When the dictator's name is typed as a part of the closing lines, it is not necessary to show his initials in the reference line, although it is not incorrect to do so. Some dictators prefer to have their name typed in the reference-initials line instead of under the complimentary close. Note some examples of the reference line:

rhv	DFH/tn	TWL/2
MJB:ej	KOS:CO	RENorman/sl

ENCLOSURE NOTATION

When other papers are enclosed with a letter, this fact is noted by typing an enclosure notation a double space below the reference initials and even with the left margin. Several common forms are:

Enclosure	Enc.	Enclosure:	Contract
Enclosures 2	Encs. 2	Enclosures:	Check Lease

CARBON COPY NOTATION

In some cases, additional carbon copies of letters are made and sent to interested persons. Use the carbon copy notation to indicate to whom copies are to be sent. Type the notation a double space below the reference-initials line or the last typed line at the left margin.

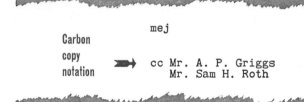

Carbon copy notation   ➡   mej

cc Mr. A. P. Griggs
   Mr. Sam H. Roth

POSTSCRIPT

Type the postscript a double space below the reference-initials line or the last typed line. The postscript need not be preceded by the letters *P. S.*; it is indented or blocked to agree with the style used in other paragraphs of the letter.

lnc

If I have not heard from the FSA by this Friday, Mr. Stein will fly to Petersburg to consult with you.

TYPING LETTERS OF TWO OR MORE PAGES

Use plain paper for the second and subsequent pages of letters. Begin the heading about an inch from the top edge of the sheet. Type the heading at the left margin in *block form* or in the *horizontal form* (one-line arrangement). The block form is preferred for its easy placement; if a page might be crowded, however, use the horizontal form.

Leave 3 blank lines between the heading and the first line of the resumed letter; use the same margins as for the preceding page.

> **NOTE** Do not resume the body of a letter with the last part of a divided word. Include at least two lines of a paragraph on the preceding page and on the succeeding page.

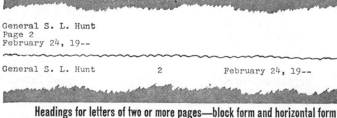

General S. L. Hunt
Page 2
February 24, 19--

General S. L. Hunt   2   February 24, 19--

Headings for letters of two or more pages—block form and horizontal form

6C ● STROKING TECHNIQUE PRACTICE *12 minutes (each line three times)*

● All letters taught are used in this practice.

1	Hold the elbows in position	p; up cup p; cap tap lap pen pan rip trip rap trap	Return carriage quickly
2		gf dug rug tug fog cog dog rig fig dig keg log fog	
3	Shift firmly	mj am jam ham ram sum rum mj me men mend make roam	
4		Pam must make much more each month than Gus makes.	Don't twist the elbow outward
5		Top men such as George and Tom Crump will help us.	

6D ● TYPING FROM DICTATION *7 minutes*

PROCEDURE Type each line once from dictation with the book open; then type each line two or three times from dictation with the book closed or with the page covered. Listen to the *word*, then type the *word*.

	to in to we of as go up to up go up as of we to in	Release the key quickly
Think the word	the for man put men put men get and top firm hands	
	with mind plan plan firm must make work plan place	

6E ● CONTINUITY PRACTICE *10 minutes (each line three times)*

PROCEDURE As you type each sentence the first time, note the awkward or difficult letter combinations. In later writings try to smooth out the typing pace so you can type these difficult combinations with continuity. A word such as *get* may need to be typed more slowly than other words because it is typed with one hand. Speed up the stroking of balanced-hand words such as *to*, *of*, *go*, and *the*.

1	Type evenly	Gus will make a good place in the firm for George.	Return carriage quickly
2		A man must plan his work and put the plan to work.	
3	Space quickly	We must train the mind just as we train the hands.	Type with the fingers—hold the arms still
4		Men with lots of get up and go can get to the top.	

. . . . 1 . . . . 2 . . . . 3 . . . . 4 . . . . 5 . . . . 6 . . . . 7 . . . . 8 . . . . 9 10

6F ● SELF-IMPROVEMENT PRACTICE *(each line three times)*

1	Hold shift key down firmly	Gene will go with Paul to get the lamp Maud wants.	Return carriage without spacing after last stroke in the line
2		Paul and Mark made good time on the trip to Maine.	
3	Release key quickly	George will go to France with Tom and Pam in June.	
4		It is just their good luck to win this first game.	

. . . . 1 . . . . 2 . . . . 3 . . . . 4 . . . . 5 . . . . 6 . . . . 7 . . . . 8 . . . . 9 10

Problem Typing Information

MAILING NOTATION IN A LETTER

If a special mailing notation is used in a letter, type it at the left margin midway between the date and the first line of the inside address. (A mailing notation may also be typed a double space below the date at the right margin.) If the notation is to be typed on the carbon copy only, insert a piece of heavy paper between the ribbon and the original (first) sheet. The paper should be thick enough to prevent the imprint of the type from showing on the original sheet.

TITLES IN THE ADDRESS

Use a personal title (*Mr., Mrs., Miss,* etc.) in the address when the letter is to an individual. An official title (indicating the position held) may be typed (1) on the line with the name, (2) on the line with the company name, or (3) on a separate line. Capitalize the title. Use the style that will give the best balanced lines.

ATTENTION LINE IN A LETTER

While the attention line is still used, there is a growing preference for addressing the letter to an individual or department rather than to the company. When the attention line is used, type it a double space below the inside address and a double space above the salutation. Since it is part of the address, the recommended placement is at the left margin. The attention line may also be centered.

SUBJECT LINE IN A LETTER

A *subject line,* when used, is typed a double space below the salutation. In the block style or AMS Simplified letter style (formerly the NOMA Simplified letter style), the subject line is typed even with the left margin. In other styles it may be typed (1) even with the left margin, (2) at paragraph point, or (3) centered.

The word *Subject* in the subject line is followed by a colon and may be typed (1) in all capitals, (2) with only the first letter capitalized, or (3) omitted (as in the AMS Simplified letter style).

REPLY REFERENCE NOTATION

Some writers ask that a reply to a letter mention a file or case number. If the letterhead indicates a printed position for this information (usually at the top of the letterhead), supply it. If not, type the reply reference notation as you would type a subject line. The word *Reference* or *Re:* may be typed before the notation.

February 23, 19--

Mailing notation   REGISTERED MAIL

Title on line with name

Mr. E. P. Carter, Manager
McKean Real Estate Company
1497 North 24th Street
Omaha, Nebraska 68112

Title on line with company name

Mr. Arnold P. Robertson
Manager, Ohio Tractors, Inc.
2200 S. Metcalf Street
Lima, Ohio 45801

Title on separate line

Miss Anne K. Taylor
Dean of Women
North Idaho Junior College
Coeur d' Alene, Idaho 83814

Left-margin placement of attention and subject lines

Maine Paper Company
3896 Eaton Boulevard
Bangor, Maine 04405

Attention Mr. R. N. Briggs, Manager

Gentlemen:

SUBJECT: Certifying Trade Name

Centered attention line

Feldt Aircraft, Inc.
562 Meadow Road
Portsmouth, Ohio 45662

        Attention Mr. V. L. Weyman, Chief Technician

Gentlemen:

    Your letter about research in adhesives has been referred to me for reply.

Centered subject line

Dear General Hunt

        SUBJECT: Bold Journey Project

    As you know, our men have been working day and night to find an answer to the adhesives problem that has been delaying

Dear Sir

        Reference: Your File #31-082

    The Federal Space Administration has granted us a 10-day extension on our contract for the Bold Journey Project. We now believe we shall be able to satisfy the contract, and assignment to you will not be necessary.

LESSON 7 | 7A ● PREPARATORY PRACTICE *8 minutes (each line three times)*

Full sheet, single spacing, 50-space line	PROCEDURE (for Lessons 7, 8, and 9)

SENTENCE 1 Type with even pacing and rhythmic stroking.

SENTENCE 3 Type a bit faster than you typed the first two sentences.

SENTENCE 2 Type with continuity, trying for improved shift-key control.

Put your improved technique to work in order to increase your speed.

● All letters taught are used in the first line of this practice.

Shift firmly

Jane said Mark would find the right place for Pam.

Return carriage quickly and smoothly

Space quickly

I can make a flight to France and Greece in March.

Quick, sharp stroking

We must hold the arms still to do this work right.

`. . . .1. . . . 2. . . . 3. . . . 4. . . . 5. . . . 6. . . . 7. . . . 8. . . . 9. . . .10`

7B ● NEW KEYS: q, y, and x *8 minutes*

Q

Y

X

1. REACH TECHNIQUE FOR Q

Reach the *left fourth finger* up to type **q** without arching the wrist or moving the other fingers from their keys. Watch your finger move up to type **q** and down to type **a** a few times.

Tryout Practice. Type the following drill twice on one line.

qa quit quack quick quote

2. REACH TECHNIQUE FOR Y

Straighten the *right first finger* slightly and move it up to type **y** without arching the wrist or moving the other fingers from their typing position. Watch your finger type **yj** a few times.

Tryout Practice. Type the following drill twice on one line.

yj yes jay yj lay day may

3. REACH TECHNIQUE FOR X

As you reach the *left third finger* down to type **x**, extend the finger for the reach-stroke without moving the hand forward. Watch your finger type **xs** a few times.

Tryout Practice. Type the following drill twice on one line.

xs lax six sx fix fox mix

BACKSPACING If you need to fill in an omitted letter or to position the carriage, depress the backspace key **30.** Find the key on the keyboard.

Nonelectric Backspacing Straighten the finger and reach directly to the key

with minimum hand motion. Learn to use the exact force needed to depress the key to backspace.

Electric Backspacing Reach with the finger and lightly depress the key. You can do this without moving the

hand from its typing position. Use a light, quick stroke and a quick release of the key to avoid a double backspace. An easy, quick, and controlled flick of the finger is all you need to backspace the electric way.

Problem 2–1: Letter on Half-Size Paper (5½″ x 8½″)
(*errors corrected*)

Half sheet	5-space ¶ indention
4-inch line (40 pica or 48 elite spaces)	● 4 blank line spaces after the date
Modified block, indented ¶s, mixed punctuation	Address an envelope

PROCEDURE Type the letter from the illustration at the right. Set a tabulator stop for the paragraph indentions and a second tabulator stop at the center point of the sheet. Tabulate to this second stop to type the return address, date, and closing lines.

Indent the quoted paragraph 5 spaces from the left and right margins. After you address the envelope, fold and insert the letter into it.

Letter typed on a half-size sheet

	Words
1027 Markham Drive	4
Akron, Ohio 44308	8
November 12, 19--	11
Science Research Associates, Inc.	18
1256 Michigan Boulevard	23
Chicago, Illinois 60607	28
Gentlemen:	30
For my term paper on "Beginning Positions for Office Workers," I am quoting Humphreys and Traxler as follows:	37 / 45 / 52
Because so much depends on impressions made by the job seeker in his interview, the guidance worker may well arrange for groups of students to learn job-finding techniques.	57 / 63 / 69 / 76 / 82 / 87
If you have other books or pamphlets on job-finding techniques for beginning office workers, please send me a price list.	95 / 103 / 110 / 112
Sincerely yours,	115
Loretta M. King	
Miss Loretta M. King	119/147

Problem 2–2: Lengthening a Letter

PROCEDURE Use Problem 1 directions. After typing the complimentary close, look at the letter to see if its placement seems too high on the sheet; if so, leave 4 or 5 line spaces between the complimentary close and the writer's name to add the appearance of length to the completed letter.

	Words
(*Return address and date of Problem 1*)	11
dr. frank e liguori teachers college university of cincinnati cincinnati, ohio 45221	20 / 29
dear dr liguori (¶ 1) You are quoted as	36
saying in your dissertation, "Few high	44
school graduates had adequate under-	51

	Words
standing of the details of the job application." (¶ 2) Will you please send me the exact reference for the quotation or tell me where I can get access to your research. I shall be most grateful for this help. sincerely yours miss loretta m king	60 / 67 / 75 / 84 / 93 / 100/129

Problem 2–3: Judgment Placement of a Letter

PROCEDURE If the letter typed as Problem 2–2 is not satisfactorily placed on the page, retype it leaving more blank line spaces between the date and the letter address.

7C ● STROKING TECHNIQUE PRACTICE *12 minutes (each line three times)*

SPACING RULE *Space once after a period used with an initial or with an abbreviation.*

● All letters taught are used in this practice.

1	Hold elbows → still as you	qa quit quit quite quack quaint quack plaque quack	Feet on floor; body erect
2	reach to q → and y and x	yj yj yes yet jay hay say pay may joy coy toy they	
3	→	xs xs ax six lax mix six fix fox sox six next next	
4		Max says I can fix up a quick game with Q. L. Poe.	Hold hands and arms
5		Mr. Young said you are quite right to quit in May.	quiet

7D ● TYPING FROM DICTATION *7 minutes*

PROCEDURE Type each line once from dictation with the book open; then type each line two or three times from dictation with the book closed or with the page covered. Think and type the *words*.

Type with a fast "getaway" stroke

go to may fix you for our tax fix may tax for form

to go form quit make four your quit play next make

will take with days quit fine play fine will queen

7E ● CONTINUITY PRACTICE *10 minutes (each line three times)*

TECHNIQUE EMPHASIS Type with continuity— just keep the stroking of the keys at a steady pace.

Hold the hands and arms quiet. Make the *fingers* work. Strike and release the keys and space bar quickly.

● All letters taught are used in this practice.

1	Make direct reach to key—	Ray Quinn may go with you to Queens for four days.	Type with the fingers—
2	don't twist your elbow	Clay may fix your tax form for Mr. Jacques to see.	hold your arms and hands quiet
3	in or out	Gayle Quill may quit the New York play next month.	
4		Fay will make a fine queen for our school May Day.	

. . . . .1. . . . .2. . . . .3. . . . .4. . . . .5. . . . .6. . . . .7. . . . .8. . . . .9. . . .10

7F ● SELF-IMPROVEMENT PRACTICE *(each line three times)*

1	Be smooth in your	My group of six hoped Jack would not just quit us.	Send carriage back quickly
2	key stroking	Rex could fix the short tax forms for you and Ray.	
3		Max says to fix your car may not take quite a day.	Keep feet on floor for
4	Double letters	Nell will soon say if she will quit your new play.	body balance

. . . . .1. . . . .2. . . . .3. . . . .4. . . . .5. . . . .6. . . . .7. . . . .8. . . . .9. . . .10

PROJECT 1 ● INVENTORYING BASIC KNOWLEDGE AND SKILL

2 full sheets   Single spacing;
1 small envelope   ●   triple-space
1½″ top margin   between items
60-space line

PROCEDURE Type the inventory item; then refer to the page number (in parentheses) for the explanation. Repeat the typing of items not typed correctly the first time. Retype selected items as time permits.

NOTE Do not type identifying numbers; ignore your typing errors temporarily.

1–1 Type the figures *1* to *10* in a column at the left margin. **(37)**

1–2 Type Roman numerals for Arabic numbers *1* to *10* at the left margin. **(109)**

1–3 Type each sentence with the figure *4, 6, 8, 10,* or *12* in the blank space.

A horizontal inch of pica type has __ spaces. **(6)**

A horizontal inch of elite type has __ spaces. **(6)**

A vertical inch has _ line spaces **(45)**

1–4 Type the symbol for the italicized words in the following sentences.

Ship McCoy *and* O'Dell 500 *pounds* at 79 **(44)** *cents* a lb. **(48)**

Use the 15 *second* call of the guide **(111)**

1–5 Type the italicized words in the following sentence as a "made" fraction.

The stock is quoted at *sixty-seven and two thirds*. **(36)**

1–6 Center and type the heading in all-capital letters.

Stocks Held in 1964 **(59)**

1–7 Use the apostrophe in the italicized words in the following sentences to show contractions and possessives. **(42, 43)**

Wont Toms wages go in *todays* payroll?

Childrens shoes and *mens* coats are on sale at *Wards* store.

I *didnt* like Mary and *Joes* research.

1–8 Complete the following sentence.

The symbol for Care of is (*type the symbol and underline it*). **(111)**

1–9 Type the periods for the abbreviations and initials in the following sentences. Use correct spacing.

Mr C M Davis used Okla for Oklahoma. **(18)**

The plane left at 9:05 a m today. **(34)**

I am working for my Ph D degree. **(34)**

1–10 Type the following titles in all-capital letters, centering by "guesstimating" (judgment placement). Double-space between the lines.

A Bird at Dawning

Inventorying Basic Manipulative Skills

Erasing

1–11 Center the lines of **1–10** by exact placement. **(59)**

1–12 Center as a "spread" heading by "guesstimating." **(108)**

PRODUCTION TYPING

1–13 Center and "spread" the heading of **1–12** by exact placement. **(59, 108)**

1–14 Type the words with a hyphen to show the first acceptable division if the bell rings on the typing of the third letter. Use judgment placement in typing the three-column tabulation. **(96, 104)**

accounted	expressed	pleased
educated	expression	steady
excelling	humiliate	wouldn't

1–15 Type the letter address and salutation in the block style with mixed punctuation. **(69, 79)**

mrs edna m paulson 619 w 34th street lima ohio 45801 dear miss paulson

1–16 Address an envelope to Miss Escoril; for the return address, use the letter address of **1–15.** **(70, 111)**

mary a escoril c/o mrs rodrigue campanille 2390 pompano drive punta gorda florida 33950

8A ● **PREPARATORY PRACTICE** *8 minutes (each line three times)*

● All letters taught are used in the first line of this practice.

Clay knew Gus Fox helped Jim for quite some weeks.

Drill on y　They may try to stay in New York for a day in May.

Fluency　The men say that I am just the man to do the work.
. . . . 1 . . . . 2 . . . . 3 . . . . 4 . . . . 5 . . . . 6 . . . . 7 . . . . 8 . . . . 9 10

8B ● NEW KEYS: b, z, and , (Comma)
8 minutes

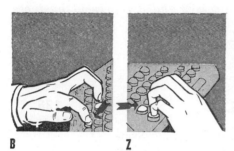

B　　　Z　　　, (Comma)

1. REACH TECHNIQUE FOR B
Reach the *left first finger* to the **b** key without moving the hand from its typing position. Watch your finger as it moves down to type **b** and up to type **f** a few times.

Tryout Practice. Type the following drill twice on one line.

2. REACH TECHNIQUE FOR z
Move the *left fourth finger* down to type **z** without moving the other fingers from typing position. Watch your finger move down to type **z** and up to type **a** a few times.

Tryout Practice. Type the following drill twice on one line.

3. REACH TECHNIQUE FOR , (Comma)
Hold the arm in position as you move the *right second finger* down to type , (comma). Watch the finger move down to type , and up to type **k** a few times. *Space once after the comma.*

Tryout Practice. Type the following drill twice on one line.

bf bug bf rub fib fob tub　　za zeal size za quiz haze　　k, Kim, Ken, or I can go.

8C ● STROKING TECHNIQUE PRACTICE *12 minutes (each line three times)*

● All reach-strokes taught are used in this practice.

1　　bf bug fob fib rub rob tub job but burn born broke

2　　za za zeal whiz daze zone zinc quiz size fizz doze

3　Work for continuity　Bob may bring Burt Grubbs to the next bridge game.

4　　Liz said she was in a daze when she took the quiz.

5　　Zoe, Rob, or Paul may go, I think; and so may Liz.

● Sit erect
● Curve the fingers
● Space quickly
● Strike the keys with quick, sharp strokes and release them quickly
● Return carriage smoothly

Contents | Special Projects

The projects listed below and presented as typewriting problems on the following pages are provided for those students who want additional applications or for those students for whom this course is the final formal instruction in typewriting. The activities presented in Projects 1 and 4 are those <u>all</u> students should be able to perform effectively. Those presented in Projects 2 and 3 represent business applications of high frequency that anyone who uses the typewriter in an office should be able to perform capably.

8D ● TAB MECHANISM CONTROL *7 minutes (three times)*

SETTING TABULATOR STOPS

1 Move the carriage as far to the left as possible.

2 Clear previous settings to eliminate false stops by depressing the tab clear key **31** as you pull the carriage all the way to the right. *To remove a single stop without canceling other stops, tabulate to the stop* and operate the tab clear key. *Smith-Corona and Olympia typewriters have a Total Tab Clear key that clears all stops at one time without moving the carriage.*

3 To set a tabulator stop, move the carriage to the desired position; then depress the tab set key **23**. Repeat this procedure for each stop needed.

TABULATING TECHNIQUE

Nonelectric Machines: Depress and hold the tab bar or key down until the carriage has completed its movement. Depress the tab bar with the right first finger.

Electric Machines: Flick the tab key lightly with the little finger; return the little finger to its home position at once.

● PROCEDURE FOR SETTING TABULATOR STOPS FOR THE DRILL

*Full sheet, single spacing,
50-space line*

1 Clear all the tab stops. (See the directions given above.)
2 For Column 2, set a tab stop 15 spaces from left margin.

3 For Column 3, set a tab stop 15 spaces from *beginning* of Column 2.
4 For Column 4, set a tab stop 16 spaces from beginning of Column 3.

Begin to type quickly after tabulating or returning the carriage		Tab		Tab		Tab		Return carriage without looking up from the copy
	and		the		with		high	
	did		mix		work		says	
	you		her		goal		must	
	set		win		club		hard	
	not		has		size		well	
	job		mix		zeal		zest	
	3	**12**	**3**	**12**	**4**	**12**	**4**	

8E ● CONTINUITY PRACTICE *10 minutes (each line three times)*

● All letters taught are used in this practice.

1 Reduce the time between strokes

2

Both Bob and Zoe do the job quite well, Burt says.   Return quickly

To win, you must mix zeal and zest with hard work.

3 Down-and-in space-bar stroke

4

Rob Zoerb did not tell the size of the club prize.

For the drill, Zoe has set more speed as her goal.

`. . . . 1 . . . . 2 . . . . 3 . . . . 4 . . . . 5 . . . . 6 . . . . 7 . . . . 8 . . . . 9 . . . . 10`

8F ● SELF-IMPROVEMENT PRACTICE *(each line three times)*

● All letters taught are used in this practice.

1 Put your techniques to work in these lines

2

3

4

5

By zeal and hard work, Burt Boyd may go quite far.

My six boys built the car, and it runs quite well.

In June, the prize was won by Zoe Barnes, of York.

The six Swiss boys swam with zest in the big meet.

A quick stroke can be my goal for the way to type.

`. . . . 1 . . . . 2 . . . . 3 . . . . 4 . . . . 5 . . . . 6 . . . . 7 . . . . 8 . . . . 9 . . . . 10`

75B ● PROBLEM MEASUREMENT *(Continued)*

Problem 4: Tabulation with Columnar Headings
(errors not corrected)

Half sheet	Center problem vertically
Double spacing	10 spaces between columns

PROCEDURE

1 Space before and after the hyphen (–) in Column 1.

2 Align the colon (:) separating the hours and minutes when typing the figures of Column 1. These figures can become a "trap" for you if you are not careful with the spacing.

		Words
S E R V I C E C L U B		5
Schedule for Week Ending April 29		12
Time	Typists	17
9:00 - 10:15	Ruth McCullough	23
10:15 - 11:00	Ida Grace Houston	29
11:00 - 12:15	Martin Broughton	35
12:15 - 1:00	Norris Threlkeld	42
1:00 - 2:30	Nancy O'Brien	47
2:30 - 3:45	Lolamae Fletcher	53
3:45 - 4:30	Frank Lowell	59

Problem 5: Rough Draft of Enumerated Items
(errors not corrected)

Half sheet
50-space line
Single spacing
1½" top margin

PROCEDURE Remember that your line of typing will not be the same as the lines in the copy.

Words

1. T his is once *when* I considr *e* it ~~best~~ *wise* to "beginthe" impos- 12
sible" and to do it ~~now.~~ *as quickly as possible.* 21

2. ~~When~~ *If* I type at my ~~fastest~~ *highest* speed, Ihave toruble in con- 33
trolling the timing of my strokes *because of tension.* 44

3. A major ity of their ofice *f* ~~men~~ *workers* have ranked "appreciation *A* 56
tion of good worker" first and "Tactful discipline" 66
~~last.~~ *tenth.* 67

4. I find that ~~most of my~~ *many* tpying errors are *errors of* ~~ins~~trans- 78
position that can be corrected by improved timing 88
of my storking techniques. 93

75C ● TYPING FOR CONTROL *5 minutes (a 1′ and a 3′ control-level writing; erase errors, unless otherwise directed)*

PROCEDURE Type at a rate that is 8 or more words lower than your highest speed. Deduct 10 words for any uncorrected error.

● **All letters are used in the paragraph.**

1.35 si
120 words

	GWAM 1′	3′	
A wit said, "The hardest thing about holding a job is the work it	13	4	44
requires." That is a clever witticism; but as an expression of the way	28	9	49
some workers feel about their jobs, it shows the tragic plight of those	42	14	54
who failed to match interest and ability with job availability at the	56	19	59
time they went to work. Whether your work is a chore or a satisfaction	70	23	63
depends on you more than on the work. If you are bored much of the time	85	28	68
with the work you do, you should change jobs. That may take courage as	99	33	73
well as demonstrated ability; but if a change in jobs will cause you to	114	38	78
realize job satisfaction, do it.	120	40	80

1′ | 1 | 2 | 3 | 4 | 5 | 6 | 7 | 8 | 9 | 10 | 11 | 12 | 13 | 14 |
3′ | 1 | 2 | 3 | 4 | 5 |

LESSON 9 | **9A ● PREPARATORY PRACTICE** *8 minutes (each line three times)*

Full sheet, single spacing,
50-space line

● All letters taught are used in the first sentence.

```
            Rex and Dick must play jazz for the big quiz show.
Drill on b  Buz brought this big book for Burt Briggs to read.
Fluency     When the word is to be typed, think it with force.
            ....1....2....3....4....5....6....7....8....9....10
```

9B ● NEW KEYS: v and ? (Question Mark)

8 minutes

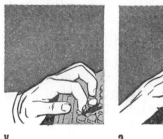

v   ?

1. REACH TECHNIQUE FOR V

Reach the *left first finger* down to type **v** without changing the hand alignment with the keyboard. Watch your finger as it moves down to type **v** and up to type **f** a few times.

Tryout Practice. Type the following drill twice on one line.

```
vf vie five vie give five
```

2. REACH TECHNIQUE FOR ?

Depress the left shift key and type **?** with the *right fourth finger* without moving the hand down and without twisting the wrist. Watch your finger type **?;** a few times.

Tryout Practice. Type the drill twice on one line. *Space twice after ? at the end of a sentence.*

```
?; ?; Is it so?  Do I go?
```

● **SUMMARY OF SPACING RULES**

1 Space once after semicolon, comma, and a period used with an abbreviation or an initial.

2 Space twice after a period at the end of a sentence, except when it comes at the end of the line; then return the carriage without spacing.

3 Space twice after **?** at the end of a sentence.

9C ● STROKING TECHNIQUE PRACTICE *12 minutes (each line three times)*

● All letters are used in this practice.

1	Quick, snap strokes	`vf vim vf van vex five have give live drive thrive`	Return without pausing
2	Shift firmly	`?; ?; Has he typed it?  Has he gone?  May I do it?`	
3		`Eve said they have moved five times in five years.`	Return without spacing after .and ?
4	Keep on!	`Does Dave live on Vine Street?  Must he leave now?`	
5		`Is Jack quite a whiz at bridge?  Do you play much?`	

75B ● PROBLEM MEASUREMENT: Manuscript; Personal Letter; Tabulations; Rough Drafts *35 minutes*

Problem 1: Unbound Manuscript Page with Footnotes
(errors corrected)

Full sheet Carbon copy Double spacing	5-space ¶ indention Type in unbound manuscript form

Words

"LOVE ME, LOVE MY DOG" · 5

(¶1) *Qui me amat, amet et canem* · 15
meum––"Who loves me will also love my · 24
dog" is a saying that is at least a thou- · 32
sand years old. According to Bartlett,[1] · 40
this was a proverb used by Saint Bernard, · 48
a medieval saint (but not the one for · 56
whom the dogs were named). It appears · 64
in the earliest collection of English col- · 72
loquial sayings by John Heywood (1497– · 80
1580). (¶2) "Love me, love my dog," a · 87
shorter and more familiar version of the · 95
Saint Bernard saying, is said to be an old · 103
Sicilian proverb. We use this and hear it · 112
often, but what does it mean? To me, it · 120
means that if you like me, you must do so · 129
in spite of my annoying habits or faults. · 137
Others may interpret this saying liter- · 145
ally––"If you love me, you'll have to love · 154
my dog." (¶3) We often fail to convey · 160
exact ideas because words do not mean · 168
the same thing to all of us. For example, · 177
a young girl when asked the meaning of · 184
the saying "If the shoe fits, wear it" re- · 193
plied: "If you've got big feet, don't wear · 202
little shoes!" No wonder there is often · 210
failure to understand what is heard. If, · 218
when we speak, "Our intention . . . is noth- · 227
ing but to unfold to others the thoughts · 235
of our minds,"[2] let's use words that say · 243
what we think we are saying. · 249
· 253

[1] Christopher Morely, Editor, and Lou- · 261
ella D. Everett, Associate Editor, *Bart-* · 269
lett's Familiar Quotations (12th ed.; · 282
Boston: Little, Brown and Company, · 289
1951), p. 17. · 291

[2] Alexander Gode "The Case for Inter- · 300
lingua," *The Scientific Monthly*, LXXVII · 311
(August, 1953), p. 82. · 312

Problem 2: Personal Letter
(errors corrected)

Full sheet No carbon 60-space line	Block style Open punctuation Current date	Your return address Envelope

SINGLE QUOTATION
To indicate a quotation within a quotation, type the apostrophe ('). (See ¶2.)

● **8 blank line spaces after the date**

Words

Professor Patrick McM. O'Leary, Jr. | Pro- · 19
fessor of Industrial Management | Univer- · 27
sity of Arizona | Tucson, Arizona 85702 | · 35
Dear Professor O'Leary | (¶1) When you · 41
spoke at our Midterm Convocation on the · 49
topic · 50

HUMAN UNDERSTANDING IN INDUSTRY · 57

you referred to a study of job conditions · 65
that were ranked by workers as leading · 73
to job satisfaction. (¶2) In my notes of · 80
your lecture, I have "Appreciation for · 88
good work," ranked first; "Feeling 'in' on · 97
things," second; "Good wages," fifth; · 104
and "Good working conditions," ninth. · 112
I failed to record the other ratings you · 120
quoted, but I would like to include these · 129
in a paper I am preparing for my seminar · 137
in industrial relations. (¶3) Will you be · 144
good enough to send me the source of your · 153
quotation. I shall be most grateful for · 161
this courtesy. | Sincerely yours | (*Your* · 167
Name) | · 170/204

Problem 3: Tabulation with Columnar Headings
(errors not corrected)

Half sheet Double spacing	Center problem vertically 10 spaces between columns

Words

AREA OF SELECTED PARKS · 5

Name	Sq. Mi.	
Yellowstone	1,213,207	15
Mount McKinley	1,939,319	20
Glacier	997,248	23
Yosemite	756,441	27
Grand Canyon	645,296	31
Great Smoky Mts.	461,004	36

● *75B is continued on page 133.*

9D ● TAB MECHANISM CONTROL *7 minutes (three times)*

Tab Bar

Tab Key

PROCEDURE
1 Clear all tabulator stops.
2 For Column 2, set a tab stop 15 spaces from left margin stop.
3 For Column 3, set a tab stop 15 spaces from beginning of Column 2.

4 For Column 4, set a tab stop 16 spaces from *beginning* of Column 3.
5 Type the first word; tabulate to Column 2; type the first word in that column; tabulate to Column 3; type; and so on.

Tabulate from column to column	the can and may but	Tab	you how now not yet	Tab	then type work this what	Tab	next move quit whiz just	Return carriage without looking up from the copy
	3	12	3	12	4	12	4	

9E ● PARAGRAPH TYPING *10 minutes*

Double spacing,
5-space paragraph indention

PROCEDURE Type the paragraphs as shown; then type one or more 1-minute writings, as time permits. Use the tabulator bar or key to indent the first line of each paragraph.

● All letters are used in the paragraphs.

	Words in Para.	Total Words
Indent ➡ If you type in the right way, you will learn	9	9
to type well. There can be no doubt of that. It	19	19
is how you type and not what you type that counts	29	29
most right now.	32	32
Indent ➡ You may not be a whiz in this work just yet,	9	41
but that is no cause for you to quit now. Strike	19	51
a key; move to the next key and type it; and then	29	61
the next; and so on. This is the way to learn to	39	71
type.	40	72

. . . . 1 . . . . 2 . . . 3 . . . . 4 . . . . 5 . . . 6 . . . . 7 . . . . 8 . . . 9 10

9F ● SELF-IMPROVEMENT PRACTICE *(each line three times)*

● All letters are used in the first sentence of this practice.

1   Did Vern Fox ask Jack to help on my big quiz show?

2   Have Burt and Van used the five quail I gave them?

3   Dave may give the first prize to Van or Eve Vance.

4   May Peg fix the prize for Burt Burns or Eve Voltz?

. . . . 1 . . . . 2 . . . . 3 . . . . 4 . . . . 5 . . . 6 . . . . 7 . . . . 8 . . . . 9 10

74C ● PROBLEM MEASUREMENT (Continued)

Problem 2: Letter with Tabulated Items
(errors corrected)

Letterhead (or full sheet) Carbon sheet File copy sheet	●	60-space line Current date	●	Modified block, blocked ¶s Mixed punctuation Envelope

Words

● 6 blank line spaces after the date

Mrs. Pierre Chaulnes | Beauport, Quebec |	11
Can. | Dear Mrs. Chaulnes (¶ 1) The	17
Boehm sculptures listed in last month's	25
issue of Antiques are some of the best-	35
known examples of his Limited Edition	42
portrayals of birds. The importance of	50
these life-size pieces is their fidelity of	59
appearance, their precise rendering of	67
spirit and personality, and the delicacy of	76
foliage and flowers. (¶ 2) Of the sculp-	83
tures we listed, only those named below	91
are now available:	95

● 4 spaces between columns

Cerulean Warblers	No. 424	$800 Each	102
Ruffed Grouse	No. 456	950 a Pr.	108
Ptarmigan	No. 463	800 a Pr.	114
Tree Sparrow	No. 468	125 Each	120

(¶ 3) "Sugarbirds" (Cyanerpes cyaneus),	131
Hallmark No. 460, of which only 100	138
were in the Limited Edition, are now val-	146
ued at $2,500 each. They are a collector's	155
item and are seldom available now. (¶ 4)	162
If you will telegraph or telephone us about	171

Words

the pieces in which you are interested, we	179
shall be glad to hold them for you. | Sin-	188
cerely yours | Wilis O. Bordeaux | Man-	195
ager | (Your Initials) |	196/205

Problem 3: Making Special Corrections

PROCEDURE Make the following corrections in the letter and envelope you typed as Problem 2. Then, fold and insert the letter into the envelope.

1 Erase the period after *Can.* in the address; then reinsert the letter and type *Canada* instead of the abbreviation. Correct *Can.* on the envelope.

2 Underline *Antiques* in Line 1 of ¶ 1.

3 Squeeze a second *l* in the dictator's given name to have it spelled *Willis*.

Problem 4: Centered Announcement on Postal Card

2 postal cards Double spacing	●	Center vertically "Spread" heading	●	Center each line horizontally

PROCEDURE Address the cards to **| Miss Mabel G. Lindsey | 4501 St. Paul Street | Baltimore, Maryland 21218 |** and **| Mrs. Thomas Heinzman, Jr. | 267 Queen's Road | Toronto, Ontario | Canada |**

Words

B O E H M S C U L P T U R E S	6

● Triple-space

At Bordeaux Galleries	11
Cerulean Warblers	14
Ruff Grouse (Pair)	18
Ptarmigan (Pair)	22
Tree Sparrow	24

Miss Lindsey's card .... *14 words*
Mrs. Heinzman's card .... *13 words*

LESSON 75 | 75A ● PREPARATORY PRACTICE *5 minutes (each line three or more times)*

Alphabetic	Hazel lacked judgment but quite excelled Winnona in brevity of speech.
Figure-symbol	The 50 gal. of Q-1762 White Enamel at $9.38 a gal. cost Mr. West $469.
Fluency	Ken Workman paid the penalty for his wrongdoing, as criminals must do.

| 1 | 2 | 3 | 4 | 5 | 6 | 7 | 8 | 9 | 10 | 11 | 12 | 13 | 14 |

LESSON 10 | 10A ● PREPARATORY PRACTICE *8 minutes* *(each line three times)*

**Full sheet, single spacing,
50-space line**

SENTENCE 1 In the first writing, type at a slow rate; emphasize rhythmic continutiy of stroking. In the second and third writings, speed up the stroking slightly.
SENTENCE 2 Strike the keys in rhythm; space quickly; return the carriage quickly and without looking up. Improve the technique of shifting for capital letters.

SENTENCE 3 Type the sentence once with a slight push for speed; type it a second time at a slower rate; and type it a third time at a well-controlled rate.

Alphabetic	Jane packed my box with five quail for Zim Briggs.
Drill on v	Would Dave give Vern a leave of five days to move?
Fluency	We can do the work well if he will lend us a hand.

`. . . . 1 . . . . 2 . . . . 3 . . . . 4 . . . . 5 . . . 6 . . . . 7 . . . . 8 . . . . 9 . . . 10`

10B ● STROKING TECHNIQUE REVIEW *10 minutes* *(each line three times)*

TECHNIQUE CONDITIONER: Quiet Hands and Arms Center the typing action in the fingers with the hands and arms as quiet as possible—almost motionless. To get this quiet stroking, curve the fingers and hold them in typing position; then when a long reach is to be made, as to **y** or **b**, straighten the finger slightly and make the reach-stroke without arching the wrist and with as little forward movement of the hand as possible. Reduce unnecessary and inefficient motions.

● All letters are used in these sentences.

1	Drill on b	Has Jane Burns a big part in the Bridge Club play?	Return without spacing at the end of the line
2	Drill on q	This queer quill pen is not quite what Clay needs.	
3	Drill on x	Did Rex fix the box for the tax forms Max may use?	
4	Drill on y	Did they say they may stay with you for five days?	
5	Drill on z	Liz is such a quiz whiz she should take the prize.	

`. . . . 1 . . . . 2 . . . . 3 . . . . 4 . . . . 5 . . . . 6 . . . . 7 . . . . 8 . . . . 9 . . . 10`

10C ● TYPING FROM DICTATION *7 minutes*

PROCEDURE Type each line from dictation with the book open; then type each line two or three times from dictation with the book closed or with the page covered.

● *Hear the word;*
    Think the word;
  Type the word.

Space quickly with right thumb

for you the fun and mix may not can but work right

it with do done is wish they when play quite comes

sure have must best both zest type well will first

Return carriage quickly

Problem 1: Leftbound Manuscript with Footnotes

2 full sheets
1 carbon copy
Leftbound manu-
   script form
Double spacing
	5-space ¶ indention
	Type on *control level*
	Errors not corrected
	   (unless otherwise
	   directed)

Words

AUTOMATION AND OFFICE WORKERS   6

(¶1) Automation has come to the office 13
because of the "alarming growth of paper 21
work in recent years."[1] Business expan- 29
sion, tax laws, and government regula- 36
tions have placed a burden of paper work 45
on business that staggers the imagination. 53
It has to withhold from the wages of 61
workers the Social Security tax and in- 69
come tax; the contribution to the pension 77
plan and group insurance; and in some 85
states, a wage or other tax, all involving 93
paper work. It is estimated that 20 billion 102
checks were written in 1963.[2] Because of 111
automation, this seemingly impossible task 119
was just routine. (¶2) Computers now do 126
much of the routine work that used to be 135
done by unskilled workers. The National 143
City Bank of New York put in electronic 151
equipment to compute overhead distribu- 158
tion and reduced computing time from 166
1,000 hours to 9½ minutes. (¶3) As 172
offices become automated and the low-level 181
jobs disappear and the higher-level jobs 189
become available, a few workers may 196
be displaced; but many will be retrained. 205
These workers must have command of the 212

FOOTNOTING

Ibid. refers to the source immediately preceding the footnote. (Footnote 2 refers to Footnote 1.)

Loc. cit. (not illustrated) refers to the same passage in a reference previously cited.

Op. cit. refers to a reference previously cited when other references intervene. (Footnote 4 refers to Footnote 1.) Both *op. cit.* and *loc. cit.* are typed with the author's name and the page number of the reference.

Words

basic tools of arithmetic, reading, and 220
writing, of course; but they must also 228
know something about economics and 235
finance and how to operate the new ma- 243
chines. There is no place in the world of 251
office work for those who do not have com- 259
mand of the fundamental tools, which are 268
basic to the use of specialized skills and 276
also basic to working under supervision or 285
working in a supervisory capacity. Morse 293
writes that one of the requirements of 301
automation is a need for more supervisory 309
personnel.[3] (¶4) In automated offices 316
electronic machines have relieved workers 325
of the drudgery of many routine tasks, 332
but they also perform many tasks that 340
could not be done otherwise. The intricate 349
calculations needed for guiding rockets, 357
manufacturing polyethylene (a soft but 365
strong plastic), and making color tele- 373
vision possible are examples of the use of 381
these machines to do "the impossible."[4] 389
(¶5) Whether automation has brought 396
the electronic machines or the machines 404
have brought automation is beside the 411
point. Automation is here to stay. It can 420
be the friend and need not be the foe of 428
workers in office or plant, for the mind of 437
man can think imaginatively, which is 445
something the most sophisticated machine 453
cannot do. 455

459

[1] Walter Buckingham, "The Human 465
Side of Automation," *Readings in Eco-* 476
nomics (Cincinnati: South-Western Pub- 485
lishing Company, 1963), p. 199. 491

[2] *Ibid.* 494

[3] Kenneth P. Morse, "Automation 500
Demands Training in Fundamentals," 507
Business Education World (December, 519
1957), p. 12. 522

[4] Buckingham, *op. cit.*, p. 200. 530

● *74C is continued on page 131.*

10D ● PARAGRAPH TYPING *10 minutes*

Double spacing,
5-space paragraph
indention

PROCEDURE

1 Type the paragraphs once at an easy pace. Type with even, continuous stroking.
2 Type each paragraph for 1 minute; then prac-tice difficult words, typing each two or three times; finally, type each paragraph again as a 1-minute writing, if time permits.

● All letters are used in the paragraphs.

	Words in Para.	Total Words

TECHNIQUE EMPHASIS

Strike and release the keys and space bar quickly, but type with quiet hands and with the action in the fingers. Keep the carriage moving at a steady pace.

	Words in Para.	Total Words
It is quite right for you to have fun in the	9	9
work you do, but be sure that you do the work and	19	19
not just have the fun. Work and fun may mix; but	29	29
when they do not, work comes first.	36	36
When you work, work as hard as you can; when	9	45
you play, play just as hard as you wish. Do both	19	55
with zest to be at your best. You have work that	29	65
must be done now. Do the work well, and you will	39	75
learn to type quite well.	44	80

. . . . 1 . . . . 2 . . . . 3 . . . . 4 . . . . 5 . . . . 6 . . . . 7 . . . . 8 . . . . 9 10

10E ● STROKING SKILL CHECKUP *10 minutes*

PROCEDURE

Type each sentence as a 1-minute writing, typ-ing it as many times as you can until time is called; then type Sentences 1, 3, and 5 for 1 minute each; compare the *gwam** for the writings.

● All letters are used in the sentences.

		Words in Line
1	There is work for each of us to do.	7
2	Do you think you can learn to type well?	8
3	Wish for what you want, but work for it, too.	9
4	The six girls do not have quite the zeal you have.	10
5	All of them know they must put first things first.	10
6	He needs to know just the way to write your check.	10

Hold your eyes on the copy as you return the carriage.

. . . . 1 . . . . 2 . . . . 3 . . . . 4 . . . . 5 . . . . 6 . . . . 7 . . . . 8 . . . . 9 10

* TO DETERMINE GWAM:

1 List the figure at the end of each complete line typed during the timed writing.

2 Note in the scale the figure directly below the point at which you stopped typing.

3 Add these figures to determine the total gross words typed. (Gross words are the same as *gwam* for a 1-minute writing.)

MEASUREMENT OF BASIC SKILL AND PROBLEM TYPING

STANDARD
PROCEDURES
FOR SECTION 12

GET READY TO TYPE

Clear the desk. Use full sheets; 70-space lines; single spacing for drills; double spacing and a 5-space paragraph indention for paragraphs. Use the line length and spacing indicated for typing the problems. Type on the *control level*. Do not try to type at your maximum speed.

LESSON 74 | 74A ● PREPARATORY PRACTICE *5 minutes (each line three or more times)*

Alphabetic   The quiet behavior of the boys amazed and pleased Judge Clyde W. Knox.

Figure-symbol   Page 293 of Catalog #B87 quotes the unit price on Item #560 as $12.45.

Fluency   All good citizens should help Mr. Clayborne in his big election fight.

| 1 | 2 | 3 | 4 | 5 | 6 | 7 | 8 | 9 | 10 | 11 | 12 | 13 | 14 |

74B ● GROWTH INDEX *15 minutes (two 5' control-level writings)*

PROCEDURE Pause 30 to 40 seconds between writings to relax. After both writings are completed, check them for *gwam* and errors.

● All letters and figures are used in the sentences.

	GWAM
	1' | 5'

¶ 1
1.35 si
76 words

The typewriter is your partner in learning to type, as it will be   13 | 3 | 49
your partner in getting and holding a good job when you have finished   27 | 5 | 51
your training. Take good care of this partner of yours, for it will pay   42 | 8 | 54
you dividends if you do. The care you must give the typewriter is really   57 | 11 | 57
quite simple, but it must be regular. You can't neglect it and expect   71 | 14 | 60
it to perform efficiently.   76 | 15 | 61

¶ 2
1.35 si
76 words

Dust the typewriter daily. Dust the top of the desk and under the   13 | 18 | 64
typewriter. Use a long-handled brush to remove all dust and eraser par-   28 | 21 | 67
ticles. If the typewriter has a movable carriage, moisten a cloth with   42 | 24 | 70
a few drops of oil and wipe off the two rails on which the carriage moves.   57 | 27 | 73
Clean the type with a stiff brush. A clean typewriter can improve the   72 | 30 | 76
quality of your typing.   76 | 30 | 76

¶ 3
1.35 si
76 words

Use oil sparingly on the carriage rails. If too much oil is used,   13 | 33 | 79
it may collect dust and the carriage may become stuck. If two keys jam,   28 | 36 | 82
untangle them gently so as not to bend the bars. The typewriter is a   42 | 39 | 85
durable machine; but when you realize the pounding it takes day after   56 | 42 | 88
day, you will understand that it is necessary to take care of it if it   70 | 44 | 90
is to give efficient service.   76 | 46 | 92

| 1' | 1 | 2 | 3 | 4 | 5 | 6 | 7 | 8 | 9 | 10 | 11 | 12 | 13 | 14 |
| 5' | | 1 | | | 2 | | | 3 | | |

STANDARD PROCEDURES FOR SECTION 2

GET READY TO TYPE

Follow the procedure given for Get Ready to Type, page 6, except that you will use a 60-space line, single spacing for drills, and a 5-space paragraph indention and double spacing for paragraphs.

SELF-IMPROVEMENT PRACTICE

Type the lines of Self-Improvement Practice, page 31, two or three times each, as time permits. If additional practice material can be used, type the lines of the Technique Practice of each lesson as directed.

Only 1-syllable words are used in the practice materials of this section.

LESSON 11 | 11A ● PREPARATORY PRACTICE *10 minutes* (each line three times)*

PROCEDURE (for each Preparatory Practice in this section)

Sentence 1 Think each letter forcefully. Type at a steady, even pace. Keep the carriage moving.
Sentence 2 Type with easy rhythm—without jerks or breaks in the typing. Speed up the stroking slightly

* The timing allows for getting ready to type and for some 1-minute writings on the last sentence of the Preparatory Practice.

when typing the sentence the second and third times.
Sentence 3 Speed up the stroking; then drop back in rate to gain control. Space quickly.

Alphabetic	My friend Jack would just love to pass up his next big quiz.
Drill on b	Babs bought a book to learn how best to bake breast of lamb.
Fluency	Find the men who will learn how to make their own good luck.

| 1 | 2 | 3 | 4 | 5 | 6 | 7 | 8 | 9 | 10 | 11 | 12 |

11B ● TECHNIQUE PRACTICE: Quiet Hands and Arms *10 minutes (each line three times)*

TECHNIQUE EMPHASIS

*Type with the fingers. Hold the arms and hands quiet—almost motionless. Make the long reach, such as **m** to **u** or **b** to **r** with the finger without moving the arm forward or arching the wrist.*

● All letters are used in the sentences.

1   Have you read the card Jane Muntz wrote Vic Fox from France?

2   Fred Burke reached the top as the sun came through the haze.

3   Is this the prize plaque Ruth Treen brought you from Greece?

4   We see the point you make, but we will not change our plans.

| 1 | 2 | 3 | 4 | 5 | 6 | 7 | 8 | 9 | 10 | 11 | 12 |

73D ● INVENTORYING PROBLEM TYPING *25 minutes*

SUPPLIES NEEDED
5 full sheets ● 4 file copy sheets
2 carbon sheets ● 1 envelope

PROCEDURE Type the inventory item; then refer to the page number (in parentheses) for an explanation and illustration. Repeat the typing of items not typed correctly the first time. Do not type identifying numbers. Retype selected items as time permits.

● TYPING SPECIAL SYMBOLS

Full sheet ● 2″ top margin ● Use correct symbol for
45-space line ● Double spacing ● each italicized item

Use a 2-*inch* top margin for the first page. (111)
Don't yell *exclamation* Speak calmly, PLEASE. (44)
Type a timed writing *dash* a 5-*minute* writing. (111)
What is the meaning of the symbol H_2SO_4? (111)
The boiling point of water is 212 *degrees* F. (111)
What is 423 *minus* 156 *times* 7 *plus* 890? (111)
Speed is important but (*underline following words*) accuracy is more so. (46)
Bill *number* 890 is for 450 *pounds* of salt. (44)
The room is 20 *feet* 6 *inches* long and 15 *feet* wide. (111)
What is 540 *times* 2 *divided* by 5? (111)

● PARTS OF A BUSINESS LETTER

2 carbon copies (97) ● Mixed punctuation (79)
60-space line ● Current date
Modified block, ● Correct errors, unless
blocked ¶s. (79) ● otherwise directed (99)

1 Type date on Line 10 to end at right margin; follow by 8 blank line spaces. (95)

2 Type this address in correct form:
elizabeth n baker 892 w 34th street (119)
paterson new jersey 07516 (95)

3 Add an appropriate salutation for Step 2. (79)

4 Type opening line, heading, column headings, and data with 8 spaces between columns. (87)

Information about the fastest growing state is given below:

PROJECTED POPULATION BY 1970
State   *1960*   *1970*
California   15,717,204   20,296,000

5 Space forward 8 times; type the closing lines in correct position with the dictator's name and title on one line.
sincerely yours t h carter manager (93)

6 Type your initials in the reference line. (79)

7 Add an enclosure notation. (117)

8 Address an envelope. (70)

9 Fold and insert letter into envelope. (84)

10 Retain one copy; hand in the extra copy.

● PARTS OF A MANUSCRIPT WITH FOOTNOTES

2 carbon copies ● Type in unbound manuscript form
Correct errors ● 5-space ¶ indention

1 Type the first-page heading:

ENTHUSIASM AND JOB SUCCESS (110)

2 Type the opening paragraphs:

For job success, you must have the skill the job requires, of course; but skill alone is not enough. Enthusiasm for the work is of importance, too. Balsley and Robinson say,

Genuine enthusiasm for one's work and for the particular task of the moment is contagious. Fellow workers gravitate toward the enthusiastic person; they shy away from (*ellipsis*) the discontented.[1] (115)

3 Space down and type the footnote in correct position to maintain a 1″ bottom margin.

[1] Irol Whitmore Balsley and Jerry W. Robinson, *Integrated Secretarial Studies* (Cincinnati: South-Western Publishing Company, 1963), p. 11. (113)

4 Number the first page of this manuscript. (113)

5 Number the second page. (113)

6 Type these closing paragraphs to begin the second page:

Promotion to a more responsible position usually follows job success on a lower level. Enthusiasm for the work and the ability to get along with others are as necessary as skill itself. As has been said,

It is your responsibility to adjust to the (*ellipsis*) surroundings in which you work. You must be able to cooperate with your supervisor and your co-workers.[2]

7 Type the second footnote to give a 1″ bottom margin.

[2] *Ibid.,* p. 371.

8 Repeat Steps 1-7, using the leftbound manuscript form. Do not make carbon copies. (118)

PROCEDURE (for each Typing from Dictation in this section)

Writing 1 Read and type the words from the book as your instructor dictates them.

Writings 2 and 3 Cover this page and get the impulse to type from your instructor's dictation.

Hear and
think
the <u>word</u>

to be if is do as it on so at of at if on it as of be do the

for set the you but can key one may let not for you all work

goal your make what gain each when have zeal just keep speed

11D ● **PARAGRAPH GUIDED WRITING** *20 minutes*

Each paragraph (¶) is marked with the 4-word count shown in figures and with an in-between count of two words shown by a dot (•) to aid you in noting your goals easily and quickly.

FOR ¶ 1 | 1 Type two 1-minute writings. Determine your *gwam* for the better writing (ignoring the errors temporarily). This will be your 1-minute base rate.

2 Divide your base rate by 2; then add 2 words. This rate will be your ½-minute goal. Type three ½-minute writings, trying to reach this goal.

3 Double your ½-minute goal for a new 1-minute goal rate. Type two 1-minute writings, trying to reach this new goal rate.

FOR ¶ 2 Type ¶ 2 as directed for ¶ 1.

FOR ¶ 1 AND ¶ 2 Type a 2- and a 3-minute writing, beginning with ¶ 1 and typing as much of ¶ 2 as you can. Type without the ½-minute or 1-minute guides. To determine 2′ *gwam*, divide 1′ *gwam* by 2.

TECHNIQUE SUMMARY Curve the fingers • Use quick, sharp strokes • Space with a down-and-in space-bar motion • Shift firmly • Return the carriage quickly and smoothly •

● All letters are used in these paragraphs.

		GWAM*		
		1′	3′	
¶ 1 44 words	Set a goal for your work. Know what you can gain from	11	4	36
	each line to be typed. If more speed is the goal you seek,	23	8	40
	make quick strokes, do not pause when you have typed a key,	35	12	44
	and keep right on, just one stroke at a time.	44	15	47
¶ 2 52 words	Let your goal be high, of course, but not too high for	55	18	50
	you to reach. A fixed goal may not be right at all times.	67	22	54
	Change the goal when you need to do so. You can do this as	79	26	58
	you work with zeal to learn to type well. Set a high goal;	91	30	62
	work for it, and gain it.	96	32	64

1′ | 1 | 2 | 3 | 4 | 5 | 6 | 7 | 8 | 9 | 10 | 11 | 12 |
3′ | 1 | 2 | 3 | 4 |

*THE FIGURES IN COLUMN 1 SHOW the total words as well as the 1-minute *gwam*. The first scale under the final paragraph indicates the 1-minute *gwam* for the incomplete line. **THE FIGURES IN COLUMN 2** show the 3-min. *gwam* for completed lines. The second scale below the paragraphs indicates the 3-min. *gwam* for the incomplete line. If you type any stroke between the vertical lines of this scale, the figure in the space between the lines indicates the 3-min. *gwam* to be added to the figure in the column for the last line completed.

72D ● INVENTORYING BASIC MANIPULATIVE SKILLS *25 minutes*

Full sheet,
60-space line,
double spacing,
1½" top margin

PROCEDURE Type the inventory item as best you can; then refer to the page number (number given in parentheses) for the explanation. After studying the explanation, repeat the typing unless you have done the typing correctly the first time and understand the procedure.

NOTE Do not type the numbers (in color); ignore your typing errors.

1 Type the sentence in correct form.

> For accuracy, type on the *control
> level.*   (71)

2 Begin 5 spaces outside the left margin and type the sentence in one line.

> I must know what I am to type and how
> I am to type it before I begin to
> type.   (59)

3 Type a 5-inch line. Remove the paper; reinsert it; gauge the line and type the sentence correctly placed on the line.

> I learn by INVENTORYING BASIC MANIPU-
> LATIVE SKILLS.   (93)

4 Repeat Step 3, but center and type only the capitalized words on the 5-inch line.   (57)

5 Type the sentence; then, double-space and center the title.

> I shall use the following title for
> my talk in Santa Monica:
>
>   SPARK PLUG OR FUEL PIPE   (61)

6 Center and type the title of Step 5 as a "spread" heading.   (108)

7 Remove the paper. Fold it lengthwise to give a 4¼" sheet. Reinsert the folded sheet; center and type your name and the current date on two lines within the 4¼" width.   (62)

8 Remove the paper; unfold it; then reinsert the full sheet. Draw an approximate 5-inch horizontal pencil line; then draw two downward vertical lines approximately 3 inches long to connect at the beginning and end of the horizontal line. Center and type the name of your school on the horizontal line; then center and type your name horizontally and vertically between the vertical lines.   (92)

9 Remove the paper; reinsert it; gauge the line and letter; and type over the sentence of Step 1 (at the left). If the alignment is not exact, remove the paper; reinsert it; and type over the sentence of Step 2; then Step 3; and so on until you demonstrate acceptable skill in typing over.   (90)

10 X-out your name typed in Step 8, and center and type the current date a double space below.   (115)

LESSON 73 | **73A ● PREPARATORY PRACTICE** *5 minutes (each line three or more times)*

Alphabetic | Objectives of this tax quiz were made clear by checking samples of it.

Figure-symbol | Kauffman's Invoice #3278 for $461.50 (less 2%) was paid on November 9.

Fluency | Work on the downtown Dickenson Building is to begin sometime in March.
| 1 | 2 | 3 | 4 | 5 | 6 | 7 | 8 | 9 | 10 | 11 | 12 | 13 | 14 |

73B ● INVENTORYING SELECTED TECHNIQUES
7 minutes

PROCEDURE Type each line of 55B, page 94, three times on the *control level*; retype selected sentences as time permits.

73C ● INVENTORYING BASIC SKILL
8 minutes

PROCEDURE Type the paragraphs of 70B, page 123, once on the *control level*. Determine *gwam* and errors.

● *Lesson 72 is continued on page 128.*

LESSON 12 | **12A ● PREPARATORY PRACTICE** *10 minutes (each line three times)*

Alphabetic   Gus Fox served with Karl and Jack in La Paz but quit in May.

Drill on **c**   The checks for the Camp Clay boys were cashed by Carl Crews.

Fluency   If we have the get up and go, can we go where we want to go?
| 1 | 2 | 3 | 4 | 5 | 6 | 7 | 8 | 9 | 10 | 11 | 12 |

12B ● TECHNIQUE PRACTICE: Direct-Reach Stroking *10 minutes (each line three times)*

TECHNIQUE
EMPHASIS

*When the same finger is to control two keys in succession,
as the right first finger controls* **mu** *in* **Munce, must,** *and* **much,**
move the controlling finger directly to the second key.

● All letters are used in the sentences.

1   June Munce must have much more work to do than Fred or Burt.

2   Art Briggs said Mr. Myles likes broiled ham with fried mush.

3   My sixth man quit the hunt just when he won the first prize.

4   Should Grace Brooks have trumped the last play by Gus Young?
| 1 | 2 | 3 | 4 | 5 | 6 | 7 | 8 | 9 | 10 | 11 | 12 |

12C ● TYPING FROM DICTATION *5 minutes*

it as to in of it as to you and top men our big are can both

the far man who job not mix for top more they read make give

when firm what grow than have know rich earn town pays prize

12D ● PARAGRAPH GUIDED WRITING *20 minutes*

In this practice activity, you will select your own speed goals and work to reach them.

Use the table shown below to select your quarter-minute goals quickly and easily.

EXAMPLE If your selected speed is 16 *gwam*, the first quarter-minute segment will end at 4; the second, at 8; the third, at 12; and the last, at 16.

TABLE OF QUARTER-MINUTE CHECK POINTS

GOAL	QUARTER	HALF	THREE-QUARTERS	ONE
12	3	6	9	12
16	4	8	12	16
20	5	10	15	20
24	6	12	18	24
28	7	14	21	28
32	8	16	24	32
36	9	18	27	36
40	10	20	30	40

PROCEDURE (for paragraphs on page 28)

1 Type ¶ 1 for 1 minute. Note the *gwam* base rate.

2 Add 4 words to base rate to get new goal. Divide this goal into quarter-minute segments, and note these quarter-minute goals in the copy.

3 Type a ½-minute writing, guided by the call of *Quarter* and *Half*. Then, type a 1-minute writing guided by the call of *Quarter, Half, Three-Quarters,* and *One* or *Time.*

4 Type two additional ½-minute writings and two 1-minute writings as directed in Step 3.

5 Type ¶ 2 as directed in Steps 1-4.

6 Finally, type a 2- then a 3-minute writing without the call of the guide, starting with ¶ 1 and typing as far as you can before time is called. Determine your *gwam* for the 3-minute writing. Note your *gwam* for comparison in Lesson 13.

INVENTORYING BASIC AND PROBLEM-TYPING SKILL

GET READY TO TYPE

Clear the desk. Use full sheets; 70-space lines; single spacing for drills; double-spacing and 5-space paragraph indention for paragraphs. Use the line length and spacing indicated for skill-performance and problem-typing inventories. Type on the *control level* without trying for maximum speed—but type!

LESSON 71 | **71A ● PREPARATORY PRACTICE** *5 minutes (each line three or more times)*

Alphabetic   Was Mavis Glenn expected to sell a dozen tickets for the July banquet?

Figure-symbol   Handley & Firth 4½% bonds (due 9/25/87) sold at 103 to 106 in October.

Fluency   Type it right the first time, and then you won't have to type it over.
   | 1 | 2 | 3 | 4 | 5 | 6 | 7 | 8 | 9 | 10 | 11 | 12 | 13 | 14 |

71B ● INVENTORYING SELECTED TECHNIQUES
10 minutes

PROCEDURE Type 45C, page 78, as directed. As time permits, retype the sentences that provide needed practice in typing capitals, figure-symbols, double letters, and one-hand words.

71C ● DISCOVERING SPEED RANGE WITH MAXIMUM ACCURACY *5 minutes*

PROCEDURE Type 67C, page 119, as four 1-minute writings. First, type at approximately 40 *gwam*; then at 50, 55, and 60 (or other appropriate rates). Determine the rate at which you maintain maximum control.

71D ● INVENTORYING BASIC SKILL *25 minutes*

PROCEDURE Type three 5-minute writings of 60B, page 103, on the *control level*. Determine errors and *gwam* after each writing and be guided by these in setting your goals for the next writing.

LESSON 72 | **72A ● PREPARATORY PRACTICE** *5 minutes (each line three or more times)*

Alphabetic   Today Frank J. McIntosh was happy to be given quite a sizable tax cut.

Figure-symbol   Your 1964 edition of the book has 3 parts, 27 chapters, and 580 pages.

Fluency   Friends sent us the ornament from an ancient temple in a foreign land.
   | 1 | 2 | 3 | 4 | 5 | 6 | 7 | 8 | 9 | 10 | 11 | 12 | 13 | 14 |

72B ● INVENTORYING SELECTED TECHNIQUES
7 minutes

PROCEDURE Type each line of 53B, page 91, three times on the *control level*. Strive to improve your typing techniques.

72C ● INVENTORYING BASIC SKILL
8 minutes

PROCEDURE Type 65B, page 114, as a 5-minute writing. Type on the *control level*. Determine *gwam* and errors.

● *Lesson 72 is continued on page 127.*

The figures in the 1' GWAM column show both the gwam for 1' writings and the total cumulative word count for both paragraphs. This word count may therefore be used to determine gwam for writings of any length:

Total words ÷ Time of writing = gwam

● All letters are used in these paragraphs.

	GWAM *	
	1'	3'

¶ 1
52 words

It pays to read. The more you read, the more you will — 11 | 4 | 40

learn and earn. A man from a big firm in our town says the — 23 | 8 | 44

top men read far more than those who are not quite tops. A — 35 | 12 | 48

big job calls for a big man, and men grow big when they can — 47 | 16 | 52

read more and learn more. — 52 | 17 | 53

¶ 2
56 words

The more you read, the more you know; and the more you — 63 | 21 | 57

know, the more you grow. You should mix the types of books — 75 | 25 | 61

you read to give breadth and depth to what you know. Prize — 87 | 29 | 65

the books you read as you prize the friends you have. Both — 99 | 33 | 69

books and friends can make life rich for you. — 108 | 36 | 72

```
1' | 1 | 2 | 3 | 4 | 5 | 6 | 7 | 8 | 9 | 10 | 11 | 12 |
3' |   1   |   |   2   |   |   3   |   |   4   |
```

LESSON 13 | 13A ● PREPARATORY PRACTICE *10 minutes*
(each line three times)

Alphabetic Was Fred quick to give him a box just the size for my plant?

Drill on m Men must try to move up and make room for more men to climb.

Fluency Do the work you like to do and like the work you have to do.
```
| 1 | 2 | 3 | 4 | 5 | 6 | 7 | 8 | 9 | 10 | 11 | 12 |
```

13B ● TECHNIQUE PRACTICE: Space Bar and Shift Keys *10 minutes*
(each line three times)

TECHNIQUE EMPHASIS: Space Bar
Strike the space bar with a quick inward motion of the thumb. Keep the hand and the elbow in good typing position to avoid spacing irregularities.

Shifting for Capitals
Hold the shift key down until the capital has been struck and released; then move *immediately* and without interrupting the stroking rhythm to the next letter.

● All reach-strokes taught are used in this practice.

1 Have they played them? Should we tell the men to stop soon?

2 Don, I see, wants to quit; and if he does, I must stop, too.

3 Keep the wrists low and the arms still. Make quick strokes.

4 Clay, Zeke, and Max will have a big day in New York in June.
```
| 1 | 2 | 3 | 4 | 5 | 6 | 7 | 8 | 9 | 10 | 11 | 12 |
```

Problem 4: Letter with Tabulated Items (*errors corrected, unless otherwise directed*)

Full sheet Carbon sheet File copy sheet	●	Use machine adjustments and letter style and punctuation you prefer Your return address; current date	●	Decide on number of spaces between columns	●	Address an envelope; fold and insert letter into envelope

	Words
United Credit Union | 926 Boynton Street |	19
Denver, Colorado 80209 | Gentlemen |	26
(¶ 1) For a class report in Banking and	33
Finance, I am preparing a paper on credit	41
unions in the United States and Canada.	49
I am writing to ask for information on	57
types of credit unions, how they are or-	65
ganized, and where and how they operate.	74
(¶ 2) It will help me greatly if you will	81
check the figures I give below and let me	89

	Words
know if they are accurate enough for me	97
to use in my paper:	101

	Number	Members	
			107
United States	18,433	10,081,113	114
Canada	4,351	2,199,119	119

(¶ 3) I shall be grateful for copies of — 125
printed bulletins you have on credit unions — 134
and for references to source material I — 142
can use for further study on this subject. \| — 151
Very truly yours \| (*Your Name*) \| — 158/170

SELF-IMPROVEMENT PRACTICE ● (*each line three or more times*)

● All letters and figures are used in the sentences.

		Words in Line	GWAM 15"	12"	10"
1	Learn how much you can do in a certain time––and do it.	11	44	55	66
2	Poise is the ability to do things well while others look on.	12	48	60	72
3	Bess will take a good look at the book Nell Briggs wants to sell.	13	52	65	78
4	Hal and Clay will go to Spain in March or April if Mat goes to France.	14	56	70	84
5	Their 5½¢ increase makes your price a 20¢-a-pound item.	11	44	55	66
6	The 5-inch writing line has just 50 pica or 60 elite spaces.	12	48	60	72
7	Keith bought Decker & Sloane 4s at 45¼ and sold on May 23 at 87½.	13	52	65	78
8	The postal card has 19 lines of 66 elite or 55 pica spaces for typing.	14	56	70	84
9	A number of men mentioned their fear of my Muncie deal.	11	44	55	66
10	We were told that we were to be rewarded for excellent work.	12	48	60	72
11	A man who pulls his weight doesn't have any left to throw around.	13	52	65	84
12	Boredom is not in the work we do, but in ourselves as we do that work.	14	56	70	78
13	Forget the faults of others, and do your own work well.	11	44	55	66
14	The 85 men, 36 boys, and 79 girls did not leave until 12:40.	12	48	60	72
15	Don't try to carve your way to success with many cutting remarks.	13	52	65	78
16	The auditor said the company will pay your men for a month's vacation.	14	56	70	84
17	This work challenges your competence, resourcefulness, and creativity.	14	56	70	84
18	Except in centers of recent revolts, we received exceptional courtesy.	14	56	70	84
19	It was decided to make a second check of the central decoding service.	14	56	70	84
20	W. K. Vance made quite a sizable fortune by exporting jade from China.	14	56	70	84

\| 1 \| 2 \| 3 \| 4 \| 5 \| 6 \| 7 \| 8 \| 9 \| 10 \| 11 \| 12 \| 13 \| 14 \|

13C ● TYPING FROM DICTATION *5 minutes (each line three times)*

to at so is on if as or up of in it be do at if up or in for

key are but you and try fix won can out use now not may down

work plan find have slow back your keep well need will worth

13D ● PARAGRAPH GUIDED WRITING *20 minutes (as directed in 12D, page 27)*

● All letters are used in these paragraphs.

	GWAM	
	1'	3'

¶ 1
52 words

You are on your way now. You have learned to type on, | 11 | 4 | 40 |
one key at a time. It is the pause that kills skill, so do | 23 | 8 | 44 |
not pause. Use a quick stroke if you can and a slow stroke | 35 | 12 | 48 |
if you must, but keep on. Fix your eyes on the word, think | 47 | 16 | 52 |
and type it; and type on. | 52 | 17 | 53 |

¶ 2
56 words

If you fail to type as well as you think you should at | 63 | 21 | 57 |
times, try to find out just what holds you back. It may be | 75 | 25 | 61 |
you will need to speed up or slow down for a time or change | 87 | 29 | 65 |
your plan of work in some way. There is a prize to be won, | 99 | 33 | 69 |
and that prize is worth the work you must do. | 108 | 36 | 72 |

1' | 1 | 2 | 3 | 4 | 5 | 6 | 7 | 8 | 9 | 10 | 11 | 12 |
3' | 1 | 2 | 3 | 4 |

LESSON 14 | 14A ● PREPARATORY PRACTICE *10 minutes (each line three times)*

Alphabetic   If my TV is fixed, can Lew look at the quiz by Judge Thorpe?

Letter p   Paul dropped the plan to put the place up for sale just now.

Fluency   A man does not have to wait for luck if he will work for it.

| 1 | 2 | 3 | 4 | 5 | 6 | 7 | 8 | 9 | 10 | 11 | 12 |

14B ● TYPING FOR CONTROL *35 minutes*

Use Lesson 12, page 27. Begin with 12B Technique Practice and type the remainder of the lesson as directed in each part. The purpose of this repetitive typing is to build typing control so that your growth index will be satisfactory when you type Lesson 15. Work for controlled, but continuous, stroking.

Problem 1: Leftbound Manuscript with Footnote (*errors corrected*)

| Page-end indicator Typed in leftbound manuscript form | ● | 1 full sheet (for elite type) 2 full sheets (for pica type) | ● | 5-space ¶ indention; double spacing Single-space; indent quoted ¶ 5 spaces from both margins |

	Words
DIPLOMAS AND CONSERVATISM	5

(¶ 1) Americans have been told for years that in the 60's a vast new crop of college students would appear on the nation's campuses––the 1945–47 "war babies." They appeared on schedule, and now we wonder what they are like. Are they surging forth to slay the dragons? Researchers say "No." After months spent talking with college seniors from coast to coast, researchers find a generation that has learned to live with the world into which they were born. Sociologists at times call this generation apathetic, but many believe the young have returned to reason. (¶ 2) Today's college student has lived relatively well all through his life. But he has also lived through what one writer calls "brinkmanship"––on the very edge of crisis and catastrophe. He has had to learn to live in a drastically insecure

	Words

world. These factors have shaped his thinking, just as they have affected the attitude of older people. (¶ 3) One writer notes that job security is important as a goal today. The young want to contribute to society––if it will pay enough. An important part of the security goal is a home. The college student wants a comfortable suburban home equipped with the best of everything. Such a home is, to be sure, a status symbol for the young married set, but it has a deeper meaning, too.

(¶ 4) . . . home is the refuge, where there is no need for pretenses, where one can teach one's children the standard virtues. . . . This kind of practical thinking is a natural enough reaction to the basic insecurity that hangs over the heads of everyone.[1]

[1] "War Babies with Diplomas," *Business Week*, Number 1763 (June 15, 1963), p. 25.

(Word counts: 12, 21, 29, 36, 44, 52, 61, 68, 77, 85, 93, 102, 110, 118, 125, 133, 142, 150, 158, 166 / 174, 182, 189, 198, 206, 215, 222, 230, 238, 247, 255, 264 / 270, 278, 286, 294, 302, 310, 315, 319, 326, 336, 337)

Problem 2: Outline from Rough Draft (*121 words*)

| Half sheet | ● | 60-space line |

PROCEDURE Type the heading IMPROVING YOUR STUDY HABITS on Line 6.

```
I.   READING IS KEY TO EFFECTIVE STUDY

     A.  Efficiency in Reading is Important.
         1.  Force yourself to read rapidly.
         2.  Grasp (first) the main thought.

     B.  Underline after You Have Read.
         1.  Use red pencil for initial
             underlining.
         2.  Use black pencil over red to
             show mastery.
         3.  Underline very important
             passages with a double line.

II.  TAKE NOTES EFFECTIVELY

     A.  Make Note of Important Points Only.
  Record 1.  Note ideas in your own words.
         2.  Avoid repetition. if possible.
     B.  Summarize What You Have Read. Not
         1.  Reread passages that are clear.
         2.  Test yourself on what is read.
                            you have
```

Problem 3: Poem (*106 words*)

| 3 half sheets 2 carbon copies | ● | Single spacing Center vertically | ● | "Spread" the heading |

PROCEDURE The following lines (in their original form) appear in Part 1 of the verse play *Paracelsus*. Center horizontally, using the longest line. Type the author's name at the extreme right. Type PARACELSUS for the title of the poem.

Truth is within ourselves; it takes no rise
From outward things, whate'er you may believe.
There is an inmost centre in us all,
Where truth abides in fulness; and around,
Wall upon wall, the gross flesh hems it in,
This perfect, clear perception––which is truth.
A baffling and perverting carnal mesh
Binds it, and makes all error: and, to KNOW,
Rather consists in opening out a way
Whence the imprisoned splendor may escape,
Than in effecting entry for a light
Supposed to be without.

● Triple-space

––Robert Browning

● *70C is continued on page 125.*

LESSON 15 | 15A ● PREPARATORY PRACTICE *10 minutes (each line three times)*

Alphabetic   Will Vic Boyd pay a good sum for Jack to fix the quaint adz?

Drill on v   Van Vaughn drove with Eve and Dave Voigt to see Vince Grove.

Fluency   Can a man grow out of a small job and come to fit a big one?
   | 1 | 2 | 3 | 4 | 5 | 6 | 7 | 8 | 9 | 10 | 11 | 12 |

15B ● TECHNIQUE PRACTICE: Tabulator and Carriage Return *10 minutes (three times)*

PROCEDURE Use double spacing. Clear all tab stops. (Review page 20.) Set a tab stop approximately 10 spaces to the right of the center of the paper. Begin the first line at this point by tabulating to this stop. Double-space after the completed drill before you type it the second time and the third.

Study your hand motions and try to make each needed motion without waste of time or effort. This is the intelligent way to build skill.

TECHNIQUE EMPHASIS: Nonelectric Return Bring the hand back to typing position immediately after the throw has been made, and start to type the new line immediatly. Hold your eyes on the copy as you return the carriage.

Electric Return Flick the little finger to the electric return key and return the finger to its typing position immediately. Hold your eyes on the copy as you return and as you start the new line.

Tab _____Hold the arms still; Return

type with a quick stroke._____Tab_____Keep the eyes on the Return

word as you type it._____Tab_____Think the word as it Return

is typed._____Hold your wrists low

as you type._____Type with ease; just

strike one key at a time._____Type on; do not stop

when you have typed a word.

15C ● TYPING FROM DICTATION *5 minutes (each line three times)*

is on it in he at if up to no is on he in if at up to no man

the get who can few for now how you job use not and has time

work next does know find hard mind have want want your right
| 1 | 2 | 3 | 4 | 5 | 6 | 7 | 8 | 9 | 10 | 11 | 12 |

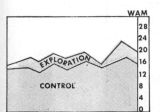

EXPLORATION LEVEL OF PRACTICE

When the purpose of your typing is to reach out into new speed areas, use the *exploration level of practice*. Take the brakes off your fingers and let them experiment with new stroking technique patterns and try out new speed areas.

CONTROL LEVEL OF PRACTICE

When the purpose of your typing is to type with ease and control, drop back in rate and type on the *control level of practice*. This drop back should be 4 to 8 words below the exploration rate; stroking should be rhythmic, continuous.

70A ● **PREPARATORY PRACTICE** *5 minutes (each line three or more times)*

Alphabetic   Jack proved quite a few girls analyzed these mixed dates and problems.

Figure-symbol   The * (asterisk) on page 978 refers to Item #52 of List 46 of Book 13.

Fluency   If you have the right worker in the right job, you are very fortunate.
| 1 | 2 | 3 | 4 | 5 | 6 | 7 | 8 | 9 | 10 | 11 | 12 | 13 | 14 |

70B ● **GROWTH INDEX** *15 minutes (two 5′ control-level writings)*

Full sheet, 70-space line,
double spacing,
5-space ¶ indention

PROCEDURE Pause 30–40 seconds between writings to relax, but do not check your writings until both are completed; then determine *gwam* and errors.

● All letters are used in the paragraphs.

GWAM | 1′ | 5′

¶ 1
1.35 si
120 words

Is it true that there is just as much competition in business today — 14 | 3 | 53
as fifty years ago? Many people do not think so. They say it is found — 28 | 6 | 56
much less now than before. They point to what they consider to be a — 42 | 8 | 58
great growth in big business, yet there has been very little real change — 56 | 11 | 61
in this growth in the past five decades. They point, also, to the in- — 70 | 14 | 64
crease in government control and in taxes, which do limit competition to — 85 | 17 | 67
some extent. It is quite true that a number of people wish to limit com- — 100 | 20 | 70
petition, and these people often have a strong urge to make their wishes — 114 | 23 | 73
known to just about everyone. — 120 | 24 | 74

¶ 2
1.35 si
132 words

Still, one fact does stand out. Competition over the years does — 133 | 27 | 77
seem to have been growing stronger. This is due to the fact that the — 147 | 29 | 79
prizes given to business are spreading and taking a number of new and — 161 | 32 | 82
better forms. One form is increased production caused by automation. — 175 | 35 | 85
The other is the fact that all new products will continue to be sold. — 189 | 38 | 88
Private business must make a fair profit. It is certain, too, that a — 203 | 41 | 91
limit will be set on the resources to be used. It is very important, — 217 | 43 | 93
then, that those that are found be made into those things that the people — 232 | 46 | 96
want and need. Competition should help bring about the goal of better — 246 | 49 | 99
goods at much better prices. — 252 | 50 | 100

1′ | 1 | 2 | 3 | 4 | 5 | 6 | 7 | 8 | 9 | 10 | 11 | 12 | 13 | 14 |
5′ | 1 | 2 | 3 |

15D ● GROWTH INDEX *20 minutes*

1 Type ¶ 1 as a 1-minute writing. Note the *gwam* base rate.
2 Set a new goal: *Deduct* 4 words from the base rate. Divide this new rate into quarter-minute segments. Make a note of the quarter-minute check points for quick reference.

3 Type a ½- and then a 1-min. *control-level* writing, guided by the call of the guide.
4 Type two additional ½-min. and then two 1-min. writings as directed in Step 3.
5 Type ¶ 2 as in Steps 1-4.

6 Finally, type two 3-minute writings without the call of the guide, starting with ¶ 1 and typing as far as you can before time is called. Determine *gwam* for the better writing. Note this rate for comparison purposes in later lessons.

● All letters are used in these paragraphs.

			GWAM	
			1'	3'

¶ 1
52 words

The job squeeze is on right now, and it will get worse — 11 | 4 | 40
in the next few years. The man who does not know how to do — 23 | 8 | 44
at least one thing well will find it hard to get work. The — 35 | 12 | 48
man who has a trained mind and skilled hands will have work — 47 | 16 | 52
he likes and can do well. — 52 | 17 | 53

¶ 2
56 words

It is up to you to train your mind and build the skill — 63 | 21 | 57
you will need for the job you want. It takes time and hard — 75 | 25 | 61
work to train the mind, and it takes time and work to build — 87 | 29 | 65
a skill you can use on the job. No one can do the work for — 99 | 33 | 69
you, but you can do it if you will start now. — 108 | 36 | 72

1' | 1 | 2 | 3 | 4 | 5 | 6 | 7 | 8 | 9 | 10 | 11 | 12
3' | 1 | 2 | 3 | 4

SELF-IMPROVEMENT PRACTICE ● *(each line three or more times)*

1	Alphabetic	Max just left my quiz show, and he gave back a prize he won.
2	Double letters	Will Bill call Miss Huss to see if Dr. Reeves took the book?
3	Double letters	Tell Bill Stull that Nell will soon get a room for the cook.
4	Home row	As we said, Hal Hall was glad to have the lad take the flag.
5	One-hand	We were as sad as you and John Hill were at your great loss.
6	One-hand	I look as old as you, but I feel quite sure you know my age.
7	Adjacent letters	We were asked if the lad has as much poise as Jane Munn has.
8	Direct reach	Burt grows the flax from which this quaint old lace is made.
9	Direct reach	A group of brave men checked the fire and saved my big barn.
10	Capital letters	Don Trigg will go to France and Greece with Ken Hunt in May.

| 1 | 2 | 3 | 4 | 5 | 6 | 7 | 8 | 9 | 10 | 11 | 12 |

69B ● PROBLEM TYPING: Composing a Letter; Check; Composing a Manuscript *25 minutes*

Problem 1: Composing and Typing a Letter

Full sheet	Current date
Carbon sheet	Modified block,
File copy sheet	blocked ¶s
50-space line	Mixed punctuation

PROCEDURE Your father has asked you to answer the letter typed as Problem 1, page 117, and to enclose his check for $100. In closing the letter, express best wishes for a successful drive for funds. Type your father's name in position for his pen signature, and type *Enclosure* at the left margin a double space below the typed name.

Problem 2: Typing a Check

PROCEDURE Before typing the check illustrated at the right, insert a drill sheet and type a 3- or 4-inch line; then type *Sylvania College Alumni Fund* on the line. Study the relation of the letters to the line, so when you type the check for $100 you will have the typed lines placed correctly in relation to the lines on the check.

A typed check

JAMES W. HARMON
1028 College Street
Memphis, Tennessee 38109

No. 346   26-2 / 840

Atlanta, Georgia_____ February 28, 19--

PAY TO THE
ORDER OF Sylvania College Alumni Fund- - - - - - - - -$100.00

One hundred and no/100- - - - - - - - - - - - -.- - - - - - - - - - -DOLLARS

THE 2d NATIONAL BANK
MEMPHIS, TENNESSEE 38104

James W. Harmon

⑈0840⑈0002⑈ 719⑈4420⑈

Problem 3: Composing a Manuscript

Page-end indicator	5-space ¶ indention
Full sheet	Type in an unbound
Double spacing	manuscript form

PROCEDURE Type the portion of the manuscript as given; then add two or more paragraphs describing your difficulty in typing without error, in proofreading, and in correcting the errors on the original and file copy. Use the title ACCURACY RANKS FIRST.

(¶ 1) Of the five most important performance traits of a competent secretary, accuracy ranks first. But what is accuracy in typewriting? Is it typing without error without regard to speed, or is it typing with reasonable control—and then finding and correcting the errors? (¶ 2) Beamer, Hanna, and Popham say, "Accuracy is careful work, carefully checked, carefully corrected, and carefully rechecked." [1] (*Continue with the two or three paragraphs you are to compose; remember to save space for the footnote reference.*)

[1] Esther Kihn Beamer, J Marshall Hanna, and Estelle L. Popham, *Effective Secretarial Practices* (4th ed.; Cincinnati: South-Western Publishing Company, 1962), p. 17.

69C ● PROBLEM TYPING REVIEW *15 minutes*

SUPPLIES NEEDED:
2 full sheets
Page-end indicator

PROCEDURE

1 Make pencil notations of the problems and page numbers given below:

67D, Problem 1, page 119
67D, Problem 2, page 120

Place the notation sheet beside the typewriter.

2 Unless otherwise directed, erase and correct all errors. After typing a problem and before removing it from the typewriter, proofread the typing and correct all errors that are correctible.

LEARNING TO TYPE FIGURES

STANDARD PROCEDURES FOR SECTION 3

GET READY TO TYPE

Adjust the paper guide and the ribbon control. Use a 60-space line; single-space the drills, double-space the paragraphs and use a 5-space paragraph indention. Type the copy line for line.

SELF-IMPROVEMENT PRACTICE

Type the lines of Self-Improvement Practice, page 41, three or more times each, as time permits. Identify each errorless line typed so that extra credit may be given for this work if your instructor desires to do so.

● **SYLLABLE INTENSITY**

Syllable intensity (si) is determined by dividing the total syllables by the total words in a paragraph. Only 1- and 2-syllable words are used in the practice materials of this section.

LESSON 16 | 16A ● PREPARATORY PRACTICE *7 minutes (each line three times)*

Alphabetic	Was the process of quick freezing explained by James Weaver?
q and u	Quentin quickly quizzed them about the plaque for Vic Quinn.
Fluency	It is the mind that makes you rich or poor, a whiz or a dud.

| 1 | 2 | 3 | 4 | 5 | 6 | 7 | 8 | 9 | 10 | 11 | 12 |

Work for continuity of stroking

16B ● NEW KEYS: 1, 3, and 7 *8 minutes*

TO LEARN TO TYPE THE NEW KEY:

1 Find the new key on the keyboard chart.
2 Find the new key on the typewriter keyboard.
3 Study the reach-stroke illustration for the key.
4 Watch your finger make the reach a few times.

Reach to 3

Reach to 7

FINGERS

1. CONTROL OF 1

Use small letter *l* for figure **1** if the typewriter does not have a special key for it. If there is a special key for **1**, reach up to it with the *left fourth finger.* Type the Tryout Practice twice on one line.

1l The 1ll men work well.

2. REACH TECHNIQUE FOR 3

As the *left second finger* moves up to type **3**, lift the first finger slightly. Type **3** without moving the hand from typing position. Watch your finger type **3d** a few times; then type the Tryout Practice twice.

3d 3 d3d 33 d3d 333 d3d 3

3. REACH TECHNIQUE FOR 7

Reach the *right first finger* up to type **7** without moving the other fingers from their home positions. Keep the wrists low. Watch your finger type **7j** a few times; then type the Tryout Practice twice on one line.

7j 7 j7j 77 j7j 777 j7j 7

Problem 1: Rough Draft of a Leftbound Manuscript Page with Tabulated Items (*errors not corrected*)

Page-end indicator • Full sheet • Leftbound manuscript form • 5-space ¶ indention • 4 spaces between columns

PROOFREADER'S MARKS: *ss* single spacing   *ss* →¹⁄₂   *¶* paragraph

	Words
ALL CAPS [Department Store Sales in Selected Areas *TRIPLE-SPACE*	8

The following data from an unpublished report shows the distribution of department store sales in a large eastern city for downtown areas in 1953, 1957, and 1958; and for selected outlying areas in 1957 and 1958 only, as data for (outlying) specific areas before 1957 are not given: *available:*

15
27
40
54
60

	1953	1957	1958	
Large downtown stores	48.0	40.6	39.4	ds	66 / 73
Small downtown stores	18.6	17.9	15.1		81
Selected shopping centers	--	12.0	12.0 9		89
Other outlying stores	--	29.5	29.6		96

ss →
ds →
ss →

ds ¶ The data reveal a *steady* decline in *the* per cent of sales by downtown stores and a gradual increase in sales for stores in outlying areas.

111
123

Problem 2: Two-Page Manuscript with Tabulated Items

Page-end indicator • 2 full sheets

PROCEDURE Type Problem 2, page 120, as directed, incorporating Problem 1, above, as part of the manuscript to follow ¶ 1; then, continue typing the rest of Problem 2. Study the guides at the right before you begin typing.

GUIDES FOR TYPING MANUSCRIPTS OF TWO OR MORE PAGES

1 Avoid having more than two consecutive lines end with a hyphened word; never end a page with a hyphened word.

2 Never have only one line of a paragraph at the bottom or at the top of a page.

3 A footnote is typed on the same page as its reference.

4 PAGE NUMBERS: *First page*, centered ½″ from bottom of page; *second page*, ½″ from top of page in upper right corner, approximately even with the right margin.

68D ● **SENTENCE GUIDED WRITING FROM CORRECTED SCRIPT** *5 minutes*

(*two 1′ control-level writings on each sentence*)

	GWAM 15″	12″	10″
If When you growl all day, you must can expect to feel dog tired by night.	52	65	78
The Thoughts and the ideas you think you hold form your the world for you.	56	70	84

LESSON 69 | 69A ● **PREPARATORY PRACTICE** *5 minutes* (*each line three or more times*)

Alphabetic   Next week qualified judges will have to analyze our club performances.

Figure-symbol   He ordered 48 boxes of #573 @ $2.69, less 10%, from O'Brien & Company.

Fluency   The very time to try again and to do our best is when we want to stop.

| 1 | 2 | 3 | 4 | 5 | 6 | 7 | 8 | 9 | 10 | 11 | 12 | 13 | 14 |

16C ● STROKING TECHNIQUE PRACTICE *10 minutes (each line three times)*

● All letters and figures taught are used in the sentences.

<table>
<tr><td>1</td><td rowspan="2">Strive for continuity of stroking</td><td>From May 1 to June 1, the 11 men have worked 111 hours each.</td><td rowspan="2">Reach to the figure</td></tr>
<tr><td>2</td><td>Max and Liza read pages 3 to 33 of the 333 pages in my book.</td></tr>
<tr><td>3</td><td></td><td>The 7 women and 17 men took Flight 777 to New York on May 7.</td><td></td></tr>
<tr><td>4</td><td></td><td>Did 3 of the 33 boys make a grade of 77 on the June 17 test?</td><td rowspan="2">Hold the wrists low</td></tr>
<tr><td>5</td><td></td><td>Could Ruth quickly give the sum of 11 and 33 and 77 and 173?</td></tr>
</table>

| 1 | 2 | 3 | 4 | 5 | 6 | 7 | 8 | 9 | 10 | 11 | 12 |

16D ● TECHNIQUE PRACTICE: Tab Mechanism and Carriage Return *10 minutes*
(twice as shown)

60-space line, 8 columns (5 spaces between)

PROCEDURE FOR SETTING TAB STOPS
1 Clear all tab stops.
2 For Column 2, set a tab stop 5 spaces from end of first column.

3 For Column 3, set a tab stop 5 spaces from end of second column.
4 Set stops for remaining columns in similar manner.

and	did	aid	rod	but	got	big	map
for	pay	wit	may	fir	rub	bid	pen

● Double-space (to leave one blank line space)

sit	dug	man	pan	cue	fit	rib	men
rub	fur	end	sir	vow	cut	woe	rug

Eyes on copy as you return the carriage

Reach to the figure

all	111	due	333	sum	777	cue	373
hue	377	end	373	sue	337	hem	773

16E ● BUILDING SPEED AND CONTROL *10 minutes*

Double spacing, 5-space paragraph indention

PROCEDURE
1 Type two 1-minute writings, the first for speed and the second for control (4 to 8 words below the *gwam* of the first writing).
2 Relax 20 to 30 seconds; then type a 2′ writing at your controlled speed.

3 Relax 20 to 30 seconds, and type a 3′ writing; then determine the *gwam* on the 3′ writing. Use this *gwam* rate as your base rate when typing 17E, page 35.

● Double-space (to leave one blank line space)

1.10 si
116 words

	GWAM	
	1′	3′

It is in the mind that you learn to type. The fingers strike the keys, of course; but it is the mind that directs them. Just before the next writing, choose a goal of speed or control and tell your fingers the goal you want to gain; then make them type as you want them to type. If your goal is more speed, tell your fingers not to freeze to a key but to move quickly from key to key. If control is the goal of your practice, drop back in speed and type with ease. Know what you are to gain from each line you type, and then tell your fingers what to do to achieve your goal.

1′	3′
11	4 / 43
23	8 / 47
35	12 / 51
47	16 / 55
59	20 / 59
71	24 / 63
83	28 / 67
95	32 / 71
107	36 / 75
116	39 / 78

1′ | 1 | 2 | 3 | 4 | 5 | 6 | 7 | 8 | 9 | 10 | 11 | 12 |
3′ | 1 | 2 | 3 | 4 |

67D ● PROBLEM TYPING *(Continued)*

Problem 2: Leftbound Manuscript Page with Footnote *(errors not corrected)*

● *Keep this problem for 68C, page 121.*

Page-end indicator	5-space ¶ indention
Full sheet ●	Type in leftbound
Double spacing	manuscript form

                                              Words

NEW LOOK IN SUBURBIA   4

(¶ 1) There is a new look in Suburbia. It   12
comes from the giant shopping centers   19
that have sprung up outside the city limits   28
all over the United States. Marketing ex-   36
perts say the automobile has much to do   44
with the phenomenon. When two or more   52
cars to a family became common, the mass   60
exodus to the suburbs was on. (¶ 2) Two   67
big problems in these giant centers are: 76
(1) How to find the car parked among the   84
rows of other cars that look so much   91
alike, and (2) What to do when the gas   99
tank is empty and a gas station is a mile   108
or more from the shopping center. "At   115

                                              Words

one Michigan center the police cars carry   124
an extra can of gas and provide a free   132
gallon to the motorist who runs out." [1]   140
(¶ 3) There is a bright side to the story.   147
The surroundings are usually very attrac-   155
tive. The landscaping is often "lavish   163
tropical planting . . . to suggest eternal   170
springtime." [2] (¶ 4) Two cars for every   179
garage in Suburbia, the family income   186
growing steadily higher, and the work   194
week growing shorter, mean more money,   202
more time, and a car at the door. Hop in;   210
let's run over to the new shopping center.   219
We can get just about everything we need   227
there without going to town!   234
                                                 237

[1] Don Wharton, "Many Shopping Cen-   244
ters," *The Reader's Digest* (May, 1963),   256
p. 184.   258

Ibid. refers to the source immediately preceding. ➡ [2] *Ibid.*, p. 183.   262

67E ● PROBLEM SKILL BUILDING *5 minutes* *(3' writing on Problem 2, above; errors corrected, unless otherwise directed)*

PROCEDURE Use the machine adjustments for which the typewriter is set.

LESSON 68 | 68A ● PREPARATORY PRACTICE *5 minutes (each line three or more times)*

Alphabetic	We expected to solve the jigsaw puzzle more quickly than Fred and Bud.
Fractions	I used 1/2 and 1/4 instead of ½ and ¼ when typing a number of carbons.
Fluency	The chairman's duties have been taken over by Elvis while Paul is ill.

| 1 | 2 | 3 | 4 | 5 | 6 | 7 | 8 | 9 | 10 | 11 | 12 | 13 | 14 |

68B ● TIMED WRITING ON A ROUGH-DRAFT TABULATION *10 minutes*
(5' writing on Problem 1, page 119)

PROCEDURE You will be given 3 minutes in which to get ready to type; read the directions, insert the paper, and adjust the machine for the four columns.

LESSON 17 | 17A ● PREPARATORY PRACTICE *7 minutes (each line three times)*

Alphabetic   Jim questioned why Phil Kortz gave six fawns to Buck Graves.   Work for

Figures   Their July 13 test will cover pages 33 to 77 and 137 to 371.   continuity
    of stroking

Fluency   Type the word; then go quickly to the next word and type it.

`| 1 | 2 | 3 | 4 | 5 | 6 | 7 | 8 | 9 | 10 | 11 | 12 |`

17B ● NEW KEYS: 9, 5, and : (Colon)

8 minutes

PROCEDURE Follow the four-step procedure
for learning new keys, page 32.

Reach to 9

Reach to 5

1. REACH TECHNIQUE FOR 9

As the *right third finger* moves up to type **9**, keep the wrist low and the elbow in position. Make the reach with minimum hand motion. Watch your finger type **91** a few times; then type the Tryout Practice twice on one line.

91 9 191 99 191 999 191 9

2. REACH TECHNIQUE FOR 5

Reach the *left first finger* to **5** without moving the other fingers from their home position or moving the hand forward. Keep the wrist low. Watch your finger type **5f** a few times; then type the Tryout Practice twice.

5f 5 f5f 55 f5f 555 f5f 5

3. CONTROL OF THE : (COLON)

Type the : (which is the shift of the ;) with the *right fourth finger. Do not space before or after the : when it separates hours and minutes.* Watch your finger type **:;** a few times then type the Tryout Practice twice.

:; :: ;:; I left at 9:15.

17C ● STROKING TECHNIQUE PRACTICE *10 minutes (each line three times)*

SPACING RULE 1 Do not space after a : (colon) used to separate hours and minutes in stating time. Space twice after : in other uses; for example, to introduce a series, a list of enumerated items, or a long quotation. See Line 3.

SPACING RULE 2 Do not space after a period used within an abbreviation, but space once after the final period used to punctuate the last letter of the abbreviation except at the end of the line; then return without spacing. See Lines 3 and 5.

● All letters and all figures taught are used in the sentences.

1 Reach—   Did 9 boys and 19 girls make 99 on the May 19 test in Latin?   Return without

2 don't "leap"   Each of the 5 boys worked 55 hours from July 5 to August 15.   pausing at the
  to the keys   end of the line

3   Type these figures: 39, 75, and 91. Jane left at 9:15 p.m.

4 Shift quickly We bought 39 cases of peas and 57 of pears in Quebec in May.

5   Max flew to Brazil at 7:35 a.m., but Ben leaves at 9:15 p.m.

`| 1 | 2 | 3 | 4 | 5 | 6 | 7 | 8 | 9 | 10 | 11 | 12 |`

Full sheet	5-space ¶
Carbon copy ●	indention
70-space line	Double spacing

PROCEDURE Correct errors as a part of the timing, unless otherwise directed. For each uncorrected error, deduct 15 words to compensate for the time it would take to erase and correct the error. Determine your corrected copy typing rate. This will give you a clue to your probable production rate when typing problems.

● All letters are used in the paragraph.

	1' GWAM
Some workers can't do anything unless they are told just what to	13
do and how to do it. They may be good in routine tasks, but they are	27
limited by their lack of imagination, creativity, and the urge to explore	42
new ways of doing things. Even great skill isn't enough, because their	56
skilled hands must be guided by reflective heads--a fact many workers	70
frequently fail to recognize.	76

1.44 si
76 words

1' | 1 | 2 | 3 | 4 | 5 | 6 | 7 | 8 | 9 | 10 | 11 | 12 | 13 | 14 |

67D ● **PROBLEM TYPING: Tabulation with Columnar Headings; Manuscript Page** *25 minutes*

Problem 1: Rough-Draft Tabulation with Columnar Headings

Full sheet	6 spaces between columns
Double spacing	Center in reading position

PROCEDURE In the last three columns, type the $ before the first amount (and the total, where given) so the $ will be one space to the left of the longest amount in the column.

PROOFREADER'S MARK:

ds double spacing *ds →* 1/2

NOTE In a list of names, titles such as *Dr., Professor,* and *Mrs.* are typed while *Mr.* and *Miss* are usually omitted.

SYLVANIA COLLEGE

ds [AMOUNTS PLEDGED TO ʌ ANNUAL ALUMNI FUND

by

(ALUMNI OF NORTH CAROLINA) Triple-space

				Words
				11
				12
				16

Name	Pledged	Paid	Balance	
Paul C. Abbott	$ 500.00	$ 250.00	$ 250.00	36
Dr. O. R. Callahan	1,250.00	700 ~~750~~.00	550.00	45
Sue A. Dahlbert	100.00	100.00	-	51
Andrew H. Garrison	7 ~~650~~.00	375.00	375.00	59
Morton W. Johnson	2,500.00	1,000.00	1,500.00	70
E. N. Lazenby	75.00	50.00	25.00	77
Mrs. Walter K. Snyder	250.00	250.00	-	85
Daniel D. Talbott	1,000.00	875.00	125.00	93
Theodore Y. Sullivan	350.00	125.00 ~~400.00~~	225 ~~200~~.00	102
Louis C. Woodward	7 ~~650~~.00	400.00	350.00	109
M. Trexler Yeager	50.00	50 ~~100~~.00	(-) ~~50.00~~	116

● *67D is continued on page 120.*

17D ● TECHNIQUE PRACTICE: Tab Mechanism and Carriage Return *10 minutes*

(twice as shown)

60-space line,
8 columns
(5 spaces
between)

PROCEDURE FOR SETTING TAB STOPS

1 Clear all tab stops.
2 For Column 2, set a tab stop 5 spaces from end of first column.

3 For Column 3, set a tab stop 5 spaces from end of second column.
4 Set stops for remaining columns in similar manner.

TECHNIQUE EMPHASIS: Manual Tabulating Depress and hold the tab bar or key down until the carriage stops. Move quickly back to home position.

Electric Tabulating Flick the tab key lightly; return the controlling finger to its home position at once.

	but	old	the	cut	got	rot	tub	map	Eyes on copy
	big	top	aid	fit	ham	pen	for	due	as carriage
	all	see	too	add	you	saw	him	lop	is returned
	● Double-space								
Reach	555	551	755	155	757	175	157	751	Keep wrists low
with the	999	991	933	391	939	193	139	937	
fingers	159	957	195	395	591	937	175	593	
	sum	775	hot	595	buy	715	cot	593	
	old	993	use	379	ton	795	rob	591	
	too	995	see	337	you	793	top	951	

17E ● PARAGRAPH GUIDED WRITING *10 minutes*

Double spacing,
5-space paragraph
indention

PROCEDURE

1 Set a new goal: Add 4 words to your 3-minute base rate recorded for 16E, page 33. Divide this new goal into quarter-minute segments, and note the check points. Type two 1-minute *exploration-level* writings, guided by the quarter-minute call; then type

two 1-minute writings on the *control level* without the call of the guide.
2 Type a 3-minute writing without the call of the guide. Determine your *gwam* and compare this with the *gwam* recorded for 16E.

● All letters are used in the paragraph.

	GWAM	
	1'	3'

1.10 si
116 words

	1'	3'
Time is the one thing we all have in equal amount. We	11	4 43
do not all show the same degree of wisdom in the way we use	23	8 47
our time, though; and it is in the way we use our time that	35	12 51
we set the extent of the success we will achieve. It takes	47	16 55
time to do things, and we must prize time highly and use it	59	20 59
wisely. It will pay to take time to do all work right, but	71	24 63
it does take time. Work is just part of the price you have	83	28 67
to pay for success. You have to think before you work, and	95	32 71
it takes time to think, but it is time well spent; so think	107	36 75
before you work and save time while you work.	116	39 78

1' | 1 | 2 | 3 | 4 | 5 | 6 | 7 | 8 | 9 | 10 | 11 | 12 |
3' | 1 | 2 | 3 | 4 |

66C ● PROBLEM TYPING (Continued)

Problem 3: Typing from a Form Letter

PROCEDURE Type the letter given as Problem 1, page 117, twice as directed, except that you will use the names and addresses given at the right. Add an appropriate salutation; use a personal title with the name in the letter. Address envelopes; for the enclosures use the two carbon copies typed as Problem 2, page 117.

Words

(*Doctor*) O. B. Norton | 2684 E. Brighton Road | Knoxville, Tennessee 37905 | . 141/154★

Amos N. Rodgers | R. 1, Box 29 | Cave City, Kentucky 42127 | . . . . . . 142/153★

★ Add 18 words to this figure if plain paper and a **plain** envelope are used.

66D ● TYPING COLUMNAR HEADINGS *5 minutes*

DETERMINING CENTER POINT OF A COLUMN (2 METHODS)

Method 1 From the point at which the column begins, space forward once for each two letters or spaces in the longest line. This will bring the carriage to the center of the column. (Disregard an odd space.)

Method 2 (1) Read and add the numbers on the scale at the left and right edges of the column; (2) Divide the total by 2 for the center point.

NOTE Use Method 2 when typing between two vertical lines or when centering a heading within a specified writing line (such as the heading for a left-bound manuscript).

TYPING A COLUMNAR HEADING

From the center of the column, backspace once for each two spaces in the heading. Begin to type where the backspacing ends.

PROCEDURE (*repeat if time permits*)

Drill 1 Use Method 1; 10 spaces between columns.

May 12	May 14
T. D. Martin, Chairman	Oliver Strong, Chairman

Drill 2 Use Method 1; 8 spaces between columns.

City	1950	1960
Los Angeles	1,970,358	2,479,015

LESSON 67 | 67A ● PREPARATORY PRACTICE *5 minutes (each line three or more times)*

Alphabetic Dick Barr from the next floor gave away juicy grapes on the quiz show.

Figure-symbol The $4\frac{1}{2}\%$ interest of $76.43 on my $1,698.50 note (dated May 25) is due.

Fluency If you are to go places in this world, you must get ready to go today.

| 1 | 2 | 3 | 4 | 5 | 6 | 7 | 8 | 9 | 10 | 11 | 12 | 13 | 14 |

67B ● TYPING HEADINGS BETWEEN VERTICAL LINES *5 minutes*

PROCEDURE (*repeat if time permits*)

Drill 1 Draw vertical pencil lines approximately 4 inches apart and 4 inches long. Center and type your name. (Use Method 2 of 66D, above.)

Drill 2 Draw vertical pencil lines approximately 2½ inches apart and 2½ inches long. Center and type the current date.

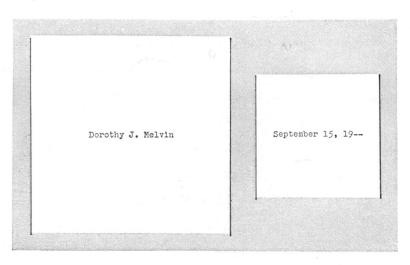

LESSON 18 | 18A ● PREPARATORY PRACTICE *7 minutes (each line three times)*

Alphabetic	Was my box packed with five dozen jugs of the liquid veneer?	Begin to
Figures	On July 15, Flight 59 left at 7:35 with 17 men and 39 women.	type slowly;
Fluency	The things that are worth doing at all are worth doing well.	gradually increase your speed

| 1 | 2 | 3 | 4 | 5 | 6 | 7 | 8 | 9 | 10 | 11 | 12 |

18B ● NEW KEYS: 6, 2, and / (Diagonal) *8 minutes*

PROCEDURE Follow the four-step procedure for learning new keys, page 32.

Reach to 6

Reach to 2

Reach to / (Diagonal)

1. REACH TECHNIQUE FOR 6
Reach to **6** with the *right first finger* straightened slightly. Make the reach with the least possible hand movement. Keep the wrist low. Watch your finger type **6j** a few times; then type the Tryout Practice twice on one line.

6j 6 j6j 66 j6j 666 j6j 6

2. REACH TECHNIQUE FOR 2
Reach the *left third finger* to **2** without changing the hand position or moving the elbow outward. Hold the wrist low. Watch your finger type **2s** a few times; then type the Tryout Practice twice on one line.

2s 2 s2s 22 s2s 222 s2s 2

3. REACH TECHNIQUE FOR /
Move the *right fourth finger* down to type **/** without moving the other fingers from their home position. Use **/** to type fractions for which there are no keyboard symbols as **2/3**. Type **/;** a few times; then type the Tryout Practice twice on one line.

/; // ;/; 1/3 1/2 2/3 1/5

18C ● STROKING TECHNIQUE PRACTICE *10 minutes (each line three times)*

SPACING RULE Space between a whole number and a fraction typed with the diagonal (/). See Line 3.

● All letters and all figures taught are used in the sentences.

1	Quiet hands and arms	Will your next science test cover pages 6, 66, 161, and 166?	Return quickly
2		The 22 girls, 12 boys, and 2 men left for Brazil on July 22.	Fingers curved; wrists low
3		My stock cost 26-2/3 in 1956. I sold it for 62-2/3 in 1962.	
4		Why did 26 or 27 men quit on April 5 and 22 or 23 on June 9?	
5		Clay is 26 years and 9 months old, and he weighs 193 pounds.	

| 1 | 2 | 3 | 4 | 5 | 6 | 7 | 8 | 9 | 10 | 11 | 12 |

66C • PROBLEM TYPING: Form Letters with Enclosures; Multiple Carbon Pack *25 minutes*

(errors corrected)

Problem 1: Typing from a Form Letter

Letterhead (or full sheet)	•	Mixed punctuation
50-space line		Current date
Modified block, blocked ¶s		Address envelope

PROCEDURE

1 *If a letterhead is used*, type the date a double space below the last line of the letterhead.

If plain paper is used, type | **Sylvania College** | **Lexington, Kentucky 40501** | as the return address, with the current date a single space below.

2 Address the letter to your father. Use his address and ZIP code number.

3 Type the word *Enclosure* at the left margin a double space below the closing line (as illustrated below).

check for this year's contribution and help Sylvania maintain its role as a college of distinction.

Sincerely yours,

Thomas A. Niemand

Student Chairman
Annual Alumni Fund

Enclosure

Enclosure notation

• 8 blank line spaces after the date

	Words
	18
Dear Mr. _____ (¶ 1) As student chair-	45
man of the Sylvania College Annual Alumni	54
Fund, I hope to interest you in joining	62
other distinguished alumni in an "invest-	70
ment in youth." This you can do through	78
your contribution to the Annual Alumni	86
Fund. (¶ 2) The enclosed copy of part of	93
an editorial from the *Alumni News* tells	103
something of our needs and our hopes.	111
Please read it; then send in your pledge of	120
support for *your* college. Better still,	129
send your check for this year's contribu-	137
tion and help Sylvania maintain its role	145
as a college of distinction.	Sincerely	153
yours	Student Chairman	Annual Alumni	161
Fund	Enclosure*		163/178**

*A small envelope is suitable for a one-page letter and a small nonbulky enclosure.

**Add 18 words to this figure if plain paper and a plain envelope are used for this problem.

Problem 2: Multiple Carbon Pack (Enclosure for Problem 1)

1 original copy		UNBOUND MANUSCRIPT FORM:
3 carbon copies	•	2" top margin;
5-space ¶ indention		1" side margins

NOTE Keep two carbon copies for Problem 3, page 118.

INSERTING A MULTIPLE CARBON PACK

1 Place the pack under an envelope flap or inside a folded piece of paper.

2 Insert pack into typewriter, releasing the paper-release lever to "start" the pack easily and to avoid wrinkling.

3 After the sheets appear at the front of the typewriter, reset the paper-release lever and remove the envelope or paper fold.

	Words
A CALL TO LOYAL ALUMNI	5
(¶ 1) Our College is going through a time	12
of "blood, sweat, and tears" because of	20
too many students for present facilities.	28
Sylvania needs more classrooms, dormi-	36
tories, laboratories, etc., to meet the needs	45
of students now enrolled and those knock-	53
ing at our doors. That "etc." is important.	62
It includes the need for more library facili-	71
ties, more professors, and—well, you name	80
it and we need it! (¶ 2) *Alumni News*	88
recently quoted our President as saying:	97

	Words
(¶ 3) Ours is a college of distinction	103
in spite of our admitted needs. We	110
maintain the high educational ideals	118
and standards set by the distinguished	126
men who studied at Sylvania before the	133
present deluge of students. Now we	141
need their help. Let's tell them so!	149
(¶ 4) The honor roll for this year's part-	156
ners in education goes to the printer soon.	165
Space has been reserved on it for *your*	173
name. Let's put it there!	179

• 66C is continued on page 118.

18D ● TECHNIQUE PRACTICE: Tab Mechanism and Carriage Return *10 minutes*
(twice as shown)

ALIGNING COLUMNS OF FIGURES AT THE RIGHT
Columns of figures are aligned at the right. At times this calls for spacing forward or for backspacing to keep the figures aligned. In adjusting your typewriter for this practice, *set the tabulator stop for the digit that will require the least forward and backward spac-* *ing in each column.* Clear all tabulator stops; then set stops for Columns 2 and 3 as follows:

Column 1 .... at left margin

Column 2 tab stop 25 spaces from end of Column 1

Column 3 tab stop 25 spaces from end of Column 2

TECHNIQUE EMPHASIS *If you are operating a manual typewriter, depress and hold the tab bar or key down until the carriage has completed its movement to the next column. A too quick release of the bar or key may result in uneven alignment of the figures in the columns. Tap and quickly release the electric key.*

● All figures taught are used in the columns.

	221		123		155	Eyes on copy
	166		266		366	as carriage
	615		772		991	is returned
Space forward once ➤	623		567		916	Reach to
	61	Space forward ➤	71	Space forward ➤	91	the figure
	26		27		29	
	612					
	675	Backspace once ◀	3699	Backspace once ◀	3615	
	723	from tab stop	2359	from tab stop	3569	
			5671		5679	

[3]   25   [3]   25   [3]

18E ● BUILDING SPEED AND CONTROL *10 minutes*

Double spacing, 5-space paragraph indention

PROCEDURE
1 Type two 1-minute writings, the first for speed and the second for control.
2 Type the second writing 4 to 8 words below the *gwam* of the first writing.

3 Relax for 20 to 30 seconds; then type a 2-minute writing at your controlled speed.
4 Relax for 20 to 30 seconds, and type a 3-minute writing; then determine the *gwam* of the 3-minute writing.

● All letters are used in the paragraph.

	GWAM	
	1'	3'
Typing is something like driving a car. You can cover	11	4 │ 43
much more ground if you go at an even pace than if you rush	23	8 │ 47
and hurry and look up to see what you have written. Pauses	35	12 │ 51
kill speed. You may not need to make your fingers move any	47	16 │ 55
more quickly than they are now moving and yet may gain more	59	20 │ 59
speed if you will only get rid of the jerks and pauses when	71	24 │ 63
you type. The secret of speed in typing is to keep on, one	83	28 │ 67
stroke at a time. When you have typed a key, do not freeze	95	32 │ 71
to it but turn loose of it quickly, and type the next key.	107	36 │ 75
Type at a steady, smooth pace to build speed.	116	39 │ 78

1.15 si
116 words

1' | 1 | 2 | 3 | 4 | 5 | 6 | 7 | 8 | 9 | 10 | 11 | 12 |
3' | 1 | 2 | 3 | 4 |

LESSON 18 | Page 37

65D ● ERROR CORRECTION: "Squeezing" Letters *5 minutes*

"SQUEEZING" AN OMITTED LETTER WITHIN A WORD

1 Erase the word.

2 Return the cylinder to writing position.

3 Operate the paper-release lever **16**, and move the paper a half space to the left or to the right.

4 Retype the word so that the first letter is in half the space following the preceding word and the final letter is in half the space following the corrected word.

NOTE Omitted stem letters *i* and *l* can often be typed between two letters without erasing. Hold the carriage in position and type the letter.

CORRECTING A WORD WITH AN ADDED LETTER

1–3 Follow Steps 1-3 for "SQUEEZING" AN OMITTED LETTER WITHIN A WORD (at the left).

4 Retype the word so that the first letter is 1½ spaces to the right of the last letter of the preceding word.

"SQUEEZING" AN OMITTED LETTER AT THE BEGINNING OR AT THE END OF A WORD

1 Move the carriage a half space before or after the word.

2 Hold the carriage in position with the hand.

3 Type the omitted letter.

PROCEDURE Type the sentences as given; then make the corrections. Repeat if time permits.

SENTENCES 1 AND 3: Erase and retype words in which errors appear.

SENTENCES 2, 4, 5: "Squeeze" in missing letters.

1 Now, type this sentnce at a fastr speed.
2 Mr. Paulson lkes the smaler publication.
3 Center the headiing on the loongest line.
4 Kay ikes the small ight for her credenza.
5 The retype letters were maile Wednesday.

> Now, type this sentence at a faster speed.
> Mr. Paulson likes the smaller publication.
> Center the heading on the longest line.
> Kay likes the small light for her credenza.
> The retyped letters were mailed Wednesday.

LESSON 66 | 66A ● PREPARATORY PRACTICE *5 minutes (each line three or more times)*

Alphabetic   Von queried Kippy and Tex about those jewel boxes for the zircon gems.

Figure-symbol   Luci's sold 3,479 meals @ $1.50 per plate and 860 pieces of pie @ 25¢.

Fluency   Claudia Ryan is the chairman for the next meeting of your study group.

| 1 | 2 | 3 | 4 | 5 | 6 | 7 | 8 | 9 | 10 | 11 | 12 | 13 | 14 |

66B ● BUILDING SPEED AND CONTROL *10 minutes (three 1' exploration-level writings; then four 1' control-level writings)*

Full sheet, 70-space line, double spacing, 5-space ¶ indention

● All letters are used in the paragraph.

1' GWAM

Striking the keys when you type is not the same as striking a golf ball, for you do not have a follow-through in typing. Rather, you must use a quick, sharp stroke and pull the finger just slightly toward the palm of your hand. Realize the power that is yours by typing with quiet, almost motionless, hands and arms; and you can expect to increase your typing skill immediately.

1.31 si
76 words

13
28
42
57
71
76

1' | 1 | 2 | 3 | 4 | 5 | 6 | 7 | 8 | 9 | 10 | 11 | 12 | 13 | 14 |

LESSON 19 | 19A ● PREPARATORY PRACTICE *7 minutes (each line three times)*

Alphabetic   Max King hopes Dick Webb can leave for quiet Zurich in July.

Figures   This stock went from 56 2/3 to 67 1/2 between 1959 and 1962.

Fluency   He can be a man of good will and also a man with good skill.
| 1 | 2 | 3 | 4 | 5 | 6 | 7 | 8 | 9 | 10 | 11 | 12 |

Work for continuity of stroking

19B ● NEW KEYS: 8, 4, and 0 *8 minutes*

PROCEDURE Follow the four-step procedure for learning new keys, page 32.

Reach to 8   Reach to 4

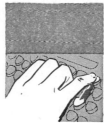

Reach to 0

1. REACH TECHNIQUE FOR 8
Keep the wrist low as you reach to **8** with the *right second finger*. Make the reach without moving the hand from its keyboard position. Watch your finger type **8k** a few times; then type the Tryout Practice twice.

8k 8 k8k 88 k8k 888 k8k 8

2. REACH TECHNIQUE FOR 4
Reach the *left first finger* to **4** without arching the wrist or moving the hand forward. Hold the wrist low to type **4** quickly. Watch the finger type **4f** a few times; then type the Tryout Practice twice on one line.

4f 4 f4f 44 f4f 444 f4f 4

3. REACH TECHNIQUE FOR 0
Reach the *right fourth finger* to **0** without twisting the elbow outward or changing the hand position. Strike and release the key quickly. Watch the finger type **0;** a few times; then type the Tryout Practice twice.

0; 0 ;0; 00 ;0; 100 ;0; 0

19C ● STROKING TECHNIQUE PRACTICE *10 minutes (each line three times)*

● All letters and all figures taught are used in the sentences.

1   What is the sum of 8 and 88 and 181 and 188 and 881 and 888?

2   Our team lost 4 games, won 16, and tied 1 during the season.

3   On March 10, Jack Baxter helped your 10 boys move 100 desks.

4   Will 10 men, 34 boys, and 39 women take the long Heinz quiz?

5   Did he add 40 and 48-5/8 and 80-3/8 and 180-1/8 and 240-7/8?
| 1 | 2 | 3 | 4 | 5 | 6 | 7 | 8 | 9 | 10 | 11 | 12 |

Fingers curved; wrists low; strike keys with tips of fingers

Problem 1: Leftbound Manuscript Page with Footnote (*errors corrected*)

Page-end indicator	5-space ¶ indention
Full sheet	2″ top margin
Carbon copy	MARGINS: Left, 1½″;
Double spacing	right, 1″ (6″ line)

PROCEDURE "Spread" and center the heading over the writing line; determine the center point as directed for centering on odd-size paper, 34D, page 62. Type the footnote in two lines at the bottom of the sheet, maintaining a 1-inch margin.

	Words
INTERLINGUA	2
(¶1) An international language is not	9
something new. During the time of Alex-	17
ander the Great, an international language	26
was introduced. It was Greek Koine. Ex-	34
pansion of religious cults helped to carry	42
Latin, the language of religion, to con-	50
quered areas; and it became the "inter-	58
national" language of religion. (¶2)	65
Interlingua is an international language	73
which is based on predominant European	81
languages. It has been used at some inter-	89
national medical congresses, and the *Jour-*	99
nal of the American Medical Association	114
has supplied summaries of some articles	122
in Interlingua. (¶3) Scientific achieve-	130
ments have made us, in effect, "citizens of	138
the world" instead of citizens of just one	147
country. As citizens of "one world," we	155
need a common language to communicate	163
with others. (¶4) Gode quotes Dante as	170
saying, "If we clearly consider what our	178
intention is when we speak, we shall find	186
that it is nothing but to unfold to others	195
the thoughts of our own minds."[1] So it	203
is; but to do this, we need a common lan-	211
guage for common understanding. This	219
is the function of Interlingua—"the best	227
hope of mankind."	231
	235

---

[1] Alexander Gode, "The Case for Inter- | 244
lingua," *The Scientific Monthly*, LXXVII | 255
(August, 1953), p. 82. | 255

Problem 2: Composing a Manuscript

Page-end indicator	2″ top margin
Full sheet	MARGINS: Left, 1½″;
Double spacing	right, 1″;
5-space ¶ indention	bottom, 1″

TYPING THE ELLIPSIS

The omission of words from a quotation is shown by an *ellipsis*, which is typed with three alternating periods and spaces, or four if the end of a sentence is included in the omission (as illustrated in the quoted paragraph of Problem 2, below).

"X-ING OUT" WORDS

As you compose at the typewriter or type a rough draft, save time by "X-ing out" unwanted words instead of erasing and correcting them. "X-out" a word by striking the *x* and *m* alternately with either the first or the second finger of each hand.

PROCEDURE Type the portion of the manuscript as given; then describe what happens to you when you type a timed writing. Make corrections; then retype the manuscript from your corrected copy.

MIND AND BODY

(¶1) If proof is needed that the mind has a far-reaching influence upon the body, just watch me type. The psychiatrists must have had my typing in mind when they wrote,

● Indent and single-space quoted ¶ 5 spaces from both margins

(¶2) The relationship between body and mind is continuous and intimate. . . . Mind and body are so closely connected . . . not even a single thought or mood can come into existence without being reflected in the physical organism.[1]

(¶3) I type quite well, as a rule; but when I hear, "Get ready for a 5-minute writing, please," my emotions take over my typing motions and (*Describe how you feel and how you type when taking a timed writing.*)

---

[1] Edward A. Strecker and Kenneth E. Appel, *Discovering Ourselves* (New York: The Macmillan Company, 1962), pp. 12-13.

19D ● TECHNIQUE PRACTICE: Tab Mechanism and Carriage Return *10 minutes (twice)*

MACHINE ADJUSTMENTS Clear all tab stops; then study the problem to be typed before setting new tabulator stops. Set the stop for the digit in each column that will require the least forward and backward spacing. Let fractions extend into space between columns.

Column 1 .... at left margin

Column 2 tab stop 25 spaces from end of Column 1

Column 3 tab stop 25 spaces from end of Column 2

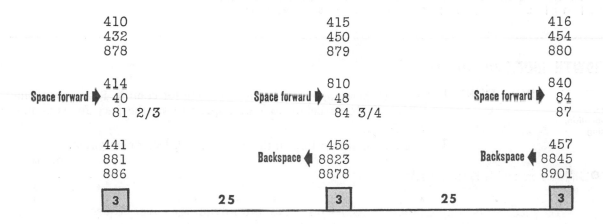

410	415	416
432	450	454
878	879	880
414	810	840
Space forward ▶ 40	Space forward ▶ 48	Space forward ▶ 84
81 2/3	84 3/4	87
441	456	457
881	Backspace ◀ 8823	Backspace ◀ 8845
886	8878	8901

| 3 | 25 | 3 | 25 | 3 |

19E ● BUILDING SPEED AND CONTROL *10 minutes*

Double spacing,
5-space paragraph
indention

PROCEDURE

1 Type two 1-minute writings, the first for speed and the second for control.

2 Type the second writing 4 to 8 words below the *gwam* of the first writing.

3 Relax for 20 to 30 seconds; then type a 2-minute writing at your controlled speed.

4 Relax for 20 to 30 seconds, and type a 3-minute writing; determine the *gwam* of the 3-minute writing. Compare it with 18E.

● All letters and all figures are used in the paragraph.

	GWAM	
	1'	3'

1.10 si
116 words

	1'	3'
Most men retire by the time they are 65 to 70 years of	11	4 | 43
age, but some do not retire until they are 75 to 80 or even	23	8 | 47
85 years of age. As a rule, a man goes to work by the time	35	12 | 51
he is 20 to 25 years old, so he has a work life of 45 to 50	47	16 | 55
years at least. Some extend their work life by 3, 5, or 10	59	20 | 59
years by starting to work quite early or by keeping on with	71	24 | 63
their work until they are 85 to 90 years of age. It is not	83	28 | 67
so much how long a man works that brings the world to prize	95	32 | 71
and honor him as it is the good he does and the joy he adds	107	36 | 75
to the lives of the men and women around him.	116	39 | 78

1' | 1 | 2 | 3 | 4 | 5 | 6 | 7 | 8 | 9 | 10 | 11 | 12 |
3' | 1 | 2 | 3 | 4 |

LESSON 65 | 65A ● PREPARATORY PRACTICE *5 minutes (each line three or more times)*

SENTENCE 2 Leave two typewriter spaces after the state name; then type the ZIP code.

Alphabetic   Don asked to have the large-sized juke box wrapped up quickly for him.

Figures   The order for $98.16 was sent to 239 Divide Road, Canton, Ohio   44705.

Fluency   A wise man said that success is to lean on but failure is to learn on.
               | 1 | 2 | 3 | 4 | 5 | 6 | 7 | 8 | 9 | 10 | 11 | 12 | 13 | 14 |

65B ● GROWTH INDEX *10 minutes*

Full sheet,
70-space line,
5-space ¶ indention,
double spacing

PROCEDURE 1 Type each paragraph as a 1-minute writing for control. Pace your typing at 8 to 10 words below your best speed to set the pace for your next writing.

2 Type a 5-minute writing on the *control level*. Determine *gwam*.

● All letters are used in these paragraphs.

	GWAM 1'	5'

¶ 1
1.35 si
116 words

If success is important to you, you have an advantage over those — 13 | 3 | 50
who have no particular feeling one way or the other. This is just as — 27 | 5 | 52
true in school as it is on the job. Your teachers can guide you, but — 41 | 8 | 55
you must do the work. History––both modern and ancient––is filled to — 55 | 11 | 58
the brim with great men who had harsh strikes against them in health, — 69 | 14 | 61
schooling, and even intelligence. But one asset they did have. They — 83 | 17 | 63
wanted to learn; they wanted to win the prize; they expected to reach — 97 | 19 | 66
their goals. Desire and action are effective qualities. Put them to — 111 | 22 | 69
work for you immediately. — 116 | 23 | 70

¶ 2
1.35 si
120 words

Have you ever felt that you were in the wrong place as you tried — 129 | 26 | 73
to master a difficult problem or succeed in a new job? Usually these — 143 | 29 | 76
feelings are caused by lack of preparation. The way to eliminate the — 157 | 31 | 78
difficulty is to concentrate on every new learning or skill that will — 171 | 34 | 81
prepare you for some goal that is ahead. Do you think you might want — 185 | 37 | 84
to have your own business some day? Then learn to analyze; learn the — 199 | 40 | 87
skills of communication; learn to make decisions. Improve in each of — 213 | 43 | 90
the skills that will be needed in the work or the study that you plan — 227 | 45 | 92
to follow. You will feel in the right place. — 236 | 47 | 94

1' | 1 | 2 | 3 | 4 | 5 | 6 | 7 | 8 | 9 | 10 | 11 | 12 | 13 | 14 |
5' | 1 | 2 | 3 |

LESSON 20 | **20A ● PREPARATORY PRACTICE** *7 minutes (each line three times)*

Alphabetic   Was Pat Longworth quizzed by Jack Hoover about his tax form?   Begin to
                                                                             type slowly;
Figures   I bought 100 shares of Maxton 4s at 58 5/8 on July 27, 1963.   increase speed
                                                                             gradually
Fluency   The man went with his friend to an ancient city by the lake.

| 1 | 2 | 3 | 4 | 5 | 6 | 7 | 8 | 9 | 10 | 11 | 12 |

20B ● NEW KEY: - (Hyphen) *3 minutes*

PROCEDURE Follow the four-step procedure
for learning new keys, page 32.

REACH TECHNIQUE FOR — (HYPHEN)
Straighten the *right fourth finger* and
move it up to type — (hyphen) without
moving the elbow outward or arching
the wrist. Watch your finger type —; a
few times; then type the Tryout Practice
twice on the same line.

-; — ;-; up-to-date model

Reach to — (Hyphen)

20C ● STROKING TECHNIQUE PRACTICE *10 minutes (each line three or more times)*

NOTE Type the dash with two hyphens (––) without spacing between the dash
and the words before and after it. See Lines 1 and 4.

● All letters and all figures are used in the sentences.

1   Strive for   An out-of-town speaker--a 37-year-old man--gave a fine talk.   Reach to
2   continuity of   Sixty-six boys took the 3- and 5-minute writings on June 13.   figures and
     stroking   hyphens
3   All up-to-date reports were sent to the out-of-town members.

4   Use a 6-inch line--60 pica or 72 elite spaces--for the quiz.

5   Did Flight 189 arrive at 6:54 p.m., or was it delayed again?

| 1 | 2 | 3 | 4 | 5 | 6 | 7 | 8 | 9 | 10 | 11 | 12 |

20D ● STROKING TECHNIQUE REVIEW *10 minutes (each line three times)*

● All letters and all figures are used in the sentences.

1   Put your   Was Buz Quinn 13 years 3 months and 7 days old on August 17?
2   best   Flight 95 arrived at 9:15 after a very hard 950-mile flight.
     techniques
3   to work   This stock sold for 66 on March 6 and for 62 2/3 on July 23.

4   The May 8 record for 80 typists: range, 40 to 80; mode, 48.

5   Larry took two 3-minute writings--six minutes in all--today.

| 1 | 2 | 3 | 4 | 5 | 6 | 7 | 8 | 9 | 10 | 11 | 12 |

Problem 1: Portion of an Unbound First Page with Footnotes

Full sheet	5-space ¶ indention
Page-end indicator ●	1″ side margins
Double spacing	(6½″ writing line)

PROCEDURE Type the first line opposite Line 18 of the bottom half of the indicator sheet to maintain a 1″ bottom margin. Follow the steps given below in typing superior figures in footnotes.

NOTE Footnote 1 is a reference to a magazine; Footnote 2, to a book.

	Words
academic economists have reassessed	7
Keynes' theory. Slichter,[1] Hazlitt,[2] and	16
others concede that Keynes ranks among	23
the greatest thinkers; but they question	32
the validity of his theory.	37
● Single-space; type a 1½″ divider line	
	41
● Double-space; single-space footnotes	
[1] Sumner Huber Slichter, "The Passing	49
of Keynesian Economics," *The Atlantic*	59
(November, 1958), pp. 141-146.	65
● Double-space	
[2] Henry Hazlitt, *The Failure of the New*	77
Economics (Princeton: D. Van Nostrand	87
Company, Inc., 1959).	91
● Type page number ½″ from bottom of page	
1	92

TYPING A SUPERIOR FIGURE

1 Move the ratchet release (line finder) forward.

2 Move the cylinder back (toward you) a half space.

3 Type the figure.

4 Return the ratchet release and cylinder to their regular positions.

Unbound first page with footnotes

Problem 2: Portion of an Unbound Second Page with Footnotes

PROCEDURE Type Problem 1, above, as directed

Unbound second page with footnotes

except that you will assume that the portion of the manuscript comes at the top of the second page. Type the page number ½ inch (on Line 4) from the top of the sheet, approximately even with the right margin; then triple-space and begin to type opposite Line 7 at the top half of the indicator sheet. Space down to Line 13 (bottom half of the indicator sheet) and type the divider line and the footnotes. This placement of footnotes will maintain a 1″ bottom margin.

NOTE Footnotes may also be typed immediately following the last line of the manuscript; it is preferable, however, to place them to end 1″ from the bottom edge of the sheet.

Problem 3: Preparing Carbon Copies

PROCEDURE Type Problems 1 and 2 as directed; make one carbon copy of each; correct errors.

64D ● PROBLEM TYPING REVIEW *10 minutes*

SUPPLIES NEEDED
2 full sheets
1 carbon sheet
2 file copy sheets

PROCEDURE

1 Make pencil notations of the problems and page numbers given below:

63C, Problem 1, page 111
63C, Problem 2, page 112

2 Make one carbon copy of each problem. Unless otherwise directed, erase and correct all errors. After typing a problem and before removing it from the typewriter, proofread the typing and correct all errors that are correctible.

20E ● GROWTH INDEX *15 minutes*

PROCEDURE

1 Type each paragraph for 1 minute. Quickly note your *gwam* for each writing.

2 Choose a goal for each paragraph that is 4 to 8 words lower than the minute *gwam*. Identify the quarter-minute goals; type each paragraph on the

control level for 1 minute, guided by the quarter-minute call of the guide.

3 Type two 3-minute writings at approximately your 1-minute control rate. Start with ¶ 1 and type as far as you can until time is called. Determine the *gwam* for the better writing.

● All letters are used in the paragraphs.

GWAM

	1'	3'	

¶ 1
1.15 si
56 words

It is right to be cautious, but it is quite foolish to · · · · 11 | 4 | 41

be fearful. Fear is a traitor. It makes us lose much good 23 | 8 | 45

that we might have as our own if we would be bold enough to 35 | 12 | 49

take one step at a time even without knowing where the next 47 | 16 | 53

step might take us. We lose from not trying. 56 | 19 | 56

¶ 2
1.15 si
56 words

Our doubts will be traitors if they cause us to be too 67 | 22 | 59

fearful to try to do something big when we know that we can 79 | 26 | 63

reach higher than we have reached before. We lose far more 91 | 30 | 68

just by not trying than by not winning, for the prize worth 103 | 34 | 71

most is coming to live without doubt or fear. 112 | 37 | 74

```
1' | 1 | 2 | 3 | 4 | 5 | 6 | 7 | 8 | 9 | 10 | 11 | 12 |
3' |     1     |     2     |     3     |     4     |
```

SELF-IMPROVEMENT PRACTICE ● *(each line three or more times)*

● All letters and all figures are used in the sentences.

1	Drill on e, i	Keith Leigh has neither the height nor the weight you think.
2	Drill on i, e	Litie Fielder tried to give a quiet series of talks in Erie.
3	Adjacent keys	A point we stress is that poise promotes power and progress.
4	One-hand words	Fred begged Ted Ward to serve in Greece with him for a year.
5	One-hand words	I look upon Jim Hull as my greatest link to my Erie friends.
6	One-hand words	Rex traced the crazed man as he raced from street to street.
7	Figure drill	On March 23 and 24, 56 boys and 90 girls must take the test.
8	Figure drill	Tom's address is 867 W. 19th Street, Eastland, Texas 76448.
9	Figure drill	I wear a size 7-3/8 hat and got it at the Niel-Marcus store.
10	Fluency	Sit well back in the chair, and keep your feet on the floor.
11	Fluency	If you put off doing this work, it will become harder to do.
12	Fluency	Drop back in speed to gain the skill of typing with control.

```
| 1 | 2 | 3 | 4 | 5 | 6 | 7 | 8 | 9 | 10 | 11 | 12 |
```

63C ● PROBLEM TYPING *(Continued)*

Problem 2: Outline in Unbound Manuscript Form

PROCEDURE Use Problem 2 directions (page 110); do not "spread" the heading.

	Words
SPACING BOUND MANUSCRIPTS	5
I. MARGINS AFFECTED BY MANU-SCRIPT BINDING	11 14
A. Manuscripts Bound at the Left	21
1. Top margin: 2 inches, first page; 1 inch, other pages	27 32
2. Side margins: 1½ inches, left; 1 inch, right	38 42
3. Bottom margin: 1 inch	48
B. Manuscripts Bound at the Top	54
1. Top margin: 2½ inches, first page; 1½ inches, other pages	61 66
2. Side and bottom margins: 1 inch	72 74

	Words
II. PAGES NUMBERED TO KEEP TEXT IN SEQUENCE	80 83
A. Placement of Page Numbers in Leftbound Manuscripts	90 94
1. First page: centered ½ inch from bottom edge of paper	101 106
2. Other pages: even with right margin ½ inch from top	113 117
B. Placement of Page Numbers in Topbound Manuscripts	124 128
1. All pages: centered ½ inch from bottom edge of paper	134 140
2. Page number separated from text or footnote by double space	146 151 152

63D ● PAGE-END INDICATOR *10 minutes*

MAKING A PAGE-END INDICATOR

Insert a full sheet of paper. At the right edge of the sheet type the figure *1* in the first line space from the top edge, the figure *2* in the next space, and so on until you type the figure *33*. In the next line space, repeat the figure *33*; in the next space type *32*, and so on down to figure *1* in the last line space on the page.

PROCEDURE

Place the page-end indicator sheet back of and extending slightly to the right of a full sheet. Insert these sheets, and type the following quotation centered on Line 12 of the bottom half of the indicator sheet.

```
"To thine own self be true."
```

● *Keep your page-end indicator sheet for the rest of the problems in this section.*

CENTER POINT

BOTTOM HALF

LESSON 64 | **64A ● PREPARATORY PRACTICE** *5 minutes (each line three or more times)*

Alphabetic	When quizzed, Val Bigner just said he expected no more work for years.
Figure-symbol	Interest accumulated in 1963 to $482.57 when the rate increased by ½%.
Fluency	As you get to know a man, you get to know his good points most of all.

| 1 | 2 | 3 | 4 | 5 | 6 | 7 | 8 | 9 | 10 | 11 | 12 | 13 | 14 |

64B ● SENTENCE GUIDED WRITING FROM CORRECTED SCRIPT *5 minutes*
(two 1′ control-level writings on each sentence)

GWAM

	15″	12″	10″
It will pays them to learn how to get along with others.	44	55	66
Keep your chin up when trouble comes, and your mouth closed.	48	60	72

LEARNING TO TYPE SYMBOLS AND FRACTIONS

STANDARD PROCEDURES FOR SECTION 4

GET READY TO TYPE

Clear desk of unneeded papers. Adjust paper-guide and paper-bail rolls. Use a 60-space line. Set line-space regulator for single spacing the drills; use double spacing when directed to do so.

SELF-IMPROVEMENT PRACTICE

Retype the first two lines of the preparatory practice three times each. Identify errorless lines, so that extra credit may be given for these. Use the third line of the preparatory practice for 1-minute writings.

LESSON 21 | 21A ● PREPARATORY PRACTICE *7 minutes (each line three times)*

Alphabetic   Zora quickly helped fix a lunch to be given to James Wilson.

Figures   Ben and I read pages 123, 167, and 189 of the 450-page book.

Fluency   The desk should be kept clear of the papers you do not need.
    | 1 | 2 | 3 | 4 | 5 | 6 | 7 | 8 | 9 | 10 | 11 | 12 |

Begin slowly; increase speed gradually

21B ● NEW KEYS: $, ' (Apostrophe), and " (Quotation) *8 minutes*

- *The symbol reach is the same as the figure reach of which the symbol is the shift character.*
- *The positions for certain symbols differ on non-electric and electric machines. Note these differences in the Reach Techniques and adapt your practice accordingly.*

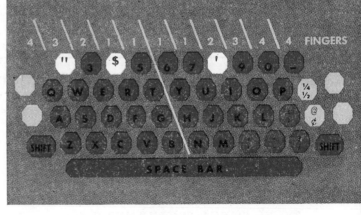

Reach to $

Reach to '

Reach to "

1. REACH TECHNIQUE FOR $

Move the *left first finger* up to type $ without moving the other fingers from their typing position. Remember to depress the right shift key to type $. Watch your finger type $f a few times; then type the Tryout Practice twice on one line.

$f $ f$f $14 f$f $94 $514

2. REACH TECHNIQUE FOR '

Nonelectric Typewriter: Depress left shift key and move the *right second finger* up to type ' (apostrophe). **Electric Typewriter:** Type ' with the *right fourth finger*; do not move other fingers from position. Watch your finger type 'k or '; then type the Tryout Practice twice.

'k ' k'k I'm Vi's cousin.

3. REACH TECHNIQUE FOR "

Nonelectric Typewriter: Depress right shift key and move *left third finger* up to type " (quotation). **Electric Typewriter:** Depress left shift key and type " with the *right fourth finger*. Watch your finger type "s or "; then type the Tryout Practice twice on one line.

"s " s"s "s He is "A-OK."

21C ● STROKING TECHNIQUE PRACTICE *10 minutes (each line three or more times)*

● SPACING RULES

1 Do not space between the $ and the following figure. See Lines 1, 4, and 5.
2 Do not space before or after the ' (apostrophe). See Lines 2 and 4.
3 Do not space between the " and the word it encloses. The quotation mark does not change the normal spacing after a word. With a punctuation mark, use the spacing that normally follows that mark. See Lines 3 and 5. (*21C continued on page 43*)

LESSON 63 | **63A ● PREPARATORY PRACTICE** *5 minutes (each line three or more times)*

SENTENCE 2 Type the abbreviation *M* directly after a figure (without a space) to indicate the word *thousand*.

Alphabetic | Mr. Ford's vim, pep, zeal, and wish to excel bring luck and quiet joy.

Figure-symbol | Wick & Rothman ordered 50M of Form CZ1234 and 9M of Form WX6789 today.

Fluency | Lean on no one, but stand near others to be ready to help when needed.

| 1 | 2 | 3 | 4 | 5 | 6 | 7 | 8 | 9 | 10 | 11 | 12 | 13 | 14 |

63B ● BUILDING SPEED AND CONTROL *5 minutes (two 1' exploration-level writings; then two 1' control-level writings—correct errors as you type)*

Full sheet
Carbon copy
70-space line

5-space ¶ indention

Double spacing

● All letters are used in the paragraph.

1' GWAM

1.35 si
76 words

Correct the errors you make as you type these writings. When you — 13
have completed each writing, proofread your typing and deduct 15 words — 27
for each uncorrected error. From this you will get a clue—just a clue— — 42
as to the cost of errors. Good typists realize how expensive errors are — 57
and learn to type with a minimum of them; but those they make, they are — 71
quite certain to correct. — 76

1' | 1 | 2 | 3 | 4 | 5 | 6 | 7 | 8 | 9 | 10 | 11 | 12 | 13 | 14 |

63C ● PROBLEM TYPING: Unbound Manuscript Pages *25 minutes*

(errors corrected, unless otherwise directed)

Problem 1: Unbound Manuscript Page

Full sheet
Double spacing
5-space ¶ indention
2" top margin

FOR 1" SIDE MARGINS:
Use a 6½" writing
line (65 pica spaces;
78 elite spaces)

● Underline italicized items.

Words

TYPING SPECIAL SYMBOLS AND SIGNS — 7

(¶ 1) Type the hyphen with a space be- — 13
fore and after it for a minus sign (6 − 2). — 22
The small x with a space before and after — 30
it can be used for the multiplication sign — 39
(2 x 6). Use the quotation mark (") for — 47
inches, seconds, and ditto; and the apos- — 55
trophe (') for feet or minutes. Type the — 64
symbol for "Care of" with the small c, — 72
diagonal, and small o (c/o). Type the — 80
dash with two hyphens without spacing be- — 88
fore or after them (May 6——Wednesday). — 96
(¶ 2) Many symbols or signs not on the — 103
standard typewriter keyboard can be made — 111
by combining characters. To type the — 119
exclamation point, type the period; back- — 127
space; and type the apostrophe (!). For — 136

a plus sign, type the diagonal; backspace; — 144
and type the hyphen (+). For a division — 153
sign, type a hyphen; backspace; and type — 161
a colon (÷). (¶ 3) Symbols are raised — 168
(superscripts) or lowered (subscripts) — 176
from the writing line by using the ratchet — 184
release and the cylinder. To type the de- — 193
gree symbol, for example: Operate the — 201
ratchet release; turn the cylinder *toward* — 210
you slightly; then type a small o (68°). — 219
(¶ 4) When typing chemistry symbols, the — 226
subscripts must be lowered from the line — 234
of writing. Type the symbol in all capi- — 242
tals, *leaving space for the subscripts*; then — 258
backspace to the space for the first sub- — 266
script; operate the ratchet release; and — 274
turn the cylinder a half space *away* from — 283
you; type the first subscript——then space — 292
to the second blank space and type the — 299
second subscript; and so on. Type the fol- — 308
lowing chemistry symbols: $MgSO_4$ and — 315
Na_2CO_3. — 318

NOTE One-page manuscripts are not numbered.

● *63C is continued on page 112.*

21C ● STROKING TECHNIQUE PRACTICE *(Continued)*

● All letters and all figures are used in the sentences.

Improve your shift-key technique

1   The April 26 check for $178.30 should have been for $187.39.

2   Zahn's work isn't right, and Len's problems aren't finished.

3   Rex Trigg quoted the following line: "No man is an island."

4   Mr. O'Neill won't pay more than $14 or $15 a day for a room.

5   I can't be sure, but I think Joe said he would "ante up" $5.

| 1 | 2 | 3 | 4 | 5 | 6 | 7 | 8 | 9 | 10 | 11 | 12 |

21D ● TYPING FROM DICTATION *5 minutes (each line three times)*

PROCEDURE For the first writing, read and type the words from the book as your instructor dictates them. For the second and third writings, cover the page and get the impulse to type from the dictation. If time permits, type a 1-minute writing from the copy in the book *without dictation*.

half most long inch size have know type just will full soon

count lines point asked quite learn which sheet paper exact

Think the phrase   to do|to be|as we|as the|on the|and the|to know|to be|as we

| 1 | 2 | 3 | 4 | 5 | 6 | 7 | 8 | 9 | 10 | 11 | 12 |

21E ● PROBLEM TYPING: Informational Memorandum *15 minutes*

Half sheet, full sheet, single spacing, 5-space ¶ indention, 10 lines in top margin

PROCEDURE

1 Type the two paragraphs on a half sheet with a top margin of 10 blank lines (space forward 11 times). Type at a rate you can maintain with ease and *continuity*.

2 Use a full sheet for typing each paragraph for two 1-minute writings (or more if time permits).

● All letters are used in the paragraphs.

		Words in Para.	Total Words
¶ 1 **1.15 si** **56 words**	Most sheets of typing paper are 11 inches long. As we	11	11
	count 6 lines to an inch, the full-size sheet has 66 lines,	23	23
	and the half sheet has 33 lines. When typing problems, you	35	35
	will need to know the number of lines on the paper you will	47	47
	use to have the problem centered on the page.	56	56

● Double-space

		Words in Para.	Total Words
¶ 2 **1.20 si** **64 words**	If you use paper that is 8-1/2 inches wide, there will	11	67
	be 102 elite or 85 pica spaces in each line. To center the	23	79
	lines of problems, as you will do quite soon, you must know	35	91
	what center point to use. You can't use the "exact" center	47	103
	point of 42-1/2 of pica type, so just use 42; and use 51 as	59	115
	the point for elite type.	64	120

| 1 | 2 | 3 | 4 | 5 | 6 | 7 | 8 | 9 | 10 | 11 | 12 |

Problem 2: Outline of Unbound Manuscripts

Full sheet,
65-space line,
single spacing,
2½" top margin

PROCEDURE After typing Roman numeral *I*, reset the left margin stop 4 spaces to the right. Set the first tab stop 4 spaces to the right of this second left margin setting. Align Roman numerals by the period that follows them. Depress the margin release key and backspace to position for typing Roman numeral *II*.

	Words
U N B O U N D M A N U S C R I P T S	8

● Triple-space

I. EASE OF READING AIDED BY MARGINS AND SPACING	17

Reset margin →

● Double-space

A. Margins	20

1st tab stop →

1. 1-inch bottom and side margins	27
2. 2-inch top margin on first page	34
3. 1-inch top margin on all other pages	42
B. Spacing	45
1. Body of manuscript double-spaced	52
2. Paragraphs indented 5, 7, or 10 spaces uniformly	63
3. Quoted material of four or more lines single-spaced	74
a. Indented 5 spaces from both margins	82
b. Quotation marks permissible but not required	92
C. Page Numbers	95
1. First page: centered ½ inch from bottom edge of paper	107
2. Other pages: even with right margin ½ inch from top	118

← Backspace

● Double-space

II. CLARITY AIDED BY HEADING AND SUBHEADINGS	128
A. Main Headings	132
1. Centered in all capital letters	139
2. Followed by triple space	145
B. First-Order Subheadings	150
1. Typed on separate line even with left margin, underlined	162
2. Preceded by triple space and followed by double space	174
C. Second-Order Subheadings	180
1. Indented as first line of paragraph, underlined	190
2. Preceded by double space	196

62D ● **USING THE RATCHET RELEASE** *10 minutes*

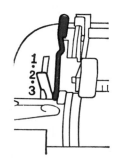

To Use the Ratchet Release (or Line Finder): Pull the lever forward, move the cylinder forward or backward to the desired position; type; then return the lever to its position.

To Type the Symbols in the Sentences: Operate the ratchet release, turn the cylinder *backward* (toward you) to type the degree symbol. Turn the cylinder *forward* (away from you) to type the chemistry symbol.

PROCEDURE

1 Type a 1-inch line, using the underline key.

2 Operate the ratchet-release lever and move the cylinder *forward* (away from you) about 1 inch.

3 Type another 1-inch line.

4 Return the lever to position and move the cylinder back to the first line and type over the line.

5 Type the sentences given below, typing the symbols as directed at the left.

Water freezes at 32° F.

The symbol for water is H_2O.

LESSON 22 | 22A ● PREPARATORY PRACTICE *7 minutes (each line three times)*

Alphabetic   Has Jimmy Vale packed my big box with the quick-frozen food?   Type with

Figure-symbol   The 1962-63 report read, "Earnings for O'Hare are $457,890."   quick, sharp strokes

Fluency   An element of doubt kept them from helping with the project.

| 1 | 2 | 3 | 4 | 5 | 6 | 7 | 8 | 9 | 10 | 11 | 12 |

22B ● NEW KEYS: # (Number), & (Ampersand), and) (Right Parenthesis)
8 minutes

Reach to #

Reach to &

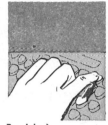
Reach to)

1. REACH TECHNIQUE FOR #
As your *left second finger* moves up to type #, lift the first finger slightly. *Do not space between # and the figure with which it is typed.* Watch your finger type **#d** a few times; type the Tryout Practice twice on one line.

#d # d#d #13 d#d #23 #143

2. REACH TECHNIQUE FOR &
Move the *right first finger* up to type & (ampersand) without arching the wrist or moving the hand forward. The ampersand (meaning "and") is used in company names. Watch your finger type **&j** a few times; type the Tryout Practice twice on one line.

&j & j&j &j& Hall & Young

3. REACH TECHNIQUE FOR)
Straighten the *right fourth finger* slightly and reach it up to type right) without twisting the elbow out of position and without moving the other fingers from their typing position. Watch your finger type **);** a few times type the Tryout Practice twice on one line.

);) ;);) ;);) ;);) ;)

22C ● STROKING TECHNIQUE PRACTICE *10 minutes (each line three or more times)*

NOTE Before a figure, # is the symbol for *No.*; after a figure, it is the symbol for *pounds*. See Line 1.

TO TYPE THE EXCLAMATION POINT: If your typewriter does not have a special key for the exclamation point, type the ' and then backspace and type the . (period). See Line 5. *Space twice after the exclamation point at the end of a sentence.*

● All letters and figures taught are used in the sentences.

1	Reach	Order #234 is for 670# of sugar. Next, pay Jay's Bill #901.	Work for
2	to the numbers	Nezi & Lee paid O'Hara & Qualls the sum of $750 on April 16.	controlled continuity
3	and symbols	The), the shift of 0, is typed with my right fourth finger.	
4		Check #978 for $342.50, dated May 16, is from Howe & Vaughn.	
5		Type right! In fact, that is how simple it is to typewrite!	

| 1 | 2 | 3 | 4 | 5 | 6 | 7 | 8 | 9 | 10 | 11 | 12 |

LESSON 62 | **62A ● PREPARATORY PRACTICE** *5 minutes (each line three or more times)*

Alphabetic — Maxine and Jack Wyllis drove by the giraffe at the quiet Arizona Park.

Roman numerals — Type Roman numerals in capital letters: one I three III five V ten X.

Fluency — You can save a lot of time and effort if you plan your work carefully.

| 1 | 2 | 3 | 4 | 5 | 6 | 7 | 8 | 9 | 10 | 11 | 12 | 13 | 14 |

62B ● ALIGNING ROMAN NUMERALS; SPACING BETWEEN RELATED AND UNRELATED COLUMNS *5 minutes*

ALIGNING ROMAN NUMERALS

Align columns of Roman numerals at the right. In the following drills, for example: To provide the proper spacing between the columns of Arabic and Roman numerals, set each tabulator stop for the number of spaces needed between columns *plus* the number of spaces required to type the longest line in the column.

SPACING BETWEEN RELATED AND UNRELATED COLUMNS

Spacing may vary between columns depending on their relationship. For example: In these drills, related columns (*1–2, 3–4, 5–6*) are typed closer together for quick identification of the relationship between the columns; but unrelated columns (*2–3, 4–5*) are more widely separated.

PROCEDURE After typing Drill 1, clear the tabulator rack of stop settings; then reset tabulator stops for Drill 2.

Half sheet
1½″ top margin ● 4 spaces between related columns
Double spacing 10 spaces between unrelated columns

DRILL 1	3 7	4	III VII	10	8 9	4	VIII IX	10	10 15	4	X XV

● 2 double spaces after Drill 1

DRILL 2	5 12	4	V XII	10	20 24	4	XX XXIV	10	30 50	4	XXX L

62C ● PROBLEM TYPING: Typing Numerals in Outlines; Outline of Unbound Manuscripts

25 minutes

Problem 1: Typing Numerals in Outlines

Full sheet ● 66-space line ● Double-spacing ● 4 spaces between related columns
3″ top margin 10-space ¶ indention 10 spaces between unrelated columns

	Words
ARABIC AND ROMAN NUMERALS IN OUTLINES	8

In typing outlines, use Roman numerals to identify major — 19
divisions; capital letters, for subheadings; and Arabic numerals, — 32
for the items under the subheadings. Type topic outlines without — 45
punctuation at the ends of lines (except abbreviations), but type — 59
sentence outlines with appropriate punctuation at the ends of lines. — 73
Study the Arabic and Roman numerals given below: — 83

1	I	6	VI	15	XV		87
2	II	7	VII	40	XL		91
3	III	8	VIII	50	L		95
4	IV	9	IX	60	LX		99
5	V	10	X	100	C		103

● *62C is continued on page 110.*

22D ● SENTENCE GUIDED WRITINGS *10 minutes*

PROCEDURE

1 Type each sentence for 1 minute, guided by the 20-second call of the line ending.

2 Type each sentence for a second 1-minute writing, guided by the 15- or 12-second call as directed by your instructor. Pace your speed so you will type each sentence in the exact time of the call of the guide.

	GWAM		
	20″	15″	12″
What is the sum of 12 and 34 and 56 and 78 and 90?	30	40	50
The man is rich who knows how to make his mind work for him.	36	48	60
This Check #2398 for $150 pays Howe & King's bill.	30	40	50

| 1 | 2 | 3 | 4 | 5 | 6 | 7 | 8 | 9 | 10 | 11 | 12 |

22E ● PROBLEM TYPING: Memorandum on the Block Style *10 minutes*

2 half sheets,
50-space line,
single spacing,
1½″ top margin,
current date

PROCEDURE

Insert the half sheet to the first line space at the top of the page; then space forward 9 times and type the current date on Line 10 (for a 1½-inch top margin).

1 Type the memorandum with 4 blank line spaces between the date and subject.

2 Type the memorandum a second time as a 3-minute writing, beginning with the date.

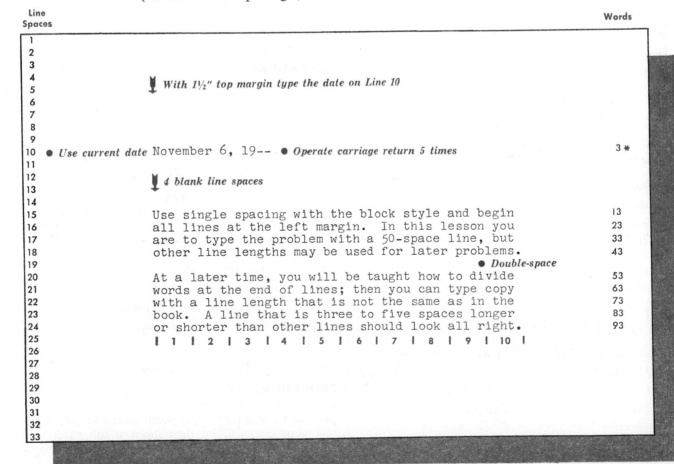

Line Spaces / Words

1
2
3
4
5 ↧ *With 1½″ top margin type the date on Line 10*
6
7
8
9
10 ● *Use current date* November 6, 19-- ● *Operate carriage return 5 times*   3 *
11
12 ↧ *4 blank line spaces*
13
14
15 Use single spacing with the block style and begin   13
16 all lines at the left margin. In this lesson you   23
17 are to type the problem with a 50-space line, but   33
18 other line lengths may be used for later problems.   43
19   ● *Double-space*
20 At a later time, you will be taught how to divide   53
21 words at the end of lines; then you can type copy   63
22 with a line length that is not the same as in the   73
23 book. A line that is three to five spaces longer   83
24 or shorter than other lines should look all right.   93
25 | 1 | 2 | 3 | 4 | 5 | 6 | 7 | 8 | 9 | 10 |
26
27
28
29
30
31
32
33

Fifteen strokes (3 words are counted for the current date even though there may be fewer or more strokes in the current date typed).

61D ● PROBLEM TYPING: Poems; Composing at the Typewriter *25 minutes*

Problem 1: Poem (89 words)

Full sheet 45-space line	●	Single spacing 3″ top margin	●	Center the title in all caps

I Asked and Received

● Triple-space

I asked for bread,
He gave me a field to plow ––
A field to seed and tend and spray,
To care for day by day ––
And I have bread now.

● Double-space

I asked for money,
He gave me work to do ––
Work most exacting, demanding,
With horizons ever expanding ––
Now I have money, too.

I asked for honors,
He gave me a choice to make ––
The easy wrong or the hard right,
Honor or honors for which to fight ––
He leadeth me: Honors without honor I forsake.

Problem 2: Poem (110 words)

PROCEDURE Use the directions for Problem 1. Use TO FIND REALITY as the title.

Let me dream again ––
Dream that life can be what I meant it to be.
If I can dream with faith again,
I'll find reality.

Dreams are the substance of things hoped for,
The evidence of things not seen;
They picture life as it may yet be,
Not life as it might have been.

Once I dreamed the world was my workshop,
And I a potter would be;
That life would be fashioned for service,
And only good would come to me.

I must dream again ––
And follow my dreams whatever they be;
I must dream again, strive again, believe again,
To find reality.

Problem 3: Centering "S P R E A D" Titles

HOW TO CENTER A "S P R E A D" TITLE

1 From the center of the paper, backspace once for each letter except the last one and once for the space between words.

2 Type the title, spacing once between the letters and three times between the words.

PROCEDURE Use a half sheet; 2″ top margin; double spacing. Center each "spread" title shown below. The first one is shown in correct form.

	Words
A B O O K R E P O R T	5
MAKING HOBBIES PAY	12
MANUSCRIPT TYPING	19
TRANSFORMED	24
I ASKED AND RECEIVED	32
TO FIND REALITY	37

Problem 4: Poem in Reading Position (73 words)

PROCEDURE Use the directions for Problem 1, except that you will type the poem in *reading position*. "Spread" TRANSFORMED as the title.

Staggering, falling, crawling ––
"What is man that thou art mindful of him."

Struggling, rising, reaching ––
"Made a little lower than the angels."

Standing straight, going on, keeping faith ––
"Transformed by the renewing of the mind."

This is man at his worst
And man at his best ––
Failing, striving, growing, giving,
Man and God together living.

Problem 5: Composing

PROCEDURE Discuss the meaning of one of the poems typed as Problems 1, 2, and 4. Criticize, interpret, and explain what the poem means to you. Correct your composition; then insert a full sheet and retype your comments in a form you consider acceptable. Type the title of the poem in "spread" form. Unless otherwise directed, erase and correct any typing errors you make.

LESSON 23 | 23A ● PREPARATORY PRACTICE *7 minutes (each line three times)*

Alphabetic	Dwight Buzwell quickly flew over the peak six times in June.
Figure-symbol	We must pay Lang & Park's Bill #2390 for $546.78 by July 10.
Fluency	Tod is the auditor for the big firm with an office downtown.

| 1 | 2 | 3 | 4 | 5 | 6 | 7 | 8 | 9 | 10 | 11 | 12 |

Control your finger and hand motions

23B ● NEW KEYS: %, _ (Underline), and ((Left Parenthesis)
8 minutes

Reach to %

Reach to _

Reach to (

1. REACH TECHNIQUE FOR %

Type % with the *left first finger* without moving the other fingers from their typing position. Do not space between the figure and the following percent sign. Watch your finger type %**f** a few times; then type the Tryout Practice twice on one line.

%f % f%f 5% f%f 4 1/2% f%

2. REACH TECHNIQUE FOR _

Nonelectric Typewriter: Reach the *right first finger* up to type the _ (underline) without arching the wrist.
Electric Typewriter: Reach the *right fourth finger* up to type _. Watch your finger type _**j** or _; then type the Tryout Practice twice.

_j _ j_j _; _ ;_; Try it!

3. REACH TECHNIQUE FOR (

Straighten the *right third finger* and reach it up to type ((left parenthesis) without twisting the elbow out of position and without moving the hand forward or arching the wrist. Watch your finger type (**l** a few times; then type the Tryout Practice.

(l (l(l (l (l (l(l(l (l

23C ● STROKING TECHNIQUE PRACTICE *10 minutes (each line three times)*

TO UNDERLINE: Backspace (or move the carriage by hand) to the first letter of the word. Type the underline once for each letter in the word.

TO UNDERLINE SEVERAL WORDS IN SUCCESSION: Depress the shift lock **29** and type an unbroken line. To release the shift lock, depress the shift key.

● All letters and all figures are used in the sentences.

1	Shift firmly	Will the 5% rate be changed to 4% or possibly 4 1/2% in May?
2		Think before you act; then quit your worrying after you act!
3	Down-and-in	Depress the shift lock (No. 29); next, type in ALL CAPITALS.
4	space-bar motion	Change the 5% rate on Jantz & Kane's note (due May 6) to 4%.
5		Clerical pay (on the average) has risen about 94% from 1944.

| 1 | 2 | 3 | 4 | 5 | 6 | 7 | 8 | 9 | 10 | 11 | 12 |

Return quickly

Do not pause

SECTION 10 | OUTLINES, MANUSCRIPTS, AND COMPOSING
Lessons 61-70

STANDARD PROCEDURES FOR SECTION 10

GET READY TO TYPE
Clear the desk. Adjust the paper guide and paper-bail rolls. Use a full sheet, 70-space line, and single spacing (unless otherwise directed).

SELF-IMPROVEMENT PRACTICE
As time permits, type the sentences of Self-Improvement Practice, page 125, three or more times each.

LESSON 61 | 61A ● PREPARATORY PRACTICE *5 minutes (each line three or more times)*

Alphabetic	Both Jay and Max received big prizes from Kyle's during the quiz show.
Figures	In 1956, 203 clerks were working here; in 1960, 734; and in 1964, 928.
Speed	Most of us, whether young or old, have potential that is never tapped.

| 1 | 2 | 3 | 4 | 5 | 6 | 7 | 8 | 9 | 10 | 11 | 12 | 13 | 14 |

61B ● TECHNIQUE PRACTICE *10 minutes (each line three or more times)*

1	Direct reach	My brother trusts the truth of the zoning decision will be made known.
2	Adjacent	Except for a deed to my house, was all property ceded to our brothers?
3	Hyphen	Joe thinks we have an up-to-the-minute plan for our out-of-town sales.
4	Combination	My Quill Club motto: "All the World's a Stage" (from As You Like It).
5	Word-recognition	Tom Hays said, "You should do a full day's work for a full day's pay."

| 1 | 2 | 3 | 4 | 5 | 6 | 7 | 8 | 9 | 10 | 11 | 12 | 13 | 14 |

61C ● TYPING FROM SCRIPT *5 minutes*

Full sheet, 70-space line, double spacing, 5-space ¶ indention

PROCEDURE Type two 2' writings on the *control level*, pausing 15-20 seconds between to relax.

Determine *gwam* and indicate errors for the better writing. Do not type at maximum rate, but type with continuity.

● All letters and an si of 1.46 are used in this paragraph.

GWAM

	1'	2'	
It pays in dollars and cents to go to college. According to the	13	7	57
Census Bureau, the average income of heads of families with college	27	14	64
degrees is fixed at $9,300 a year. Heads of families with just high	40	20	70
school diplomas and no college credit average $6,300 a year. The size	55	28	78
of your income increases the further you go in college. Also, annual	69	35	85
income tends to rise at a faster rate for workers with a college degree.	83	42	92
Put luck on your side. Get the best education you can--both in quality	98	49	99
and quantity.	100	50	100

| 1' | 1 | 2 | 3 | 4 | 5 | 6 | 7 | 8 | 9 | 10 | 11 | 12 | 13 | 14 |
| 2' | 1 | | 2 | | 3 | | 4 | | 5 | | 6 | | 7 |

23D ● SENTENCE GUIDED WRITINGS *10 minutes*

PROCEDURE

1 Type each sentence for 1 minute, guided by the 30-second call of the line ending.

2 Type each sentence for a second 1-minute writing, guided by the 20- or 15-second call as directed.

NOTE Type the dash with two hyphens (--). See Lines 2 and 3.
To type the exclamation point, type the ' and backspace and type the period. See Line 2.

		GWAM 20"	15"	12"
1	"Cash Harris & Norton's Check #1789," the auditor said.	33	44	55
2	Change--like it, hate it, or prize it, but get ready for it!	36	48	60
3	Joe's fare is $234.50 (less 6%)--a net cost of $220.43.	33	44	55
4	Hold the arms as quiet as you can and let your fingers type.	36	48	60

| 1 | 2 | 3 | 4 | 5 | 6 | 7 | 8 | 9 | 10 | 11 | 12 |

23E ● PROBLEM TYPING: Memorandum with Subject Line *10 minutes*

2 half sheets,
50-space line,
single spacing,
1" top margin,
current date

PROCEDURE

Insert the half sheet to the first line space at the top of the page; then space forward 6 times and type the current date on Line 7 (for a 1-inch top margin).

1 Type the memorandum with 4 blank line spaces between the date and subject. Type SUBJECT in all capital letters followed by a colon and 2 spaces.

2 Type the memorandum as a 3-minute writing, beginning with the current date.

NOTE To type in all capital letters, depress the shift lock 29 and type.
To release the shift lock, depress the shift key.

	Words
Current Date = 10ᵗʰ 5ᵗ	3

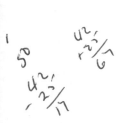

▼ Operate carriage return 5 times to leave 4 blank line spaces

SUBJECT: Informational Memorandum	10
You can fold a full-size sheet of paper and get a	20
half sheet of 33 lines. You can type four of the	30
short memos on the one folded sheet. This is for	40
practice typing only, of course; and it would not	50
be the way in which to type memos you want to use.	60
You can have equal top and bottom margins, or you	70
can begin three lines higher on the page and have	80
more space for the bottom margin than for the top.	91
This memo is typed in the block style. This is a	101
style that is used in business letters, too. The	111
lines are 50 spaces long. All lines begin at the	121
left margin. This is featured in the block style.	131

. . . . 1 . . . . 2 . . . . 3 . . . . 4 . . . . 5 . . . . 6 . . . . 7 . . . . 8 . . . . 9 10

SELF-IMPROVEMENT PRACTICE: Action Typing ● *(each ¶ twice on the control level—without timing)*

10 half sheets,
70-space line,
double spacing,
5-space ¶ indention,
1½" top margin

PROCEDURE In Action Typing you must pay attention to what is typed and do what you are told to do in the sentence you type. Always type the entire sentence before you follow any directions given in the sentence you are typing.

For example, the second sentence of Action Typing 1 directs you to type the first sentence again at a speed slower than your first typing. As the third sentence, then, retype the first sentence; then continue to type the paragraph.

1 Type at a speed that is well within your zone of control. Type the first sentence again, but type at a speed that is 8 to 10 words slower than your first typing. Type with quiet, even stroking. Underline the preceding sentence with an unbroken line; then start a new paragraph. Center and type the next sentence in all capital letters on a separate line, with a blank line space before it, and without typing the period. Think as you type.

2 Pay attention to what you type. Move the carriage to the first word of the paragraph, and type over the first sentence. Without changing the margin stops, type the next sentence on one line to begin 5 spaces outside the left margin and with a double space before it. It is the duty of a typist to check each typed page and to correct all errors.

3 Center ACTION TYPING 3 as a heading a triple space above this line, remembering to release the shift lock before typing the figure 3. When typing, underline words that are printed in *italics*, so underline the italicized word in this sentence. Beginning at the left margin a double space below this completed sentence, type the alphabet in all capitals and the figures 1 to 10, with a space after each letter and figure; then remove the paper, reinsert it to type on the reverse side, and type your own return address and current date in correct position for a 60-space line personal letter.

4 Lock the shift key when you type the next sentence in all capital letters. Type with ease. Add an exclamation point to the preceding sentence. Position the carriage and underline the second sentence; then reposition the carriage and continue to type the paragraph. As you type the next sentence, correct the misspelled words. The reply to our questionaire does not warrant our reccommending him for promotion. Remove the paper, reinsert it, and type over the first word of the paragraph.

5 Center and type your name in all capital letters a triple space above this line. Type the following sentence as rapidly as you can type with a sense of ease and control. It is up to me to build my skill in typing to as high a level as possible. Remove the paper, reinsert it, and type over your name centered above the paragraph; then continue to type the remainder of this paragraph. Center and type the current date a double space below this line.

LESSON 24 | 24A ● PREPARATORY PRACTICE *7 minutes (each line three times)*

Alphabetic	Lew very quickly mixed a big jar of soap for the next prize.	**Improve your stroking technique**
Figure-symbol	Paul's 4% note (for $750) was paid on May 26 by Check #1389.	
Fluency	The way you read what you type may control the way you type.	
	| 1 | 2 | 3 | 4 | 5 | 6 | 7 | 8 | 9 | 10 | 11 | 12 |	

24B ● NEW KEYS: * (Asterisk), ½-¼, and ¢-@ (Cent or Cents and At) *8 minutes*

- *The keys taught in this lesson are seldom used except in typing bills, invoices, and the like. In later lessons the symbols will be used in typing problems, at which time intensive drill will be given.*

Reach to *

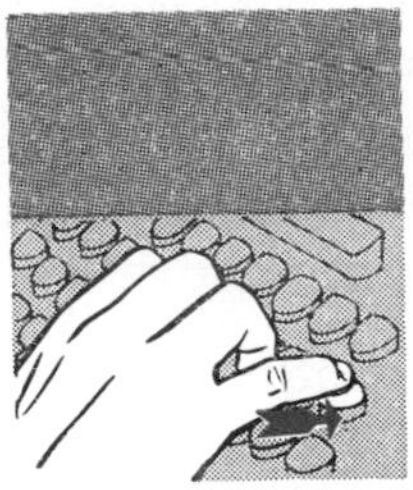
Reach to ½-¼

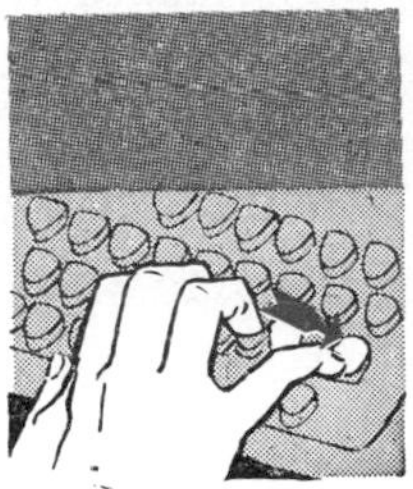
Reach to ¢-@

1. REACH TECHNIQUE FOR *

Nonelectric Typewriter: Straighten the *right fourth finger* and type * (asterisk) without swinging the elbow outward. **Electric Typewriter:** Type * with the *right second finger*. Watch your finger type ***;** or ***k**; then type the Tryout Practice twice on one line.

*; * ;*; * k*k *k *k* k*k

2. REACH TECHNIQUE FOR ½–¼

The shift of ½ is ¼. Reach the *right fourth finger* up to type ½ and depress the left shift key to type ¼. Make the reach-stroke without change of hand position. Watch your finger type **½ ¼;** a few times; then type the Tryout Practice twice on one line.

$\frac{1}{2}$; $\frac{1}{2}$;$\frac{1}{2}$; $\frac{1}{2}\frac{1}{4}$; $\frac{1}{2}\frac{1}{4}$; $\frac{1}{4}$;$\frac{1}{4}$; $\frac{1}{4}$;

3. REACH TECHNIQUE FOR ¢–@

Nonelectric Typewriter: Type **¢-@** with the *right fourth finger*. **Electric Typewriter:** Shift and type **¢** with the *right first finger* and type @ with the *left third finger*. Watch your finger type **¢ @** a few times; then type the Tryout Practice twice on one line.

¢ @ Use ¢ and @ in bills.

24C ● STROKING TECHNIQUE PRACTICE *10 minutes (each line three or more times)*

1	**Type with sure, sharp strokes**	You can use * for a footnote and ** for the second footnote.	**Return without looking up**
2		Be uniform when you type fractions: $\frac{1}{2}$ and $\frac{1}{4}$ or 1/2 and 1/4.	
3		Use ¢ and @ when typing bills; as, Ship 467 lbs. @ 98¢ a lb.	
4		Shift to type the symbols *, @, #, and % on this typewriter.	
5		Space after @, but not between the figure and #, ¢, *, or $.	
		| 1 | 2 | 3 | 4 | 5 | 6 | 7 | 8 | 9 | 10 | 11 | 12 |	

Problem 2: Three-Column Tabulation

			Words
Full sheet, double spacing, center problem in reading position, 10 spaces between columns	WORD DIVISION		3

PROCEDURE Type each word only once, adding a hyphen to show the *preferred* division after the typing of the second letter.

			Words
achieved	fluency	mimeograph	9
amounted	fundamental	mortgage	15
career	glacial	nominal	20
commonly	guessing	probable	26
creating	historical	profit-sharing	34
daily	hypnosis	reclassify	39
digest	impartial	sciences	45
elaborate	implicate	secured	51
evaluation	improper	stepped	57
expelling	insinuation	unable	63
explicit	instances	upon	68
expressions	interim	waivers	73

Problem 3: Letter with Tabulated Items

Letterhead (or full sheet) Carbon sheet File copy sheet Current date	60-space line Modified block, blocked ¶s Mixed punctuation 10 spaces between tabulated items Address an envelope

● 8 blank line spaces after the date

Words

Mrs. T. Morgan Childs | 89 Phoenix Road | — 11
Glendale, Arizona 85301 | Dear Mrs. — 18
Childs | (¶1) Our yearly preinventory — 24
sale which was announced in today's — 31
papers features many big savings. As an — 40
example, our Carlin bedspreads of antique — 48

satin, rayon and acetate, trimmed with — 56
matching double-loop edge, will be priced — 64
as follows: — 67

39″ twin spread	$34.50 — 71
54″ double spread	44.50 — 76

(¶2) The spreads come in rose, beige, — 83
French blue, gold, and white colors. (¶3) — 91
Visit our store soon and take advantage — 99
of the many big savings you will find here. | — 108
Sincerely yours | Ralph S. Quigley | Sales — 116
Manager | (*Your initials*) | — 118/130

Problem 4: Three-Column Tabulation

			Words
Half sheet, double spacing, center problem vertically, decide number of spaces to be left between columns	*UNITED FUND COMMITTEE*		4
	Clay, Enos (Chairman)	Purchasing Department	Room 1601	15
	Gatewood, Dennis	Engineering "	" 28	23
	Jessup, Robert	Marketing "	" 145	29
	LeClair, Jessica	Accounting "	" 102	36
	Orbutt, James C.	Advertising "	" 136	44
	Regan, Norah Ann	Maintenance "	" 615	51
	Spencer, Sarah	Communications "	" 19	59

24D ● STROKING TECHNIQUE REVIEW *20 minutes*

Full sheet,
60-space line,
single spacing,
2" top margin

PROCEDURE

1 On a drill sheet make pencil notations of the assignments listed below. Place the sheet on the desk near your typewriter where you can refer to it easily.

21C (page 43); 22C (page 44); 23C (page 46)

2 You will be timed for 15 minutes. When directed to begin typing, type each line of each practice twice on the *control level*. Double-space after the second typing of the line. Extra credit will be given for each errorless line.

LESSON 25 | ## 25A ● PREPARATORY PRACTICE *7 minutes (each line three times)*

Alphabetic	Will Jim Quill help fix a package as my prize to Don Beaver?	Read carefully;
Figure-symbol	Young & Johnson's Bill #4598 (dated July 26) totals $137.90.	strike surely
Fluency	Do not put off until tomorrow what should be done right now.	

| 1 | 2 | 3 | 4 | 5 | 6 | 7 | 8 | 9 | 10 | 11 | 12 |

25B ● TECHNIQUE PRACTICE: Response Patterns *10 minutes (each line two or three times)*

STROKE RESPONSE You type by *stroke (or letter) response* when you see, think, and type stroke by stroke, as you typed in your early practice. This is the "slow but sure" typing response.

Stroke — You are in

Word-recognition — When the work

Combination — The statement

WORD-RECOGNITION RESPONSE When you see and think words as words without thinking the letters, you type by *word-recognition response*—a quicker and higher form of typing than when you type by stroke response. For example, when you see the word *he*, you should think the word and not the letters *h e* and your fingers will move into position for typing the word with ease, certainty, and continuity.

COMBINATION RESPONSE When the copy has some easy and some difficult stroking sequences, use a *combination response*, typing as many words as you can by word-recognition response but dropping back to stroke response when an awkward sequence of letters or a difficult or unfamiliar word is to be typed. The combination response will evolve naturally as you practice copy of mixed difficulty.

● **SPACING REMINDER** Space once after a period following an initial.

● All letters and all figures are used in the sentences.

	RESPONSE		
1	Stroke	The executive expected the experts to explain their actions.	Listen for
2	Stroke	In my opinion, this reward should be given to J. O. Quenzer.	the difference
3	Word-recognition	Tod makes the forms for the men to use for their field work.	in response
4	Word-recognition	Now and then it is right to work with no speed gain in mind.	patterns
5	Word-recognition	It is up to me to know how to do this work in the right way.	
6	Combination	It seldom helps to stress too many skill elements at a time.	
7	Combination	It is a fact that the opinion of the workers was considered.	
8	Combination	The 53 men and 70 women sailed for Norway on April 28, 1964.	

| 1 | 2 | 3 | 4 | 5 | 6 | 7 | 8 | 9 | 10 | 11 | 12 |

Problem 1: Memorandum with Tabulated Items

Full sheet	8 spaces between 1st
65-space line	set of tabulated
Single spacing ●	words; use same
5-space ¶ indention	tab stops for 2d and
2" top margin	3d sets of words

NOTE After typing the first line of the numbered ¶, reset the left margin stop 9 spaces in from the outside margin; then when Figures 2 and 3 are to be typed, release the margin stop and backspace into the left margin 4 spaces before typing the figure.

Words

PROBLEMS IN WORD DIVISION   5

    To avoid dividing words at the end of lines, you can have a   17
line that is approximately 5 strokes longer or shorter than the   30
desired line ending. Always put enough of the word on the line to   43
suggest what the completed word will be.   53

    Guides 1 and 2, below, are positive DO's of word division;   64
Guide 3, a negative DON'T; Guide 4, an AVOID-IF-POSSIBLE. Know   76
these guides and use them so your typed page will be well balanced.   90

1. If a word is to be divided where two vowels that are   102
    pronounced separately come together, divide between   112
    the vowels.   115

| SYLLABLE ▶ | grad-u-a-tion | gradu-ation | ◀ CORRECT POINT | 120 |
| IDENTIFICATION | hu-mil-i-a-tion | humili-ation | OF DIVISION | 126 |

2. Divide hyphenated or compound words at the hyphen only.   139

        self-re-spect   self-respect   144
        self-com-mand   self-command   150

3. DO NOT divide   154
   a. a four-letter word   159
   b. a one- or two-letter syllable at the end of a word   170
   c. a one-letter syllable at the beginning of a word   181
   d. a contraction   184
   e. the last word of a paragraph or the last word on   195
      a page   196

4. AVOID, if possible, dividing   204
   a. words of five or six letters   211
   b. a two-letter syllable at the beginning of a word   221
   c. figures or abbreviations   227
   d. titles, initials, or degrees from a surname   237
   e. words at the ends of more than two consecutive   247
      lines of typing   250

        on-ly   only   252
        read-y   ready   255
        a-round   around   258
        di-vid-ed   divided   261
        should-n't   shouldn't   266
        de-gree   degree   268

60-space line,
  double spacing,
  5-space paragraph
  indention

PROCEDURE

1 Type each paragraph for 1 minute on the *control level*. Quickly note your *gwam* for each writing.

2 Type three 3-minute writings at approximately the 1-minute control rate. Determine the *gwam* for the best writing.

● All letters are used in the paragraphs.

| | GWAM | |
| | 1' | 3' |

¶ 1
1.15 si
68 words

When you believe you can't do a thing, the chances are   11 | 4 | 49
you won't be able to do it well; but if you believe you can   23 | 8 | 53
do what is to be done, you can work with sureness. If fear   35 | 12 | 57
and doubt are big enough, your mind and muscles can be tied   47 | 16 | 61
in knots, but a little doubt of yourself may spur you on to   59 | 20 | 65
do things. Be sure--only don't be cocksure.   68 | 23 | 68

¶ 2
1.15 si
68 words

If you are asked to do something you don't know how to   79 | 26 | 71
do, learn what you can from those around you--then get busy   91 | 30 | 75
and do it quickly, using your best judgment, of course. If   103 | 34 | 79
you get in a dither and don't know what to do next, you can   115 | 38 | 83
waste a lot of time and then sizzle and worry. Do what you   127 | 43 | 88
can just as well as you can, and don't worry.   136 | 45 | 90

1' | 1 | 2 | 3 | 4 | 5 | 6 | 7 | 8 | 9 | 10 | 11 | 12
3' | 1 | 2 | 3 | 4

25D ● PROBLEM TYPING: Memorandum with Subject Line *13 minutes*

2 half sheets,
  50-space line,
  single spacing,
  1" top margin

PROCEDURE Have a 1' top margin (6 blank line spaces) and 6 blank line spaces between the date and subject. You will be timed for 10 minutes. If you complete the second typing of the memorandum before time is called, use the back of that sheet to type the memorandum a third time. Type on the *control level*. Work rapidly but carefully.

| | Words |

Current Date   3

SUBJECT: Informational Memorandum   10

Move the chair so you are 8 to 10 inches from the   20
base of the machine. Sit well back in the chair,   30
your feet on the floor, and your eyes on the copy.   40

A full-size sheet of paper is 11 inches long with   50
66 lines. A half sheet is 5½ inches long and has   60
33 lines. As there are 6 lines to an inch, a top   70
margin of 1½ inches has 9 lines. From the top of   80
the page, you must space down 10 times to type on   90
the tenth line, leaving 9 lines in the top margin.   100

. . . . 1 . . . . 2 . . . . 3 . . . . 4 . . . . 5 . . . . 6 . . . . 7 . . . . 8 . . . . 9 10

| **60A ● PREPARATORY PRACTICE** *5 minutes (each line three or more times)*

Alphabetic   Fred Wilcox thinks every boy or girl can be made quite a "jazzophile."

Figure-symbol   Order #890 reads: "Ship 34 doz. #561 ** Bolts @ 70¢ a doz. on May 2."

Fluency   The chairman said a large bequest had been made to the endowment fund.

| 1 | 2 | 3 | 4 | 5 | 6 | 7 | 8 | 9 | 10 | 11 | 12 | 13 | 14 |

NOTE Remove the paper; then reinsert it, gauge the line and letter, and type over the first line.

60B ● GROWTH INDEX *10 minutes*

Full sheet,
  70-space line,
  double spacing,
  5-space ¶ indention

PROCEDURE

1 Type a 1-minute writing on the *control level*. Try to find the rate at which you can type with maximum ease and control. Determine your *gwam*.

2 Type a 5-minute writing on the *control level*, typing well below your maximum speed. Determine your *gwam*.

● All letters are used in the paragraphs.

GWAM
1' 5'

¶ 1
1.30 si
80 words

It has been said that 33 percent of the jobs of the future will require one to three years of schooling beyond high school and that 24 percent will take four or more years of college work. In the working world of tomorrow, workers must know more and be more flexible and ready to adapt to change, for change is sure to come. It will take brains and imagination to fit into tomorrow's world of work.

	1'	5'	
	13	3	51
	27	5	53
	41	8	56
	56	11	59
	70	14	62
	80	16	64

¶ 2
1.30 si
80 words

In tomorrow's world of work, the race will not be so much to the swift as to the competent. Success will come to those who earn it, not to those who just yearn for it. Skill by itself won't be enough, for skilled hands must be guided by reflective heads. It won't be a matter of skill or the ability to think; it will be skill and the ability to think. Education will be more important than ever.

	93	19	67
	107	21	69
	121	24	72
	136	27	75
	150	30	78
	160	32	80

¶ 3
1.30 si
80 words

Whitehead says, "What we should aim to produce is men who possess both culture and expert knowledge. Their expert knowledge will give them the ground to start from, and their culture will lead them as deep as philosophy and as high as art." Men need specialized skill "as the ground to start from" and learning that is "as deep as philosophy and as high as art" for their working world of tomorrow.

	173	35	83
	187	37	85
	201	40	88
	216	43	91
	230	46	94
	240	48	96

1' | 1 | 2 | 3 | 4 | 5 | 6 | 7 | 8 | 9 | 10 | 11 | 12 | 13 | 14 |
5' | 1 | 2 | 3 |

BUILDING BASIC SKILL

STANDARD PROCEDURES FOR SECTION 5

GET READY TO TYPE

Clear desk of unneeded papers. Adjust paper guide and paper-bail rolls. Use a 60-space line. Set line-space regulator for single spacing the drills; use double spacing when directed to do so.

SELF-IMPROVEMENT PRACTICE

As time permits, retype the lines of the technique practices (26B, 27B, 28B, and 29B) three or more times. Identify errorless lines so that extra credit may be given for them. Type on the *control level*.

LESSON 26 | **26A ● PREPARATORY PRACTICE** *7 minutes (each line three or more times)*

PROCEDURE (for each Preparatory Practice in this section)

Sentence 1 Type by *stroke response* and with even stroking. Maintain rhythmic continuity.
Sentence 2 Improve the technique conditioners: Low wrists, curved fingers, quiet hands and arms, eyes on the copy.

Sentence 3 Type once for speed—think the word; type a second time at a slightly slower rate and with emphasis on smooth, even typing; and type the sentence a third time on the *control level*.

Alphabetic	Pam and Jeff Wycox quickly read the big novels by Zola Munn.
Drill on c	Carl will call the new clerks to check these cuts with care.
Fluency	Either the men will do more work or they must quit this job.

| 1 | 2 | 3 | 4 | 5 | 6 | 7 | 8 | 9 | 10 | 11 | 12 |

26B ● TECHNIQUE PRACTICE: Direct-Reach Stroking *10 minutes (each line three or more times)*

TECHNIQUE EMPHASIS

When the same finger is used to strike two keys in succession, move the finger directly to the second key without returning the finger to home position and without pausing between strokes.

● All letters are used in the sentences.

1	Eyes on copy	My truck hauled hundreds of pounds of freight for Frederick.	● Curve the fingers
2		Quite a number of hunters went hungry when hunting with Ike.	● Strike sharply
3	Do not pause	Mr. Sexton told Myna he sold five hundred old desks in June.	● Space quickly
4		The role of queen was won by Myrtle, who got our five votes.	● Shift firmly
5		Ruth Tracey went to Sweetbriar to visit Zola for the summer.	● Return smoothly

| 1 | 2 | 3 | 4 | 5 | 6 | 7 | 8 | 9 | 10 | 11 | 12 |

26C ● TYPING FROM DICTATION *5 minutes (each line three times as directed in 21D, page 43)*

Think the word	to as by do on if the you may not can and but add with type
Think the phrase	work some your keys best with also copy able easy copy easy
	to do|as you|on the|and do|you can|to type|to your|to think

| 1 | 2 | 3 | 4 | 5 | 6 | 7 | 8 | 9 | 10 | 11 | 12 |

LESSON 59

59A ● PREPARATORY PRACTICE *5 minutes* *(each line three or more times)*

Alphabetic   After breaking the error jinx, Dave Zell quickly typed six words more.

Figure-symbol   The * (asterisk) refers to page 234 of Volume 18; ** to pages 567-590.

Fluency   Our ancient ornaments found by the workmen have been proved authentic.

    | 1 | 2 | 3 | 4 | 5 | 6 | 7 | 8 | 9 | 10 | 11 | 12 | 13 | 14 |

59B ● SENTENCE GUIDED WRITING FROM CORRECTED SCRIPT *5 minutes* *(1' control-level writing on each line)*

PROCEDURE   Before beginning to type, read through the sentences to be sure you understand these "script rough-draft" sentences, which provide a first, simple practice in typing corrected handwritten manuscripts.

	GWAM		
	15"	12"	10"
If (you do succeed at first), try something a bit harder.	44	55	66
No one can jump down your throat if your mouth is shut.	44	55	66
You will keep others off your toes, if you will keeping on them.	48	60	72
Humility is God's gift to man; conceit is man's own mistake.	48	60	72

59C ● BUILDING CONTROL *10 minutes* *(5' control-level writing on ¶ of 58C, page 101)*

Full sheet,
carbon sheet,
file copy sheet,
70-space line,
double spacing,
5-space ¶ indention

PROCEDURE

Erase and correct all errors at the time they are made and as a part of the timing. For each uncorrected error, deduct 15 words to compensate for the time it would take you to erase and correct the error on the original sheet and the file copy sheet. Determine your corrected copy typing rate, and use the results of the writing to guide your further practice. Type with your best accuracy. *As errors go down, watch speed go up.*

59D ● PROBLEM TYPING REVIEW *25 minutes* *(20' timing)*

SUPPLIES NEEDED
3 full sheets,
2 letterheads
(or 2 full sheets),
1 envelope
1 carbon sheet
1 file copy sheet

PROCEDURE

1 Make pencil notations of the problems and page numbers given below:

53C, Problem 1 . . . . page 91
54B, Problem 1 . . . . page 92
54B, Problem 2 . . . . page 93
56C, Problem 3 . . . . page 97
58B, Problem 2 . . . . page 100

Place the notation sheet beside the typewriter. Work rapidly, but not hurriedly.

Know what you are to do before you begin to type. This will add to the accuracy with which you type.

2 Unless otherwise directed, erase and correct all errors. After typing a problem and before removing it from the typewriter, proofread the typing and correct any errors not yet corrected.

3 Address an envelope for 54B, Problem 2, page 93. Fold and insert the letter into it.

26D ● BUILDING SPEED AND CONTROL *23 minutes*

2 full sheets,
60-space line,
double spacing,
5-space ¶ indention

PROCEDURE
1 Type the ¶s quickly on a drill sheet. Identify and practice the difficult words.

2 Type two 1-minute writings on each ¶, typing on the *exploration level*.
3 Type three 3-minute writings, two on the *exploration* and one on the *control level*.

● All letters are used in the paragraphs.

	GWAM	
	1'	3'

¶ 1
1.15 si
52 words

	1'	3'	
You will add to your typing speed if you will type the	11	4	40
word as a word and not type it letter by letter. Think the	23	8	44
word with vigor. Strike and release the keys as quickly as	35	12	48
you can, but type without jerks. Be zealous to learn to do	47	16	52
all your work just right.	52	17	53

¶ 2
1.25 si
56 words

	1'	3'	
You should also keep your eyes on the copy as you type	11	21	57
the words. You may not be able to type every word with the	23	25	61
same even stroking you can maintain when typing some simple	35	29	65
and easy words, but keep your eyes fixed on the copy and do	47	33	69
the best you can to type without long pauses.	56	36	72

```
1' |  1  |  2  |  3  |  4  |  5  |  6  |  7  |  8  |  9  |  10  |  11  |  12  |
3' |        1        |        2        |        3        |        4        |
```

LESSON 27 | 27A ● PREPARATORY PRACTICE *7 minutes (each line three or more times)*

Alphabetic   Ezra must have six Yale men do a quick broad jump for wages.

Drill on **b**   Both boys brought five bright blue balls with brown binding.

Fluency   It is well for us to do all we can in the best ways we know.

```
|  1  |  2  |  3  |  4  |  5  |  6  |  7  |  8  |  9  |  10  |  11  |  12  |
```

27B ● TECHNIQUE PRACTICE: Space Bar and Shift Keys *10 minutes*
(each line three or more times)

TECHNIQUE
EMPHASIS

Space Bar *Strike the space bar with a quick down-and-in motion of the right thumb. Keep the hands and arms quiet and the elbows in.*
Shift Key *Hold the shift key down until the letter has been struck and released.*

● All letters are used in the sentences.

1   Type it right. Jim types well. Tom Young may see Sue soon.

2   If Sam tries hard, can he win a prize? I know Fran can win.

3   Miss Moss will tell Bill Cook how soon he may have the book.

4   The names of the winners are these: Van, Kay, Rex, and Jen.

5   Do the work as well as you can; then quit worrying about it!

```
|  1  |  2  |  3  |  4  |  5  |  6  |  7  |  8  |  9  |  10  |  11  |  12  |
```

58C ● BUILDING CONTROL *10 minutes (two 1' control-level writings; then two 3' control-level writings)*

Full sheet,
  70-space line,
  double spacing,
  5-space ¶ indention

PROCEDURE Pace your typing at a rate you can control with a high degree of typing accuracy. After each writing, determine an appropriate goal—fewer words and greater accuracy or more words with the same accuracy—and type to achieve that goal.

GWAM

● All letters are used in the paragraph.

	1'	3'	5'*
A good way to learn the "time cost" of correcting typing errors	13	4	3
is to have a check made of the time you require to erase and correct	27	9	5
an error on an original and carbon copy. When this was done with some	41	14	8
typists, it was found that the most expert took 26 seconds, most took	55	18	11
about 45 seconds, and some took a full minute to erase and correct an	69	23	14
error on an original and one carbon copy. It is fair to assume, then,	83	28	17
that it will take you an average of 30 seconds to make each correction.	98	33	20
If you take a 3-minute writing and type at 48 words a minute but make	112	37	22
and correct 2 errors, your actual typing time will be just 2 minutes.	126	43	25
Then instead of typing 144 words, as you would if you typed without	139	46	28
having to erase and correct any errors, you would type just 96 words,	153	51	31
or 32 instead of 48 words a minute. You must realize the high price you	168	56	34
pay for the errors you make, and then you must learn to type with a high	183	61	37
degree of accuracy. You will type more when you type with control even	197	66	39
though you may seem to be typing at a slower speed. You should type as	211	70	42
fast as you can and just as slow as you must to type with accuracy.	225	75	45

1.30 si
225 words

```
1' |  1  |  2  |  3  |  4  |  5  |  6  |  7  |  8  |  9  |  10  |  11  |  12  |  13  |  14  |
3' |       1       |       2       |       3       |       4       |       5       |
5' |         1         |         2         |         3         |
```

* The 5-minute GWAM count is to be used for 59B, page 102.

58D ● TIMED DRILL ON ERASING *5 minutes (one 1' control-level writing on ¶ of 58C, above; then a 3' control-level writing)*

PROCEDURE

Use the directions given for 58C, above, except that you will make a *carbon copy of each writing.* Erase and correct each error you make at the time you make it. For each uncorrected error, deduct 15 words to compensate for the time it would take you to erase and correct the error on the original sheet and the file copy sheet.

The purpose of this drill is to give you a clue as to the cost of an error. This is not an exact indication of the "cost" of your errors, of course, because some errors can be corrected in less than the standard correction time and other errors will take more than the standard correction time. Use the results of this drill as guidance for your further practice and for your appropriate goal setting.

27C ● TYPING FROM DICTATION *5 minutes (each line three times as directed in 21D, page 43)*

when best that will keep ever goal more only rule path help

Think the
phrase

quick games found tense tried being relax about doing think

to do|to do it|if you|if you can|if you are|of what|of your
| 1 | 2 | 3 | 4 | 5 | 6 | 7 | 8 | 9 | 10 | 11 | 12 |

27D ● PARAGRAPH GUIDED WRITING *15 minutes*

Drill sheet, full sheet,
60-space line,
double spacing,
5-space ¶ indention

PROCEDURE

1 Type the ¶s quickly on a drill sheet. Identify and practice the difficult words.
2 Type two 1-minute writings on each ¶, typing on the *exploration level.*

3 Type three 3-minute writings, one on the *exploration* and two on the *control level.* Select a goal for the control writings that is 4 to 8 words below your best rate.

● All letters are used in the paragraphs.

	GWAM	
	1'	3'

¶ 1
1.17 si
52 words

If you are quick at games and in sports, you will find — 11 | 4 | 40
that it is best if you can keep from being tense. Have you — 23 | 8 | 44
ever tried to relax and found yourself even more tense? If — 35 | 12 | 48
you will just gaze at something restful, you will have help — 47 | 16 | 52
in your efforts to relax. — 52 | 17 | 53

¶ 2
1.18 si
56 words

When you have a job to do, try to think only about the — 63 | 21 | 57
way you are to do it. Do not think about the end result of — 75 | 25 | 61
what you are doing. There is an old saying about this, and — 87 | 29 | 65
it will help you if you follow the rule. This saying is to — 99 | 33 | 69
think about the path and not about your goal. — 108 | 36 | 72

1' | 1 | 2 | 3 | 4 | 5 | 6 | 7 | 8 | 9 | 10 | 11 | 12 |
3' | 1 | 2 | 3 | 4 |

27E ● DRILL ON CONTROL OF TAB MECHANISM *8 minutes (type twice)*

8 columns,
5 spaces between
columns,
60-space line

PROCEDURE

1 Clear all tab stops.
2 *Column 2:* Set tab stop 5 spaces from end of first column.

3 *Column 3:* Set tab stop 5 spaces from end of second column.
4 Set stops for the remaining columns in a similar manner.

(Script: copy written with pencil or pen and ink)

the	for	and	fit	did	map	but	got
aid	fur	dot	urn	big	coq	wit	bug
can	one	not	top	old	run	let	met
are	you	was	him	get	hum	red	ill

Eyes on copy
as carriage
is returned

| 58A ● **PREPARATORY PRACTICE** *5 minutes (each line three or more times)*

Alphabetic	Jack Maxwell gave this lovely box as a prize to our "Queen for a Day."
Figure-symbol	Net income for the year 1963 credited to earned surplus is $2,547,980.
Fluency	To handle the situation requires vision and the determination to work.

| 1 | 2 | 3 | 4 | 5 | 6 | 7 | 8 | 9 | 10 | 11 | 12 | 13 | 14 |

58B ● PROBLEM TYPING: Tabulations; Letters with Tabulated Items *25 minutes*

Full sheet,
double spacing,
center problem in
reading position,
4 spaces between
columns

Problem 1: Four-Column Tabulation

				Words
SUMMARY OF ADVERTISING COSTS				6
● Double-space				
Department, Item, Amount Budgeted, and Amount Spent				16
● Triple-space		Tab ↓	Tab ↓	
Sales	Circulars	$23,435.00	$18,902.75	25
"	Direct Mail	6,450.00	4,327.50	31
"	Awards to Salesmen	750.00	550.00	39
Engineering	Exhibits and Dues	1,765.00	1,346.00	48
Credit	Letters and Notices	1,500.00	817.68	57
Executive	Customer Gifts	350.00	150.00	66
"	Donations	2,500.00	1,275.00	72

11	4	19	4	10	4	10

Problem 2: Interoffice Letter with Tabulated Items

Letterhead (or full sheet) Carbon sheet	●	File copy sheet Current date 60-space line	●	Modified block, blocked ¶s Mixed punctuation

● 8 blank line spaces after the date

	Words
Mr. Walter N. Zielman	Sales Manager		10
Dear Mr. Zielman:	(¶ 1) A summary of	17
advertising costs for the Sales Depart-	24
ment shows	the amount budgeted and	31
the amount spent for your three main	39
items of expense, as listed below:		46
(Tabulate "Sales" data from Problem 1, above; 4 spaces between columns.)	67
(¶ 2) Please estimate your probable ex-	74
penditure for the remainder	of the year	82
for the three items budgeted, and let me	90
know	as soon as possible whether the	98

➤ *Erase and correct errors unless otherwise directed.*

	Words
balance left from what was	budgeted	105
will meet your needs.	Very truly yours,		113
K. C. Lanning	President	(*Your ini-*	118
tials)		

Problem 3: Letter with Tabulated Items

PROCEDURE Type Letters 1 and 2 from the copy in the letter of Problem 2 with these changes:

	Words
Letter 1 . . . Mr. Roscoe L. Biggs, Manager	Engineering Department	106
Letter 2 . . . Mr. W. N. Boswell	Credit Manager	102

For each letter: Leave 9 blank lines after the date; add an appropriate salutation. In ¶ 1 change the reference to name the appropriate department; change "three main items" to "main item" in ¶ 1 and "three items" to "main item" in ¶ 2; use the correct tabulated item for the named department.

| **28A ● PREPARATORY PRACTICE** *7 minutes (each line three or more times)*

Alphabetic	Will Maryjo pack and move the quite large-sized box of food?
Figures	The girls typed 20, 36, 48, and 57 words a minute by May 19.
Fluency	She paid for the work with her half of the sale of the land.

| 1 | 2 | 3 | 4 | 5 | 6 | 7 | 8 | 9 | 10 | 11 | 12 |

28B ● TECHNIQUE PRACTICE: Tab Mechanism and Carriage Return *10 minutes (three times)*

Space forward once ➡	616 23	765 45	609 Reach to the 67 figure
	69 2/3 582 709	Backspace once ◄	169 3/4 3456 6789	354 6890 9160

| 3 | 25 | 3 | 25 | 3 |

28C ● SENTENCE GUIDED WRITING *5 minutes*

PROCEDURE Type a 1-minute writing on the *control level*, guided by the call of the line ending. Then type a 1-minute writing on the sentence in which an error was made or the sentence that seemed more difficult, guided by the call of the line ending.

	GWAM		
	20″	15″	12″
The 23 men, 67 women, and 145 children left today.	30	40	50
Think the word vigorously, and type it "right" to typewrite.	36	48	60

28D ● BUILDING CONTROL *23 minutes*

Half sheet, full sheet, 1½″ top margin (9 lines), single spacing, 5-space ¶ indention

PROCEDURE

1 Type the ¶s on the *control level* on a half sheet.
2 Practice difficult words and figures.

3 Type two 1-minute writings on each ¶, typing on the *control level*; then type three 3-minute writings on the *control level*. Determine the *gwam* of the best writings.

● All letters are used in the paragraphs.

		GWAM		
		1′	3′	
¶ 1 1.23 si 52 words	Education pays. When you realize this fully, you will	11	4	40
	know that each day you spend in study can be worth a lot to	23	8	44
	you later. What you might earn as an untrained worker will	35	12	48
	be less than what you can expect to earn when you have just	47	16	52
	a year more of schooling.	52	17	53
¶ 2 1.25 si 56 words	It pays to learn all you can. In 1939 the men who had	11	21	57
	finished college earned 57 percent more than those who quit	23	25	61
	high school before being graduated. College-trained men in	35	29	65
	1958 had 65 percent more income than those who had quit. A	47	33	69
	man who learns more now will earn more later.	56	36	72

| 1′ | 1 | 2 | 3 | 4 | 5 | 6 | 7 | 8 | 9 | 10 | 11 | 12 |
| 3′ | 1 | | 2 | | 3 | | 4 |

Problem 3: Letter with Tabulated Items

Letterhead (or full sheet)	60-space line
Carbon copy (carbon sheet, file copy sheet)	Modified block, blocked ¶s, mixed punctuation
Current date	Address an envelope

● **8 blank line spaces after the date**

Words

Mrs. J. B. Knight | 396 Stanwix Street | 10

Yuma, Arizona 85364 | Dear Mrs. Knight | 18

(¶ 1) Our yearly preinventory sale will be   26

announced in the newspapers on Tuesday of   34

next week. This sale features savings——big   43

savings. For example, Swiss embroidery-   51

trimmed percale sheet sets (1 sheet and   59

2 cases) will be priced as follows: 66

● 10 spaces between tabulated items   Words

    72″ x 108″ $17.50   70

    90″ x 108″   23.75   74

● Underline italicized words

(¶ 2) A sale for our *regular customers*   84

only will be held on Monday, the day before   93

the public announcement. We hope you   101

will be among our first customers at this   109

special one-day sale. Please bring this let-   118

ter with you. No one will be admitted to   127

the store on Monday without a special   134

invitation letter. | Sincerely yours | Ralph   143

S. Quigley | Sales Manager | (*Your initials*) | 148/160

57D ● DRILL ON ERASING ORIGINAL AND FILE COPIES *5 minutes*

Full sheet, carbon copy (carbon sheet, file copy sheet) 65-space line

TRYOUT DRILL Type the sentence in the form given below; then read Guides 1 and 2 of 57E, below, and erase and correct the errors on the original. Read Guide 3 and erase and correct the errors on the carbon copy.

Place a card in front of teh first carbon sheet befoer erasing.

57E ● GUIDES FOR ERASING ORIGINAL AND FILE COPIES *5 minutes*

Full sheet	65-space line
Carbon copy (carbon sheet, file copy sheet)	Single spacing 3″ top margin

PROCEDURE Erase and correct any errors you make as you type the Guides. Before removing the paper from the typewriter, proofread; then correct any errors not yet corrected.

Words

GUIDES FOR ERASING ORIGINAL AND FILE COPIES   9

1. Pull the original sheet forward and place a card (5 x 3 inches,   23
   or slightly larger) in front of the first carbon sheet.   34

2. Flip the original sheet back and make the erasure. Brush the   48
   eraser crumbs away from the typewriter.   56

3. Remove the protective card (unless more than one carbon copy is   71
   being made, in which case the card is placed in front of the   83
   second carbon sheet). With a soft eraser, erase the error on   95
   the carbon copy.   99

LESSON 29 | **29A ● PREPARATORY PRACTICE** *7 minutes (each line three or more times)*

Alphabetic   Jim gave K. P. Dietz a quarter for carrying the jewel boxes.

Figure-symbol   Can you make 10% profit on #3489 @ $6.72 a dozen (56¢ each)?

Fluency   The ropes held the rod to the big oak and also held it firm.

| 1 | 2 | 3 | 4 | 5 | 6 | 7 | 8 | 9 | 10 | 11 | 12 |

29B ● TECHNIQUE PRACTICE: Typing Double Letters and Numbers *13 minutes*
(each line five or more times)

NONELECTRIC STROKING Strike the double letters in "double time," which must be learned through experimenting with double-letter stroking. Do not allow the full return of the key to its normal position after the first stroke before striking the key for the second (doubled) letter. This will shorten the time lapse between strokes.

ELECTRIC STROKING Allow the key to return after it has been struck for the first of the double letters before you type the second letter. Experiment with this stroking. You should try to shorten the time lapse between the double strokes slightly, but this calls for precise timing of the strokes to avoid omitting one of the letters.

● All letters and all figures are used in the sentences.

		Words
1	Lex will sell the mill all the green tweed wool on the loom.	12
2	Look at the good wool dress; it will look well on cool days.	12
3	Will the Queen's press keep boosting their brass hobby show?	12
4	Zora Jennings spoke to 266 women, 199 men, and 100 children.	12
5	Flight 344 left Greece at 7:00 a.m. and arrived at 5:38 p.m.	12

29C ● BUILDING CONTROL *25 minutes*

3 half sheets,
  1½″ top margin,
  single spacing,
  5-space ¶ indention,
  double-space
    between
  paragraphs

PROCEDURE

1 On a drill sheet make pencil notations of the assignments listed below. Place the sheet on the desk near your typewriter where you can refer to it easily.

26D (page 52); 27D (page 53);
28D (page 54)

2 You will be timed for 20 minutes. When directed to begin typing, insert a sheet of paper and type each assignment in single-spaced form. If you complete the assignments before time is called, retype the last one on the back of the half sheet. Do not hurry, but don't waste time. Type on the *control level*—but type!

LESSON 30 | **30A ● PREPARATORY PRACTICE** *7 minutes (each line three or more times)*

Alphabetic   Eva Wells fixed quite a big prize for Hal Jackson on Monday.

Figure-symbol   Howe & North's bonus in 1957-8 was 34¢; in 1962, it was 57¢.

Fluency   The eight men who worked on the dock came in during the day.

| 1 | 2 | 3 | 4 | 5 | 6 | 7 | 8 | 9 | 10 | 11 | 12 |

LESSON 57 | 57A ● PREPARATORY PRACTICE *5 minutes (each line three or more times)*

Alphabetic   Six jet planes flew quickly over Bowden through the azure morning sky.

Figure-symbol   The 5¼% rate on my $870 note due on July 23, 1969, was changed to 4½%.

Fluency   Len found that the elements of the problem are difficult to determine.

     | 1 | 2 | 3 | 4 | 5 | 6 | 7 | 8 | 9 | 10 | 11 | 12 | 13 | 14 |

57B ● BUILDING SPEED AND CONTROL *5 minutes (one 1' exploration-level writing; then three 1' control-level writings)*

Full sheet   ●   Double spacing
70-space line   5-space ¶ indention

● All letters are used in the paragraph.

	1' GWAM
1.38 si Office typists are expected to correct their errors. This takes	13
72 words time and skill. The greater the skill, the less time the correction	27
requires. It pays to be skillful in correcting errors––but it will pay	41
better to learn to type with accuracy and not have to correct errors.	55
Realize this now, and learn to pace your typing at just the speed you	69
can control.	72

1' | 1 | 2 | 3 | 4 | 5 | 6 | 7 | 8 | 9 | 10 | 11 | 12 | 13 | 14 |

57C ● PROBLEM TYPING: Tabulations *25 minutes*

Problem 1: Two-Column Tabulation

Half sheet,
   double spacing,
   center problem vertically,
   decide number of spaces to
     be left between columns

PROCEDURE For the heading, type
U. S. PRESIDENTS SINCE 1901

NOTE Type the second column of the tabulation with a space before and after the hyphen.

		Words
		6
Theodore Roosevelt	1901 – 1909	12
William Howard Taft	1909 – 1913	18
Woodrow Wilson	1913 – 1921	24
Warren G. Harding	1921 – 1923	30
Calvin Coolidge	1923 – 1929	35
Herbert C. Hoover	1929 – 1933	41
Franklin Delano Roosevelt	1933 – 1945	49
Harry S Truman	1945 – 1953	54
Dwight D. Eisenhower	1953 – 1961	61
John F. Kennedy	1961 – 1963	67
Lyndon B. Johnson	1963 –	71

Problem 2: Three-Column Tabulation

● *57C is continued on page 99.*

PROCEDURE Use the directions for Problem 1 except that you will retype Problem 1 in three columns, adding as your third column the party affiliation (*Republican* or *Democrat*) of each president. (*94 words*)

30B ● SENTENCE GUIDED WRITING *5 minutes* *(1' writings with the call of the line ending)*

	GWAM		
	20"	15"	12"

Don't put your trust in money -- just put your money in trust! 36 | 48 | 60

Their Check #4367 for $582.90 is dated August 21, 1964. 33 | 44 | 55

30C ● GROWTH INDEX *15 minutes* *(three 3' control-level writings)*

60-space line, 5-space ¶ indention, double spacing   ● All letters are used in the paragraphs.

	GWAM	
	1'	3'

¶ 1
1.25 si
68 words

How will a worker keep his job if a machine can do the — 11 | 4 | 49
work just as well as he can? This is one of the hardest of — 23 | 8 | 53
all our problems of automation. It isn't the worker who is — 35 | 12 | 57
fired who is the real victim but the one who is never hired — 47 | 16 | 61
in the first place. The answer to this question may lie in — 59 | 20 | 65
the area of far more and far better training. — 68 | 23 | 68

¶ 2
1.25 si
68 words

What is the right amount of work for each of us who is — 79 | 26 | 71
in the labor force? There is no really right answer to the — 91 | 30 | 75
question, most people now realize; but the question must be — 103 | 34 | 79
answered to the extent that work must be provided for those — 115 | 38 | 83
who want to work and can work. Jobs must be made available — 127 | 43 | 88
to men of good skill and to men of good will. — 136 | 45 | 90

1' | 1 | 2 | 3 | 4 | 5 | 6 | 7 | 8 | 9 | 10 | 11 | 12 |
3' | 1 | 2 | 3 | 4 |

30D ● PROBLEM TYPING: Memorandums *18 minutes*

3 half sheets, 50-space line,
single spacing, 1" top margin,
current date

PROBLEM 1 Type 23E once, as directed on page 47.

PROBLEM 2 Type the following memorandum twice.

	Words
Current Date	3

⬇ Operate carriage return 5 times to leave 4 blank line spaces

SUBJECT: Summary of Spacing Rules	10
Space once after a comma, semicolon, and a period	20
used with an abbreviation. Space twice after the	30
mark of punctuation used at the end of a sentence	40
except when the mark comes at the end of the line	50
of writing; then make your return without spacing.	60
Do not space between the figure and the following	70
symbols: #, $, %, /, ¢ (cents), and * (asterisk).	80

. . . . 1 . . . . 2 . . . . 3 . . . . 4 . . . . 5 . . . . 6 . . . . 7 . . . . 8 . . . . 9 10

Problem 2: Three-Column Tabulation

Half sheet		Center problem vertically
Double spacing	●	10 spaces between columns

PROCEDURE

1 Count the strokes in the longest word.

2 Determine syllables; then count the strokes including the hyphen for *each* syllable. Type the word in Column 2 with hyphens to show each syllable.

3 Determine the first acceptable division if the bell rings on the typing of the first letter. (If a word cannot be divided, type it in solid form.) Count the strokes with the hyphen to show the division. Set margin and tab stops for the columns.

Col. 1	Col. 2	Col. 3	Words
compelled	com-pelled	com-pelled	6
copyright			13
crucial			18
definite			24
graduate			30
logical			36
predicate			42
problems			48
reference			55
speculate			61
tabulate			67
thrilled			72

Problem 3: Three-Column Tabulation

Full sheet		Center in reading position
Double spacing	●	10 spaces between columns

PROCEDURE Use the procedure given for Problem 2, except that you will type WORD DIVISION as the main heading and assume that the bell rings on the typing of the fourth letter.

Col. 1	Col. 2	Col. 3	Words
changeable	change-a-ble	change-able	3 / 10
comparisons			18
conferring			25
contraction			33
controlled			40
dropped			45
education			51
feasible			57
minimum			63
photographed			71
possessed			77
preferred			83
preferring			91
preventive			98
professing			105
profession			112
prominence			119
promotion			126
pronounced			133
suggestions			141
suspicion			147
syllables			153

56D ● DRILL ON ASSEMBLING AND INSERTING A CARBON PACK *10 minutes*

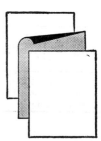

Full sheet		Single spacing
65-space line	●	3″ top margin

PROCEDURE

1 Read ¶ 1 and assemble a carbon pack as directed.
2 Read ¶ 2 and insert the pack as directed.
3 Type the following instructions.

	Words
ASSEMBLY AND INSERTION OF A CARBON PACK	8

After typing the first line, reset the left margin stop 4 spaces in. →

1. Place the sheet on which the file (or carbon) copy is to be made flat on the desk; then place a sheet of carbon paper, glossy side down, on the paper; finally, place the sheet for the original on top of the carbon paper. — 21 / 33 / 48 / 56

2. Pick up the papers and tap them lightly on the desk (with the glossy side of the carbon paper toward you); then insert the pack into the machine (glossy side toward you as papers are inserted). Roll the pack in far enough for the feed rolls to grip the papers; finally, operate the paper-release lever to release the pressure and eliminate the wrinkles. — 70 / 82 / 102 / 116 / 128 / 137

| 1 | 2 | 3 | 4 | 5 | 6 | 7 | 8 | 9 | 10 | 11 | 12 | 13 |

CENTERING, PERSONAL NOTES, AND POSTAL CARDS

STANDARD PROCEDURES FOR SECTION 6

GET READY TO TYPE

Clear the desk of unneeded papers. Adjust paper guide and paper-bail rolls. Use a 70-space line and single spacing for drills. Use double spacing for paragraph timed writings.

SELF-IMPROVEMENT PRACTICE

As time permits, type the sentences of Self-Improvement Practice, page 67, three or more times. Type on the *control level*. Identify each sentence typed without error.

LESSON 31 | **31A ● PREPARATORY PRACTICE** *5 minutes (each line three or more times)*

Alphabetic — Frank may have expected J. W. Ziegler to answer the questions by mail.

Figures — My address after May 28, 1964: Box 50, R. 3, Glasgow, Kentucky 42127.

Fluency — The element of danger on this job may make the workmen rather careful.

| 1 | 2 | 3 | 4 | 5 | 6 | 7 | 8 | 9 | 10 | 11 | 12 | 13 | 14 |

31B ● BUILDING SPEED AND CONTROL *10 minutes*

PROCEDURE Type the paragraphs of 30C, page 56, as two 3-minute writings. Use a 60-space line. Type the first writing on the *exploration level*; then drop back in speed and type on the *control level* for the second writing. Decrease your drive for speed and increase your typing control. Determine *gwam* and number of errors.

31C ● PROBLEM TYPING: Memorandum on Horizontal Centering *15 minutes*

Half sheet	●	60-space line	●	1½″ top margin	●	Block style
Full sheet		Single spacing		(9 lines)		Current Date

Add the following subject line:
SUBJECT: Memorandum on Centering

PROBLEM 1 Type the memorandum on a half sheet. Use the shift lock to underline the paragraph headings.

PROBLEM 2 Using a full sheet, type each paragraph as a 1-minute writing; then type a 3-minute writing on the entire problem, adding the current date and the subject line.

		GWAM	
		1′	3′
*Three words are added for the date and seven words are added for the subject line.			3 *

¶ 1
1.35 si
40 words

<u>Get Ready to Center</u>. Move both margin stops to the ends of the scale. Clear the tabulator stops; move the carriage to the center of the paper; set a tabulator stop at this point.

	1′	3′
	16	9
	28	13
	40	17

¶ 2
1.40 si
55 words

<u>Steps for Centering</u>. Tabulate to the center of the paper. From this center point, backspace once for each two letters (or letter and space) in the line. If the line has one odd or leftover letter, disregard it and start typing where the backspacing ends.

	1′	3′
	16	22
	28	26
	40	30
	52	34
	55	35

PREPARATORY PRACTICE *5 minutes (each line three or more times)*

Alphabetic	The audience was amazed by the report John F. Maxwell gave so quickly.
Figure-symbol	Jones & Norton's Bill #789 for $450 was paid by Check #2365 on May 16.
Fluency	The worker ranks appreciation of his good work as of first importance.

| 1 | 2 | 3 | 4 | 5 | 6 | 7 | 8 | 9 | 10 | 11 | 12 | 13 | 14 |

56B ● GUIDED WRITING *5 minutes*

PROCEDURE

1 Type a 1-minute writing on each ¶ of 55C, page 94. Type on the *exploration level*. Determine your *gwam*.

2 Set a goal for each ¶ that is 4 to 5 words higher than your *gwam*; then type a 1-minute guided writing on each ¶ to achieve your goal.

56C ● PROBLEM TYPING: Word Division—A Communication Aid *25 minutes (errors corrected)*

Problem 1: Memorandum with Tabulated Items

Full sheet
65-space line
Single spacing ●
5-space ¶ indention
2" top margin

8-spaces between 1st
set of tabulated
words; use same
tab stops for 2d and
3d sets of words

NOTE After typing the first line of the numbered ¶, reset the left margin stop 9 spaces in from the outside margin; then when Figures 2 and 3 are to be typed, release the margin stop and backspace into the left margin 4 spaces before typing the figure.

	Words
GUIDES FOR WORD DIVISION	5

● *Triple-space*

	Words
Pronounce the word carefully as an aid to the identification	17
of syllables. Use a dictionary, but remember that it shows <u>all</u>	31
syllables in a word--not the <u>preferred</u> division. Study and use	45
the following guides for dividing words when typing.	56

	Words
1. Divide words only between syllables. Type such syl-	67
Reset margin ➤ lables as <u>cial</u>, <u>tial</u>, <u>cion</u>, <u>sion</u>, <u>tion</u> as a unit.	82

		Words
suppression	sup-pres-sion	87
stopped	stopped	91
partial	par-tial	94

	Words
2. To divide a word of three or more syllables at a one-	106
letter syllable, type the one-letter syllable on the	116
first line, unless it is a part of a word with an end-	127
ing such as <u>able</u>, <u>ible</u>, <u>ical</u>--two-syllable endings	140
that must be kept as a unit.	146

		Words
separation	sepa-ra-tion	151
physical	phys-ical	155
commendable	com-mend-able	160

	Words
3. When a root word ending in a single consonant is	171
doubled in adding a suffix, type the added letter with	182
the suffix; but when the root word ends in a double	192
letter, divide between the double letters and the	202
added suffix.	205

		Words
compel	com-pel-ling	209
dismiss	dis-miss-ing	214
control	con-trol-ling	218

● *56C is continued on page 97.*

31D ● DRILL ON HORIZONTAL CENTERING *10 minutes*

Place your typed copy of 31C Memorandum on Horizontal Centering on the desk beside your typewriter so you can follow the directions as you type the drill given at the right.

Full sheet, double spacing, 3" top margin

PROCEDURE

1 Get ready to center (see ¶ 1 of 31C).
2 Center and type each line given at the right.
3 Double-space, center, and type:
   a. your name;
   b. the name of your school;
   c. the current date.

GET READY TO CENTER

            ● Triple-space

Move the margin stops to the ends of the scale

Clear the tabulator stops

Move the carriage to the center of the paper

Set a tabulator stop

Backspace once for each two letters or spaces

Type the line

31E ● SENTENCE GUIDED WRITING *5 minutes (each line as a 1' writing, guided by the 20" call of the line ending)*

Copy that is corrected with pencil or pen and ink is called a *rough draft*. Some of the most common proofreader's marks are illustrated at the right.

PROOFREADER'S MARKS

∧ means **insert**   ℰ means **delete**   ∩ or *tr* means **transpose**

l.c. means **lower-case letters**   ⊂ means **close up space**

70-space line, single spacing

		GWAM		
		20"	15"	12"
1	It is man's mind that makes him great.	30	40	50
2	An 11-inch sheet is 66 lines; long (half a) sheet, 33	33	44	55
3	We all need above all else in this day real wisdom.	36	48	60
4	This edition of the book has 3 parts, and 26 chapters,	42	56	70

LESSON 32 | 32A ● PREPARATORY PRACTICE *5 minutes (each line three or more times)*

Alphabetic	David Kingsman expects Dr. J. W. Hazard to apply for quite a big loan.
Figure-symbol	Item #6789 refers to page 453 of Section 12, Volume 10, of <u>Estate Law</u>.
Fluency	This audit of their books proves that they have done their work right.

| 1 | 2 | 3 | 4 | 5 | 6 | 7 | 8 | 9 | 10 | 11 | 12 | 13 | 14 |

32B ● SENTENCE GUIDED WRITING *5 minutes*

PROCEDURE Type each sentence of 31E, above, as a 1-minute writing with the call of the 15" or 12" guide, as directed. Type on the *exploration level*.

Problem 1: Article with Tabulated Items

Full sheet,
65-space line,
5-space ¶ indention,
double spacing,
3" top margin,
6 spaces between
columns

Words

THE ZIP CODE SYSTEM | 4

The ZIP Code (Zoning Improvement Plan) divides the country | 16
into delivery units, each designated by a five-digit number. The | 29
first digit represents one of ten geographic areas; the second, a | 42
specific portion of a geographic area; the third, one of the 553 | 55
Sectional Center areas for sorting mail; and the last two, today's | 69
delivery zone number. Here are some examples of the ZIP numbers: | 82

Reset left
margin stop

Cave City	Kentucky	42127	Single-space	87
Midland	Texas	79701	tabulated	91
New York	New York	10005	items	96

Type the ZIP number on the line with the state name, with at | 108
least 2 spaces between them. Include the ZIP number in the letter | 121
address as well as the envelope address. | 129

Problem 2: Tabulation with Three-Line Heading

Full sheet · 8 spaces between columns
Double spacing · Center in reading position

Words

ALL CAPS *of Vocational Traits*
Charters and Whitley Frequency | 10
OUTSTANDINGLY of *DOUBLE-SPACE*
SUCCESSFUL SECRETARIES | 18
^ *TRIPLE-SPACE*

Accuracy *leness*	1	21
Responsibility	2	24
Dependability	3	27
Intelligence	3	30
Courtesy	5	33
Initiative	5	35
Judgement *Tact*	8,5	39
Personal pleasantness	9	44
Personal appearance	9	48

Problem 3: Composing a Letter

PROCEDURE Use modified block style with blocked paragraphs; mixed punctuation. Type your return address and the date as illustrated at the right.

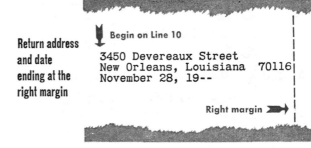

Return address and date ending at the right margin

Begin on Line 10

3450 Devereaux Street
New Orleans, Louisiana 70116
November 28, 19--

Right margin ➤

Compose a letter to your instructor saying that you found a reference to the 1924 study typed as Problem 2 (*Frequency of Vocational Traits of Outstandingly Successful Secretaries*) and that the study is now out of print. Tabulate the first four traits and their ranking and indicate your amazement that "Honesty" is not among these.

Add a final paragraph to state your personal opinion that the businessmen interviewed must have thought everyone would agree "Honesty" is a trait that no other trait can replace; and they did not, therefore, mention it frequently enough to be ranked among the first four traits. Type your name below the complimentary close.

Make pencil corrections as needed; then retype the letter in acceptable form.

32C ● TECHNIQUE PRACTICE: Stroking *10 minutes (each line three or more times)*

● All letters and figures are used in this practice.

1	Upper row	Pete says that Patty Wirtz may be "Queen for a Day" on your quiz show.
2	Home row	Is Gladys glad that Jake Jessel has a big flag for Jasper's classroom?
3	First row	Max and Zelda will stay in Vera Cruz, Mexico, for a month next spring.
4	Figures	On June 12, 34 girls, 56 boys, 78 men, and 90 women will go to France.
5	One-hand	I look upon my jump in rank as the minimum recognition that is due me.

| 1 | 2 | 3 | 4 | 5 | 6 | 7 | 8 | 9 | 10 | 11 | 12 | 13 | 14 |

32D ● PROBLEM TYPING *20 minutes*

Problem 1: Centered Lines

Half sheet, 1" top margin, double spacing

PROCEDURE

Read through the problem before beginning to type it; then center each line horizontally and type it. Triple-space between the main heading and the next line.

```
HORIZONTAL CENTERING

Check the placement of the paper guide
Move the margin stops to the ends of the scale
Clear the tabulator rack
Move the carriage to centering point and set a stop
Backspace once for each two spaces (or space and letter)
Disregard single leftover letter
Begin to type where backspacing ends
Type the line
Tabulate to center and center and type next line
```

Problem 2: Centered Lines from Rough Draft

PROOFREADER'S MARK: ## means **add space**

Half sheet, 1½" top margin (9 lines), double spacing

PROCEDURE

Type each line centered horizontally.

```
PARTS OF THE LESSON
    Preparatory Practicing
    Sentences for Guided Writing
    Technique Practices
    Drill on Typing Problem
    Typing Outside the Margins
```

32E ● DRILL ON TYPING OUTSIDE THE MARGINS *5 minutes*

PROCEDURE Set the margin stops for an exact 60-space line (*Do not add 5 spaces for the ringing of the bell.*) To begin typing the 73-space sentence outside the left margin, depress the margin-release key **25** and move the carriage 5 spaces outside the left margin. Type until the carriage locks (ignoring the ringing of the bell); then depress the margin release and type the rest of the word.

When the carriage locks, depress the margin release (No. 25) and type on.

LESSON 55 | 55A ● PREPARATORY PRACTICE *5 minutes (each line three or more times)*

Alphabetic   Jack Pew requested a large-size box and vat for the chemical analysis.

Figure-symbol   Is the up-to-date report on Bill #6753-48 on <u>Profits</u> due May 19 or 20?

Fluency   The auditor said the profit due you should have been paid much sooner.

| 1 | 2 | 3 | 4 | 5 | 6 | 7 | 8 | 9 | 10 | 11 | 12 | 13 | 14 |

NOTE Remove the paper; then reinsert it, gauge the line and letter, and type over the last line.

55B ● TECHNIQUE PRACTICE *10 minutes (each line three or more times)*

1   One-hand words   A few dead trees were scattered among the great grove of orange trees.

2   One-hand words   Lolly Polk gathered the vegetables we were to serve for Lily's dinner.

3   Direct-adjacent   Three trucks hauled several hundred pounds of freight to the railroad.

4   Direct   Many hundreds of old people received their first pension checks today.

5   Drill on SW   The Swede swore he saw their Swiss sword swung swiftly at the swimmer.

| 1 | 2 | 3 | 4 | 5 | 6 | 7 | 8 | 9 | 10 | 11 | 12 | 13 | 14 |

55C ● BUILDING CONTROL *5 minutes*

Full sheet, 70-space line,
double spacing,
5-space ¶ indention

PROCEDURE Type a 3-minute writing on the *control level.*
Determine your *gwam* and the number of errors. If time permits, type a 1-minute writing on the *control level.*

● All letters are used in the paragraphs.

		GWAM 1'	3'

¶ 1
1.30 si
72 words

You can make a copy of a typed paper by using a carbon sheet of   13   4   52
appropriate weight. A standard-weight carbon sheet can be used if you   27   9   57
want to make from one to four carbon copies; but if you are to make more   42   14   62
than four carbon copies, use a lightweight carbon sheet. If you are to   56   19   67
make ten to a dozen copies at the same time, use extra lightweight   69   23   71
carbon paper.   72   24   72

¶ 2
1.30 si
72 words

When you use a carbon "pack," your copies may at times have dark   13   28   76
lines or "trees" on them. These may be caused by the use of carbon paper   28   33   81
that is too soft or just by not releasing the pressure, which can be   42   38   86
done quite simply by operating the paper-release lever after the feed   56   43   91
rolls have gripped the papers and before the pack is rolled into writing   70   47   95
position.   72   48   96

1' | 1 | 2 | 3 | 4 | 5 | 6 | 7 | 8 | 9 | 10 | 11 | 12 | 13 | 14 |
3' | 1 | 2 | 3 | 4 | 5 |

| **33A ● PREPARATORY PRACTICE** *5 minutes (each line three or more times)*

Alphabetic   N. B. Powers made five or six quick jet flights to Germany via Zurich.

Figure-symbol   Clay & Lang's note of $38,765 (plus 4½% interest) is due May 19 or 20.

Fluency   Entry forms for the next event can be mailed to you on or about May 2.

| 1 | 2 | 3 | 4 | 5 | 6 | 7 | 8 | 9 | 10 | 11 | 12 | 13 | 14 |

33B ● BUILDING SPEED AND CONTROL *10 minutes*

60-space line,
double spacing
5-space ¶ indention

PROCEDURE

Type two 3-minute writings, the first on the *control level* and the second on the *explora-* *tion level*. Type line for line as shown in the copy. Determine *gwam* and number of errors.

● All letters are used in the paragraphs.

	GWAM	
	1'	3'

¶ 1
1.30 sl
68 words

Work hard, of course; but hard work of itself will not   11 4 49
be enough. Think smarter, and you can let the other fellow   23 8 53
work harder--for he will be working for you in due time. A   35 12 57
man who realizes the power that comes from thinking smarter   47 16 61
will work at the job of learning how to control his mind as   59 20 65
an athlete practices the control of his body.   68 23 68

¶ 2
1.16 si
68 words

It requires time and work to learn to control the mind   79 26 72
just as it does to learn how to control the body. The mind   91 30 76
has to solve problems--problems big enough to make you want   103 34 80
to solve them--if it is to grow in the power to think. The   115 38 84
mind grows through use just as muscles grow through use; so   127 43 88
prize mind and body, and expect much of both.   136 45 90

1' | 1 | 2 | 3 | 4 | 5 | 6 | 7 | 8 | 9 | 10 | 11 | 12 |
3' | 1 | 2 | 3 | 4 |

33C ● DRILL ON LISTENING FOR THE BELL *10 minutes*

Half sheet,
70-space line,
double spacing,
1" top margin

PROCEDURE

1 Type the paragraphs of 33B, above. You will not type the copy line for line as shown. Instead, listen for the ringing of the bell to tell you that you are typing near the end of the 70-space writing line. When the bell rings, type the remainder of the word; then return the carriage and continue typing. If the carriage locks before you type the word, depress the margin release key and finish typing it. Type on the *control level*.

2 Type a 1-minute writing on each paragraph, typing on the *control level*. (Listen for the ringing of the bell to warn you of the line ending.)

33D ● SENTENCE GUIDED WRITING *5 minutes (two 1' guided writings on each line)*

	GWAM		
	20"	15"	12"

This line has 85 pica spaces. [8½-inch or 102 elite]   30 40 50

Work Try to increase your (speed/typing) and decrease your errors.   36 48 60

Problem 2: Letter with Tabulated Items
(errors corrected)

Letterhead (or full sheet) Current date	●	Modified block, blocked ¶s Mixed punctuation	●	60-space line Address an envelope

PROCEDURE Date the letter *July 12*; leave 8 spaces between the columns of tabulated items. Note the illustration of the dictator's name and title typed on the same line.

● 8 blank line spaces after the date

	Words
Mr. Samuel P. Clayton │ 2390 W. Newton	10
Street │ Tulsa, Oklahoma 74106 │ Dear Mr.	18
Clayton │ (¶ 1) A resolution to change the	25
Corporation's name from "National Trans-	33
port Signal Company" to "National Signal	42
Corporation" was approved at the meeting	50
of stockholders held on July 9. The fig-	58
ures given below indicate the number of	66
shares voted in favor of and the number	74
voted against the change in name:	81

		Words
For	1,306,815	84
Against	4,016	87

	Words
(¶ 2) The common stock of the Corpora-	94
tion remains the same, and the certificates	103
you hold need not be exchanged for new	110
ones.	112

Cordially yours,

Dictator's name and title typed on the same line

P. W. Owens, President

	Words
(¶ 3) I am glad to give you this informa-	119
tion as requested in your recent letter. │	127
Cordially yours │ P. W. Owens, President │	135
(*Your initials*) │	136/149

Problem 3: Letter with Tabulated Items
(errors corrected)

PROCEDURE Use Problem 2 directions.

● 10 blank line spaces after the date

	Words
July 12, 19-- │ Mrs. Elsa M. Rogers │ 826	8
Exeter Drive │ Hot Springs, Arkansas	15
71901 │ (*Add appropriate salutation; type*	20
¶s 1 and 2 of the letter given as Problem	111
2.) │ Cordially yours │ P. W. Owens, Presi-	118
dent │ (*Your initials*) │	120/131

54C ● SENTENCE GUIDED WRITING *5 minutes*

PROCEDURE Type each sentence as two 1-minute writings. Type on the *exploration level*.

	GWAM		
	15"	12"	10"
Ned will be ~~about~~ 8 23 years, old on May 1. 5. [6 months and 19 days]	44	55	66
It is quite right that men must be worth more than they are paid.	52	65	78

54D ● TYPING ON RULED LINES *10 minutes*

1 Type the following heading and underline it.

          Typing on Ruled Lines

NOTE Study the relation of the bottom of the letters to the typed underline.

2 Make an approximate 3-inch pencil line; then remove the paper, reinsert it, operate the variable line spacer and move the cylinder so the line is in correct relation to the aligning scale.

3 Center and type the heading given in **1** above the 3-inch pencil line drawn as directed in **2**. Have the bottom of the letters in correct relation to the line. (See 34D, Centering Lines on Odd-Size Paper, page 62.)

4 Repeat **1** and **2**.

6 lines per inch (handwritten)

33E ● PROBLEM TYPING: A PERSONAL NOTE _15 minutes_

2 full sheets
Single spacing
PROBLEM 1: 50-space line, 7 blank lines between date and salutation
PROBLEM 2: 60-space line, 9 blank lines between date and salutation

PROCEDURE

Type Problems 1 and 2 as directed at the left. When you have completed both problems, compare the vertical and horizontal placement of the letters and determine your preference.

Line Space			Words
12		▼ Leave a 2" top margin (12 lines)	
13	Date		3
14		_address_ (handwritten)	
15		_Current Date_	
16			
17			
18		▼ Leave 7 blank line spaces	
19			
20			
21	Salutation	Dear Professor Shanahan	8
22		● Double-space	
23		This is the first time I have been bold enough to	18
24		write a professor to comment on a class lecture,	28
25		but you interested me greatly this morning in your	38
26		lecture on	40
27		● Double-space	
28		THE NEXT BUSINESS DOWNTURN	45
29		● Double-space	
30		A summary of business cycles in the United States	55
31		from 1854 indicates a rhythm in timing which cannot	66
32		be shrugged off. I want to make a careful study of	76
33		these cycles; and with your approval, I shall use	86
34		this topic for my midterm paper.	93
35		● Double-space	
36	Complimentary close	Sincerely yours	
37		◄— Leave 3 blank line spaces	
38		_Alvin M. Speers_	
39			
40	Writer's name	Alvin M. Speers	99
41			

(handwritten margin notes: 32, 60, 42 35/67, 42, 16/6, paper width acceptable, 2 spaces, ag d: AC 0, final doesn't make much difference)

(handwritten right margin notes: on envelop, 11 spaces from top, left on center 5 spaces (27); 3 lines = double space, 9 from bottom)

LESSON 34 | **34A ● PREPARATORY PRACTICE** _5 minutes_ _(each line three or more times)_

Alphabetic Miss Flynn expects to drive to Quebec with Mrs. G. K. Dalzell in July.

Figure-symbol Marked items—26-A, 345-X, and 789*—sell at 10% discount until May 6.

Fluency Some of the workmen for Manaheid & Henry are paid $150 or more a week.

| 1 | 2 | 3 | 4 | 5 | 6 | 7 | 8 | 9 | 10 | 11 | 12 | 13 | 14 |

Problem 3: Three-Column Tabulation

		Words
RESULTS OF SALES APTITUDE TEST		6
Scores and Ratings		10

Full sheet,
  double spacing,
   center problem in
    reading position,
   decide spaces to be
    left between columns

PROCEDURE For Column 2, set tab stop to take care of greatest number of items in the column.

Name	Score	Rating	Words
Bowers, Paul R.	68	Poor	15
Gross, J. Fred	115	Excellent	21
Harman, Louis F.	92	Fair	26
McLean, Gilpin M.	103	Good	31
Porter, Lowell S.	74	Poor	37
Richman, Ned P.	87	Fair	41
Shepard, Rex N.	109	Excellent	48
Updyck, Keith L.	98	Good	52

53D ● HORIZONTAL AND VERTICAL PENCIL LINES *5 minutes*

HORIZONTAL LINES ➡

Place the pencil point on the type bar guide above the ribbon, in the cardholder notch, or against the alignment scale. Hold the pencil against the paper; depress the carriage-release lever; draw the carriage across to make the line.

Drill 1 Make three pencil lines about 3 inches long. Repeat the drill if time permits.

VERTICAL LINES

Operate the ratchet release (or line finder **6**). Place the pencil point on the type bar guide, the cardholder notch, or against the alignment scale; turn the cylinder forward. When all vertical lines have been made, return the line finder to its normal position.

Drill 2 Make three vertical lines about 3 inches long. Repeat the drill if time permits.

LESSON 54 | 54A ● PREPARATORY PRACTICE *5 minutes* *(each line three or more times)*

Alphabetic	We expected to solve the jigsaw puzzle more quickly than Bud Franklin.
Figure	In 1958 Lock & Black had 123 salesmen; in 1960, 147; and in 1964, 210.
Fluency	The chairman thought the audience should take part in the discussions.

| 1 | 2 | 3 | 4 | 5 | 6 | 7 | 8 | 9 | 10 | 11 | 12 | 13 | 14 |

54B ● PROBLEM TYPING: Tabulation; Letters with Tabulated Items *25 minutes*

Problem 1: Two-Column Tabulation

Full sheet   ●   Reading position
Double spacing   12 spaces between columns

PROCEDURE Center and type SYLLABLE IDENTIFI-CATION as the heading. Type the first word in Column 1; then type the word in Column 2 with the hyphen to show *all* syllables.

● *54B is continued on page 93.*

		Words
		5
amenable	a-me-na-ble	9
chemical		13
comparable		18
contractual		23
correction		28
crucible		32
feasible		36
mystical		40
possible		44
primary		48
syllable		52

34B ● TECHNIQUE PRACTICE: Stroking *10 minutes (each line three or more times)*

● All letters are used in this practice.

1	1st & 2d fingers	Jeff Briggs may fly with my brother rather than take the flight alone.
2	3d & 4th fingers	As was pointed out by six of the seniors, the quiz questions are easy.
3	Double letters	Will Bill sell his sleek-looking car to Miss Nell Brooks of Tennessee?
4	One-hand words	As Frederick Webster swears, they were regarded as brave but defeated.
5	Direct reach	Mike Bixler visited briefly with his grieving friend Frank Huntington.

| 1 | 2 | 3 | 4 | 5 | 6 | 7 | 8 | 9 | 10 | 11 | 12 | 13 | 14 |

34C ● PROBLEM TYPING: Personal Note with Quoted Paragraph *20 minutes*

2 full sheets,
  single spacing,
  2″ top margin,
  current date

Type the name *Al Speers*
3 blank line spaces
below complimentary
close

PROBLEM 1: 60-space line,
  9 blank line spaces
  between date and
  salutation

PROBLEM 2: 50-space line,
  7 blank line spaces
  between date and
  salutation

PROCEDURE FOR PROBLEMS 1 AND 2: Type the note, using the spacing indicated at the left for each problem.

To Type the Quoted ¶: Reset the margin stops 5 spaces in from the left and right margins. Double-space before and after typing the ¶; then reset the margin stops to their original setting.

	Words
Practice	3
Dear Paul	5
I'm on a reading binge for the midterm paper for Econ. 285.	17
Prof. Shanahan's lecture on business cycles (one of the best	29
he's given--and you missed it) started me on this spree. He	42
said:	43
A study of business cycles in the U. S. shows that	53
expansion periods have been growing shorter. The	63
1945-48 expansion lasted 37 months; the 1954-57	73
expansion, 35 months; and the 1958-60 expansion,	83
25 months.	85
Are you interested in teaming up with me on this reading so	97
we can do two separate but related papers on these cycles?	109
We may not be able to predict the time of the next business	121
downturn, but we'll have the facts to signal its approach.	133
How about this joint effort?	139
Yours	140
	142

34D ● DRILL ON CENTERING LINES ON ODD-SIZE PAPER *10 minutes*

TO DETERMINE CENTER POINT OF ODD-SIZE PAPER (OR CARD):

1 Read and add the numbers on the scale at the left and right edges of the paper or card.

2 Divide the total by 2 to get the center point.

DRILL 1 Insert a half sheet with the long edge at the left. Use double spacing and a 2½″ top margin. Determine the center point of the paper. Center *horizontally* and type the four headings for the parts of this lesson (34A through 34D). Steps in horizontal centering are explained in 32D, page 59.

DRILL 2 Fold the half sheet used in Drill 1 from bottom to top. Insert the sheet with the creased edge at the left. Determine the center point of the paper; then center *horizontally* and type:

a the name of your school

b the name of your instructor

c your name

d the current date

53A ● PREPARATORY PRACTICE *5 minutes (each line three or more times)*

Alphabetic	Rex was amazed at the volume of quince jelly Kate bought in September.
Figure	I paid 76 3/8 for L & B on May 10 and sold it for 95 2/3 on October 4.
Fluency	It is now thought that the men who read more achieve more in business.

| 1 | 2 | 3 | 4 | 5 | 6 | 7 | 8 | 9 | 10 | 11 | 12 | 13 | 14 |

NOTE Remove the paper; then reinsert it, gauge the line and letter, and type over the first line.

53B ● TECHNIQUE PRACTICE: Stroking *10 minutes (each line three or more times)*

1	3d and 4th fingers	People quite frequently play the quiz game with plenty of zeal to win.
2	Adjacent	We truly hope you were pleased with the glass dish we sent for a gift.
3	Home row	Hal Hall said that he had a slight headache all day while at the lake.
4	Figure	There were 927 men, 364 women, and 580 children at the afternoon game.
5	Figure-symbol	Should the 3½% rate on Long's $7,250 note (dated July 8, 1964) be 4¼%?

| 1 | 2 | 3 | 4 | 5 | 6 | 7 | 8 | 9 | 10 | 11 | 12 | 13 | 14 |

NOTE Remove the paper; then reinsert it, gauge the line and letter, and type over the first line.

53C ● PROBLEM TYPING: Tabulations *25 minutes*

Problem 1: Two-Column Tabulation in Reading Position

Full sheet
Double spacing
12 spaces between columns

● Center problem in reading position (explained below)

CENTERING IN READING POSITION

1 Count lines to be centered.
  a Count 2 for triple-space after secondary heading.
  b Count 1 for each blank line space in double-spaced copy.
2 Subtract total lines from 66 (full sheet) or 33 (half sheet).
3 Divide by 2 to determine top and bottom margins. (If fraction results from dividing, disregard it.)
4 Subtract 3 from top margin for placement in *reading position* (off-center).
5 Space down from top edge of paper 1 more than lines in top margin.

		Words
WORD STUDY		2
Words Frequently Misspelled		8
controllable	counterpart	13
description	designate	17
enclosure	extension	21
indispensable	interminable	27
occasion	occurrence	31
perpetuate	preferred	35
precede	preferential	39
prefer	pretense	42
preference	proceeding	47
preferring	proportionate	52
procedure	possessions	56
qualitative	quinine	60
quasi-judicial	quizzical	65
succession	successive	69
vacuum	various	72
Wednesday	welfare	76
wherever	wherein	79
wherewithal	whereupon	84

Problem 2: Syllable Identification

PROCEDURE Use the directions given for Problem 1. Type the words of the second column of Problem 1 as the first column for this problem. For the second column, type these words with the hyphen to show all syllables. Verify your syllable identification, make corrections as needed, and retype the problem. Use the same headings. (*90 words*)

● 53C is continued on page 92.

| **35A ● PREPARATORY PRACTICE** *5 minutes (each line three or more times)*

Alphabetic   W. K. Clay made several quick jet flights to Mexico, Brazil, and Peru.

Figure-symbol Today's sales of #147, #205, and #398 "Specials" brought a 6¼% profit.

Fluency   I shall use the money for further study if I win the Quill Club prize.
               | 1 | 2 | 3 | 4 | 5 | 6 | 7 | 8 | 9 | 10 | 11 | 12 | 13 | 14 |

HOW TO ADDRESS A POSTAL CARD

Type your return address in the upper left corner of the card: Begin on the second line space from the top and two spaces from the left edge of the card.

Begin the card address a triple-space below the printed address identification and 5 to 8 spaces to the left of horizontal center.

● Type a 3-line address with double spacing; a 4-line address with single spacing.

NOTE Type the ZIP code number on the line with the state name with a minimum of 2 spaces between.

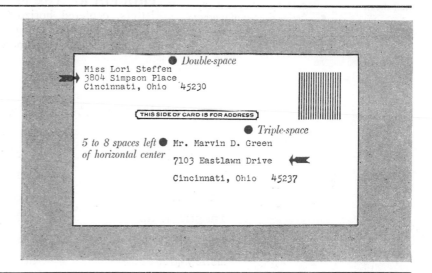

35B ● PROBLEM TYPING: Postal Cards *20 minutes*

Problem 1: Centered Announcement on a Postal Card

½" top margin, double spacing

PROCEDURE Use a postal card or paper cut to the size of a 5½- by 3¼-inch card. Center each of the following lines horizontally.

MEETING OF DELTA PI EPSILON
Wednesday, (*next week's date*)
to hear
Dr. Stefano Fedorczyk
speak on
"Devaluation of the Dollar: When?"
Science Lecture Hall, 4:15 p.m.

Problem 2: Message Typed on a Postal Card

48-space line, single spacing, block style

PROCEDURE Type the current date on Line 3. Omit the complimentary close. *DO NOT* type line for line.

● Triple-space

Dear Norman

A distinguished economist, Dr. Stefano Fedorczyk, will be the speaker at the next Delta Pi Epsilon meeting on Wednesday, (*next week's date*).

The meeting will be in Science Lecture Hall at 4:15 p.m. Be sure to hear this eminent scholar.
                    ● Triple-space
Charles Northrup, President

Problem 3: Addressing Postal Cards

PROCEDURE Read *How to Address a Postal Card;* then, using the cards typed in Problems 1 and 2, address the cards to **Mr. Norman Stanley** | **3190 Beechwood Road** | **Cincinnati, Ohio 45227** and **Miss Lizbeth Bragdon** | **68 Oak Grove Place** | **Cincinnati, Ohio 45216.**

35C ● BUILDING SPEED AND CONTROL *5 minutes (each sentence as two 1-minute writings)*

Speed up the typing by thinking the word––not the letters of the word.

It is time for me to learn to type with control as well as with speed.
| 1 | 2 | 3 | 4 | 5 | 6 | 7 | 8 | 9 | 10 | 11 | 12 | 13 | 14 |

Problem 2: Two-Column Tabulation

PROCEDURE Retype Problem 1 in two columns, omitting the second column (the population figures for 1950). For the secondary heading, type *Population for 1960*. Use the directions for Problem 1 except that you will have 18 spaces between columns. (*44 words*)

Problem 3: Two-Column Tabulation with Double Headings

Half sheet

Double spacing

● Center problem vertically
● Decide number of spaces to be left between columns

PROCEDURE Type the first heading (the *main heading*) in capital letters, centered horizontally. Double-space between the first and second (*secondary*) headings. Triple-space between the secondary heading and the first line of the columns.

		Words
A WORD STUDY		3
Expressions Written as Two Words		9
all right	bank draft	13
bona fide	curb market	18
en route	good morning	22
inasmuch as	insomuch as	27
in order	list price	31
money order	no one	35
order blank	postal card	40
parcel post	price list	44
post office	some day	48
stock market	vice versa	53

Problem 4: Four-Column Tabulation with Double Headings

PROCEDURE Using the directions for Problem 3, retype Problem 3 in four corumns, alphabetizing the words (*53 words*)

52D ● DRILL ON ALIGNING AND TYPING OVER A WORD *5 minutes*

PROCEDURE **1** Type the word *align*—do not return the carriage.

2 Find the aligning scale **33**.

3 Move the carriage so the word *align* is above the scale. Note the relation of the

Use the alignment scale to align your copy.

top of the scale to the bottom of the letters. Also, note that one of the white lines points to the center of the letter *i*.

4 Remove the paper; reinsert it. Gauge the line so the bottom of the letters is in correct relation to the top of the scale. Through the use of the variable line spacer **3**, the paper can be moved forward or backward a fraction of a space.

5 Operate the paper-release lever **16** and move the paper to the left or right (as necessary), and gauge the correct letter spacing by centering the letter *i* over one of the white lines on the scale. Test the accuracy of your alignment by setting the ribbon control **22** for stencil position and typing over one of the letters. If necessary, make further alignment adjustments.

6 Retype the word *align* over the first writing.

7 Repeat the drill two or three times.

35D ● TECHNIQUE PRACTICE: Shift-Key Control *10 minutes (each line three or more times)*

● All letters are used in this practice.

1	Left shift	Mary and Harry will go to Maine in May, but Pauline is going to Italy.
2	Right shift	Clay Ward left for Spain, but Edward Sprague went to France with Carl.
3	Both shifts	Were Jack and George told to imitate Lillian's typewriting techniques?
4	Both shifts	"Build speed WITH accuracy," Mr. Verner said, "for real typing power."
5	Both shifts	Clint and Floyd spent April in Brazil and May and June in Mexico City.

| 1 | 2 | 3 | 4 | 5 | 6 | 7 | 8 | 9 | 10 | 11 | 12 | 13 | 14 |

35E ● DRILLS ON VERTICAL CENTERING *5 minutes*

STEPS IN VERTICAL CENTERING

1 Count the lines in the copy.

2 Subtract from 66 for a full sheet or 33 for a half sheet.

3 Divide by 2; if a fraction results, disregard it.

4 Space down from the top edge of the paper 1 more than the number of lines in the top margin.

Full sheet, single spacing, 60-space line

PROCEDURE

Drill 1 Center and type *vertically* at the left margin of a 60-space line the figures **1** to **40**. Align the figures at the right. (Follow the steps for vertical centering at the left.)

Drill 2 Fold the paper in half (or use a half sheet); set the left margin stop at 50. Center *vertically* the days of the week and the months of the year; double-space between the final day and the first month.

LESSON 36 | **36A ● PREPARATORY PRACTICE** *5 minutes (each line three or more times)*

Alphabetic	Judge Quentin Weaver realized he must back F. H. Bixley for the place.
Figure-symbol	Ship Order #762-B (for 34 dozen Model #58 @ 90¢ a dozen) on August 16.
Fluency	It takes time to learn to do things right--but it will save time, too.

| 1 | 2 | 3 | 4 | 5 | 6 | 7 | 8 | 9 | 10 | 11 | 12 | 13 | 14 |

36B ● TECHNIQUE PRACTICE: Shift-Key Control *5 minutes*

PROCEDURE Type each line of 35D, above, twice on the *control level*.
Try to type without error.

36C ● PROBLEM TYPING REVIEW *25 minutes*

SUPPLIES NEEDED
1 half sheet
2 full sheets
3 postal cards

PROCEDURE

1 Make pencil notations of the problems and page numbers given below:

32D, Problem 1 .... page 59
33E .... page 61
35B, Problems 1–2 .... page 63
34C .... page 62

2 With this notation sheet beside the typewriter, type each problem *once only* and in the order listed. After typing a problem, proofread it and circle any errors you have made. You will be timed for 20 minutes. Work rapidly but not hurriedly.

● *Lesson 36 is continued on page 65.*

52B ● BUILDING SPEED AND CONTROL *10 minutes*

PROCEDURE

1 Type a 1-minute writing on each of the paragraphs given below. Type on the *control level*.

2 Type a 5-minute writing, beginning with the paragraph of 51D, page 88. After typing that paragraph, flip the page, indent, and type ¶s 2 and 3 below. If you complete these paragraphs before time is called, retype them; but do not turn back to page 88.

● All letters are used in the paragraphs.

	GWAM 1'	5'*
Use all parts of your typewriter with exactness to speed up your 93	19	48
typing without speeding up your fingers. The right use of the tab key 107	22	50
¶ 2 1.30 si 72 words or bar and a quicker carriage return will add much to your manipulative 122	24	53
skill. You don't have to agonize over this typing––just do what you 135	27	56
have to do as well as you can do it now. It's just that simple––or is 150	30	59
that simple? 152	31	60
Type with continuity––that merely means to keep the carriage moving 166	33	62
along smoothly and without pauses. To type at high speed, break through 180	36	65
¶ 3 1.30 si 72 words your zone of control and force the fingers to work out new patterns of 194	39	68
high-speed stroking. To type with good control, find the rate at which 209	42	71
you can type with confidence. Then try to hold yourself to just that 223	45	73
speed. 224	46	74

```
1' |  1  |  2  |  3  |  4  |  5  |  6  |  7  |  8  |  9  |  10 |  11 |  12 |  13 |  14 |
5' |       1        |          2          |         3         |
```

* The 1' and 5' GWAM counts include ¶ 1 of 51D, page 88.

52C ● PROBLEM TYPING: Tabulations *25 minutes*

Problem 1: Three-Column Tabulation

Half sheet,
double spacing,
center problem vertically,
10 spaces between columns

PROCEDURE For Columns 2 and 3, set a tab stop for each column at the point that will require the least forward and backward spacing.

● *52C is continued on page 90.*

			Words
MAIN HEADING ➤ EIGHT LARGEST CITIES IN THE UNITED STATES			8
		● Double-space	
SECONDARY HEADING ➤ Population for 1950 and 1960			14
	Tab ↓	● Triple-space	
New York	7,891,957	7,781,984	20
Chicago	3,620,962	3,550,404	26
Los Angeles	1,970,358	2,479,015	32
Philadelphia	2,071,605	2,002,512	39
Detroit	1,849,568	1,670,144	44
Baltimore	949,708	939,024	50
Houston	596,163	938,219	56
Cleveland	914,808	876,050	62

36D ● DRILL ON VERTICAL CENTERING *7 minutes*

Full sheet,
double spacing

VERTICAL CENTERING

PROCEDURE Read the drill through; then center it *vertically* (as directed in the lines of the drill) and center each line *horizontally*.

Count the lines to be centered
Count 2 for triple-space after heading
Count 1 for each blank line space in double-spaced copy
Subtract total lines from 66 (full sheet) or 33 (half sheet)
Divide by 2 to determine top and bottom margins
If fraction results from dividing by 2, disregard it
Space down from top edge of paper 1 more than lines in top margin
Center main heading horizontally and type it
Triple-space between main heading and first line
Center first line horizontally
Continue in similar manner until all lines are typed

36E ● SENTENCE GUIDED WRITING *3 minutes (1' writings with the call-of-the-line ending; exploration level)*

65-space line, single spacing

	GWAM		
	20"	15"	12"
K now the speed *at which* you can type best with con trols.	33	44	55
l.c. Be glad for *all* what you have no matter *what* more y ou want	39	52	65

LESSON 37 | 37A ● PREPARATORY PRACTICE *5 minutes (each line three or more times)*

Alphabetic   Prizes for Albuquerque's next track meet were given by Dick J. Whaley.

Figure-symbol My wire read: "We sold Munson at 89 2/3, ICM at 456, AP&T at 70 1/8."

Fluency   More good will come from a little praise than from a lot of criticism.
               | 1 | 2 | 3 | 4 | 5 | 6 | 7 | 8 | 9 | 10 | 11 | 12 | 13 | 14 |

37B ● SENTENCE GUIDED WRITING *10 minutes*

70-space line, single spacing

PROCEDURE Type each sentence as two 1-minute writings, once guided by the 20- or 15-second call of the line ending and once by the 12-second call. Type on the *control level.*

	GWAM		
	20"	15"	12"
The *right* best kind of rhythm builds *will* speed *and accuracy.*	33	44	55
Your speed will go up as you get rid of the jerks in typing.	36	48	60
Y ou can move a finger *your* quicker *more ly* than *you can* move the hands.	39	52	65
l.c. *Good* Typing isn't so much rapid stroking as *it is* continuous stroking.	42	56	70

Problem 2: Three-Column Tabulation

FREQUENTLY MISSPELLED WORDS

Half sheet, single spacing,
center problem vertically,
8 spaces between columns

PROCEDURE Type the first word in Column 1; tabulate to Column 2 and type the first word; then tabulate to Column 3 and type the first word. Type the remaining words in a similar way.

			Words
already Tab	altitude Tab	allowance	11
announced	ancient	boundary	16
centralize	circuit	claimant	22
miscellaneous	municipal	occasion	29
occurrence	permissible	personnel	35
precede	proceed	questionnaire	41
queue	receiving	referring	47
resistance	repetitious	secretary	53
siege	similar	singular	58
soluble	skiing	surveillance	63
succession	symmetry	transferred	70
transposition	transcript	unnumbered	77
vehicular	vicinity	zoology	82

Problem 3: Two-Column Tabulation

Half sheet,
single spacing,
center problem
vertically,
12 spaces between
columns

PROCEDURE Use SYLLABLE IDENTIFICATION for the heading. As the first column for this problem, type the words of the first column of Problem 2, above. For the second column, type the words with the hyphen to show all syllables.

For example, type: Then, tab to Col. 2:

miscellaneous   Tab   mis-cel-la-ne-ous

When you have completed the typing, verify your syllable identification; make pencil corrections as needed, and retype the problem.

51D ● BUILDING SPEED AND CONTROL *5 minutes (two 1' control-level writings; then two 1' exploration-level writings)*

Full sheet   ●   Double spacing
70-space line   5-space ¶ indention

GWAM

The 5-minute GWAM count is to be used for 52B, page 89.

	1'	5'*

¶ 1
1.30 si
80 words

It is good sense to put first things first in all you do, but it is   14   3

of utmost importance to do this when trying to improve your typing skill.   29   6

Of the many things that go into the making of expertness in typing, the   43   9

"first" is the use of right techniques in each day's practice; and this   57   11

includes the efficient use of operative parts of the machine as well as   72   14

striking the keys with speed and control.   80   16

1' | 1 | 2 | 3 | 4 | 5 | 6 | 7 | 8 | 9 | 10 | 11 | 12 | 13 | 14 |
5' | 1 | 2 | 3 |

LESSON 52 | 52A ● PREPARATORY PRACTICE *5 minutes (each line three or more times)*

Alphabetic   J. V. Packard may excel in law, but Hal Ford is quite good in zoology.

Figure-symbol   The Idaho Utility 3 3/4% bonds (due June 20, 1975) now sell at 86 2/3.

Fluency   We do not need a lot of luck nearly so much as we need a lot of pluck.

| 1 | 2 | 3 | 4 | 5 | 6 | 7 | 8 | 9 | 10 | 11 | 12 | 13 | 14 |

Full sheet, 70-space line,
double spacing,
5-space ¶ indention

PROCEDURE Type a 3-minute writing on the *control level*. Determine your *gwam* and the number of errors. If time permits, type a 1-minute writing on the *control level*.

● All letters are used in the paragraphs.

	GWAM	
	1'	3'

¶ 1
1.25 si
68 words

A pilot won't fly a plane until he knows how to control it. A trucker wouldn't want to take his truck on the highway until he knows just how to handle it. To realize the most from your typewriter, you should know it as the pilot knows his plane or the trucker his truck-- and you must use it as wisely; it is a partner in learning to type.

	1'	3'
	13	4 · 49
	27	9 · 54
	41	14 · 59
	55	18 · 63
	68	23 · 68

¶ 2
1.25 si
68 words

Try to do your work a little better each day. In time this can add up to quite a lot of typing skill. Sometimes it is difficult to see how so much skill can come from so little extra effort; but if you make the effort to know the typewriter you use as the pilot knows the plane he flies, your typing speed and control can improve greatly.

	1'	3'
	13	27 · 72
	27	32 · 77
	41	36 · 81
	55	41 · 86
	68	45 · 90

```
1'  | 1 | 2 | 3 | 4 | 5 | 6 | 7 | 8 | 9 | 10 | 11 | 12 | 13 | 14 |
3'  |       1       |       2       |       3       |       4       |       5       |
```

Problem 1: Memorandum with a Subject Line

Half sheet ● 60-space line ● Single spacing ● Space once between number in parenthesis and topic

	Words
Type on Line 7 *Current date*	3

● Triple-space

SUBJECT: Understanding Our Foreign Policy ... 12

Phi Eta Sigma will sponsor a Forum each Thursday of the next ... 24
three weeks for the purpose of ... 30

UNDERSTANDING OUR FOREIGN POLICY ... 37

Topics: (1) Foreign Aid ... 42
(2) New Approaches to Disarmament ... 48
(3) The UN in Crisis ... 53

The meetings will be in Science Hall at 4:15 p.m. ... 63

Lois Charlton

● 3 blank line spaces

Lois Charlton, Secretary ... 68

● *Problems 2 and 3 are on page 67.*

SECTION 9

Lessons 51–60

TABULATION AND WORD DIVISION

STANDARD PROCEDURES FOR SECTION 9

GET READY TO TYPE

Clear the desk. Use full sheets, a 70-space line, and single spacing—except when otherwise directed.

Use double spacing and a 5-space ¶ indention for paragraphs.

SELF-IMPROVEMENT PRACTICE

As time permits, type each of the Action Typing paragraphs of Self-Improvement Practice, page 106, as directed. For additional practice, type the lines of 53B, page 91, and 55B, page 94.

LESSON 51 | 51A ● PREPARATORY PRACTICE *5 minutes (each line three or more times)*

Alphabetic   The unexpected freezing weather killed Robert Quigley's jasmine vines.

Figures   Type page 12 on May 9, page 34 on May 10, and page 56 on May 17 or 18.

Fluency   Henry quoted, "What you do speaks so loud I cannot hear what you say."

| 1 | 2 | 3 | 4 | 5 | 6 | 7 | 8 | 9 | 10 | 11 | 12 | 13 | 14 |

51B ● DRILL ON TABULATING: Horizontal Placement *5 minutes*

RECALL ➡ 10 pica spaces

||||||||||||||||||||||||||||| 1

12 elite spaces

An 8½" line =

85 pica spaces
or
102 elite spaces

● **SPACING BETWEEN COLUMNS**

Have an even number of spaces between columns (4, 6, 8, 10, 12, etc.). Reduce or increase space as needed for easy reading.

PROCEDURE

Drill 1 Use single spacing; 10 spaces between columns. Set the margin and tab stops as directed at the right. Tabulate from Column 1 to Column 2.

```
misspelled          description
believed            uncontrollable
```

Drill 2 Type Drill 1 with 20 spaces between columns.

Drill 3 Have 12 spaces between columns.

```
12,345      56,789      90,109
54,321      76,543      89,706
 2,134       4,567       7,890
```

HORIZONTAL PLACEMENT OF COLUMNS

To Set the Left Margin Stop:

1 Move the margin stops to the ends of the scale.

2 Backspace from the center of the page 1 space for each 2 letters and spaces in the longest line of each column and for each 2 spaces left between columns. Set the *left margin stop* at this point.

To Set Tab Stops:

1 Clear the tabulator rack.

2 From the left margin stop, space forward *once* for each letter and space in the longest line of the first column and for each space to be left between the first and second columns. Set a *tab stop* at this point for the second column. Follow a similar procedure for any additional columns.

51C ● PROBLEM TYPING: Tabulations *25 minutes*

Problem 1: Two-Column Tabulation

Half sheet
Single spacing
12 spaces between columns

●

Center problem vertically
Do not type line numbers
Tabulate to Column 2

Backspacing for Horizontal Placement of Columns
When backspacing, carry forward to the next column the extra space that may occur at the end of the longest line of a column. (For example, in this tabulation carry over 1 space for the letter *y* in *accessibility* to the second column.) If an extra space occurs at the end of the longest line of the final column, drop it.

LINE			Words
12	WORDS COMMONLY MISSPELLED		5
13		● Triple-space	
14			
15	accessibility ⎯Tab⎯	accommodate	10
16	already	benefited	14
17	bookkeeping	consistency	19
18	definitely	discernible	23
19	existent	gauge	26
20	guarantee	immediate	30
21	indispensable	inoculate	35
22	insistence	judgments	39

● *51C is continued on page 88.*

37D ● PROBLEM MEASUREMENT *(Continued)*

Problem 2: Announcement Typed on a Postal Card

½-inch top margin, 48-space line, single spacing

PROCEDURE

1 Place the copy typed as Problem 1 on the desk in position for easy reading. Type the announcement in a form appropriate for a postal card with the following changes: (a) Omit the date and subject line; and (b) add an appropriate salutation.

2 Address the card to **Miss Evelyn N. Bradford** | **3790 Hyde Park Drive** | **Cincinnati, Ohio 45216.**

Problem 3: Centered Announcement on a Postal Card
PROCEDURE

1 Use double spacing. Center the problem vertically, and center each line horizontally. Triple-space between the main heading and the first line.

UNDERSTANDING OUR FOREIGN POLICY
Foreign Aid
New Approaches to Disarmament
The UN in Crisis
Thursday, 4:15 p.m., Science Hall
Sponsored by PHI ETA SIGMA

2 Address the card to **Mr. Ralph O. Wallace** | **678 W. Mason Drive** | **Cincinnati, Ohio 45213.**

5¢

SELF-IMPROVEMENT PRACTICE ● *(each line three or more times)*

● All letters, figures, and symbols are used in the sentences.

#	Sentence	Words in Line	GWAM 20″	15″	12″
1	Lead a boy to college where they try to make him think.	11	33	44	55
2	With faith enough and work enough, we can do about anything.	12	36	48	60
3	He may not be born great, but he can try to work up to greatness.	13	39	52	65
4	A good many of the workers of this world need to have a faith lifting.	14	42	56	70
5	Use * for a footnote, and use ¢ and @ in typing a bill.	11	33	44	55
6	He wrote, "Sam's Policy 765432, due in 1980, is for $2,500."	12	36	48	60
7	Check #453 (dated July 29) is for $167.80, but Paul owes $176.80.	13	39	52	65
8	Lane & Roth gave a 2% discount on Bill #345 (dated May 6) for $789.10.	14	42	56	70
9	Do some distance thinking--far ahead of where you are!	11	33	44	55
10	A man may be down, but he's never OUT until he gives up.	12	36	48	60
11	The next goal to be realized: a gain of a word or two each week.	13	39	52	65
12	James has quite as much zeal for his work as he has for his pay check.	14	42	56	70
13	The year's high for Manox was 89½; it sold at 82 today.	11	33	44	55
14	Be uniform in typing fractions: 1/2 and 1/4--not 1/2 and ¼.	12	36	48	60
15	May I use * to identify the footnote? When should I use ¢ and @?	13	39	52	65
16	You must try hard enough--but not too hard--to do what has to be done.	14	42	56	70
17	My card has 13 to 15 lines that can be used for typing.	11	33	44	55
18	Clint and Floyd will go to Spain, but Pam will go to Norway.	12	36	48	60
19	My brother brought many more bright labels for my excess baggage.	13	39	52	65
20	Ken expects and exacts expert work of himself, and he excels in typing.	14	42	56	70
21	Even small men have some elements of bigness when we get to know them.	14	42	56	70
22	When you lose your way, you can be very sure you have lost your faith.	14	42	56	70
23	Liberty is the one thing you cannot have unless you give it to others.	14	42	56	70
24	Tell the fingers what you want them to do, and they will always do it.	14	42	56	70

| 1 | 2 | 3 | 4 | 5 | 6 | 7 | 8 | 9 | 10 | 11 | 12 | 13 | 14 |

50D ● PROBLEM MEASUREMENT *25 minutes*

PROBLEMS 1 AND 2	2 full-sheet letterheads or plain paper Modified block; blocked ¶s Mixed punctuation 60-space line	Current date followed by 6 or 7 blank line spaces ● Address an envelope

➤ *Do not erase and correct errors unless you are directed to do so by your instructor.*

Problem 1: Letter with Centered Line

Words

Dr. J. Walter McDonald | 450 East 4th   10
South | Salt Lake City, Utah 84102 | Dear   18
Dr. McDonald: | (¶1) You will soon re-   24
ceive for your signature copies of our   32
E64 | contract. This contract, specifying   40
the royalty rate of | 7½ percent, is for   48
the preparation of the first ten chapters | 57
of the manuscript for | 61

NEW DIRECTIONS IN ECONOMIC THOUGHT≠134   68
(¶2) A statement of citizenship, which is   75
required when we apply | for a copyright,   83
and the Internal Revenue Service Form   91
3435 | will also be sent to you for your   99
signature. These should | be returned   106
with your signed copy of the contract. | 114
(¶3) I am very happy to have this oppor-   121
tunity to make official | your affiliation   129
with us in an author-publisher relation-   137
ship. | I am confident the relationship will   146
prove both pleasant and | profitable for   154
you and for us. | Sincerely yours, | Everett   162
Leigh Hunter | Editor in Chief | (*Your*   169
initials)   183

Problem 2: Letter with Centered Line

Words

Professor Charles Kiehley | 367 West 19th   11
Street | Montclair, New Jersey 07042 | 18
Dear Professor Kiehley: | (¶1) Contract   25
E64, which will be sent to you for your   33
signature, specifies a royalty rate of 7½   41

percent for the preparation of the last ten   50
chapters of the manuscript for   56

NEW DIRECTIONS IN ECONOMIC THOUGHT   63
(¶2) Your coauthor is responsible for the   71
preparation of the manu- | script for the   79
placement and achievement tests that cor-   87
relate with the first ten chapters and you   96
for the manuscript for the correlating   103
tests for the final ten chapters of the   111
book. You have joint responsibility for   120
the preparation of the manual. (¶3) I be-   127
lieve the new book will be a contribution   135
of worth to the literature on economics   143
and will be well received by college   151
teachers and students. | (*Problem 1 closing*)   167/182

Problem 3: Letter with Changes

PROCEDURE Use a 50-space line. Type a letter to Dr. McDonald, whose address is given in Problem 1. Use ¶s 2 and 3 of Problem 2, changing ¶2 to show the coauthor responsible for the *final ten chapters* and Dr. McDonald responsible for the *first ten chapters* and changing the words "the book" at the end of Sentence 1 to NEW DIRECTIONS IN ECONOMIC THOUGHT.

Problem 4: Postal Card

PROCEDURE Address a postal card to Professor Kiehley. Type the current date on Line 4; use an appropriate salutation, and type this message:

Words

Announcement will be made later this   15
month of the | early Spring publication of   23
NEW DIRECTIONS IN | ECONOMIC THOUGHT.   31
The book will be available | for your class-   39
room use in the summer session. | Ever-   47
ett Leigh Hunter | Editor in Chief   53/69

SELF-IMPROVEMENT PRACTICE ● *(each line three or more times)*

● All letters and figures are used in the sentences.

		Words in Line	GWAM 20″	15″	12″
1	Ben expected the quiz to be very hard for the nine men.	11	33	44	55
2	The article "World Neighbors" was written in May, 1963.	11	33	44	55
3	Can your van move the six heavy zinc boxes for Max Buchanan?	12	36	48	60
4	The 4½% rate charged Burton & Wick should be changed to 5¼%.	12	36	48	60
5	The poet quietly worked on in spite of the riots in many streets.	13	39	52	65
6	Their Order #736 amounts to $528.90 and must be shipped by May 9.	13	39	52	65
7	Most men will turn in a better job performance if you believe in them.	14	42	56	70
8	My street number is 1839; my ZIP code, 25764; and telephone, 621-3909.	14	42	56	70

| 1 | 2 | 3 | 4 | 5 | 6 | 7 | 8 | 9 | 10 | 11 | 12 | 13 | 14 |

PERSONAL LETTERS, THEMES, AND COMPOSING

STANDARD PROCEDURES FOR SECTION 7

GET READY TO TYPE

Clear the desk. Adjust the paper guide and paper-bail rolls. Use a 70-space line; single spacing, unless otherwise directed.

SELF-IMPROVEMENT PRACTICE

As time permits, type the sentences of Self-Improvement Practice, page 77, three or more times. Type on the *control level*. Identify error-less lines.

LESSON 38 | 38A ● PREPARATORY PRACTICE *5 minutes (each line three or more times)*

Alphabetic	Ben Jackson will save the money required for your next big cash prize.
Figure-symbol	Order #678 for 24 chairs (at $10.35 each) was shipped to you on May 9.
Fluency	Why will a man stay in a rut when he can walk along the broad highway?

| 1 | 2 | 3 | 4 | 5 | 6 | 7 | 8 | 9 | 10 | 11 | 12 | 13 | 14 |

38B ● BUILDING SPEED AND CONTROL *5 minutes*

PROCEDURE Use each of the sentences for two 1-minute writings. Type the first writing on the *exploration level* and the second writing on the *control level*.

The more a man leaves to chance, the less chance he has of getting it.

Don't lean on others, but stand near enough to be of help when needed.

| 1 | 2 | 3 | 4 | 5 | 6 | 7 | 8 | 9 | 10 | 11 | 12 | 13 | 14 |

38C ● GROWTH INDEX *10 minutes*

PROCEDURE 1 Use 37C Growth Index, page 66. Type a 1- and a 3-minute writing on the *exploration level*.

2 Set a goal that is 8 words slower than your 1-minute rate. Type a 1- and a 3-minute writing on the *control level* trying to type at the exact goal rate. Determine the *gwam* and errors for the 3-minute writing.

38D ● PROBLEM TYPING: Personal Letter in Block Style *25 minutes*

Problem 1: Learning the Nature of the Problem

PROCEDURE

1 Study Style Letter 1, page 69. Note the characteristics of the *block style* (all lines begin flush with the left margin).

2 Study the spacing directions between letter parts (shown in color).

3 Study the placement of the *return address* and *date, letter address, salutation,* and *complimentary close.*

4 Read the brief explanation of *open punctuation.*

5 Type the letter. Use a full sheet and a 60-space line. Type the first line of the return address on Line 10 (to have a 1½-inch top margin and to type the date on Line 12).

Problem 2: Building Letter-Typing Skill

PROCEDURE

1 Type two 1-minute writings on the opening lines (return address through salutation). If you complete this typing before time is called, retype the lines.

2 Type a 3-minute writing on the paragraphs.

Problem 3: Timed Writings on a Style Letter

PROCEDURE Type Style Letter 1, page 69, as a 3- and a 5-minute writing. Start with the return address and type at a controlled speed. If you complete the typing before time is called, remove the paper, re-insert it to type on the back, and retype as much of the letter as you can. Determine your *gwam* for the 5-minute writing.

| **50A ● PREPARATORY PRACTICE** *5 minutes (each line three or more times)*

Alphabetic	The day in June was quite bright except for a very bleak morning haze.
Figure-symbol	Did Ned pay $4.81 to $4.95 (less 6% discount) for 37 ft. of #260 wire?
Fluency	Begin the day with a smile in the eyes as well as a smile on the face.

| 1 | 2 | 3 | 4 | 5 | 6 | 7 | 8 | 9 | 10 | 11 | 12 | 13 | 14 |

50B ● GUIDED WRITING *5 minutes*

Full sheet,
70-space line,
double spacing,
5-space ¶ indention

PROCEDURE Choose a goal that is 4 to 8 words below your best speed. Type a 1-minute writing, guided by the 15-second call. Then type a 2-minute writing at approximately the same rate but without the call of the guide. Type on the *control level*.

● All letters are used in the paragraphs.

1.16 si
72 words

	2″ G W A M	
How well do you write? Is it hard for you to put your thoughts in	7	42
words? If so, you must learn to use words with ease. Choose your words	14	50
with care. Some men feel that they must use complex terms to impress	21	57
others with their knowledge. Be as concise as possible in your quest	28	64
to improve your writing. Write just what you mean in words most will	35	71
recognize.	36	72

2' | 1 | 2 | 3 | 4 | 5 | 6 | 7 |

50C ● GROWTH INDEX *10 minutes*

PROCEDURE Use the machine adjustments made for 50B, above. Type two 3-minute writings on the *control level*. Hold your typing to a rate that you can maintain with ease and accuracy.

● All letters are used in the paragraphs.

	G W A M		
		1'	3'
There are many kinds of business letters. There are letters of	13	4	52
inquiry and their replies; sales and credit letters; adjustment and other	28	9	57
specialized letters. Each should have a purpose. Before you start to	42	14	62
write, you should have this purpose clearly fixed in your mind. When	56	19	67
you know what you want to say and why you want to say it, you can start	70	23	71
to write.	72	24	72
Words are the tools used to convey thought or lead to action. They	86	29	77
must be used wisely and with care. The simple word and short sentence	100	33	81
are usually more effective than the big word and involved sentence, but	114	38	86
don't be afraid of the big or unusual word if it means just what you want	129	43	91
to say. Know what you want to say––and say it with simplicity and clarity.	144	48	96

¶ 1
1.30 si
72 words

¶ 2
1.30 si
72 words

1' | 1 | 2 | 3 | 4 | 5 | 6 | 7 | 8 | 9 | 10 | 11 | 12 | 13 | 14 |
3' | 1 | 2 | 3 | 4 | 5 |

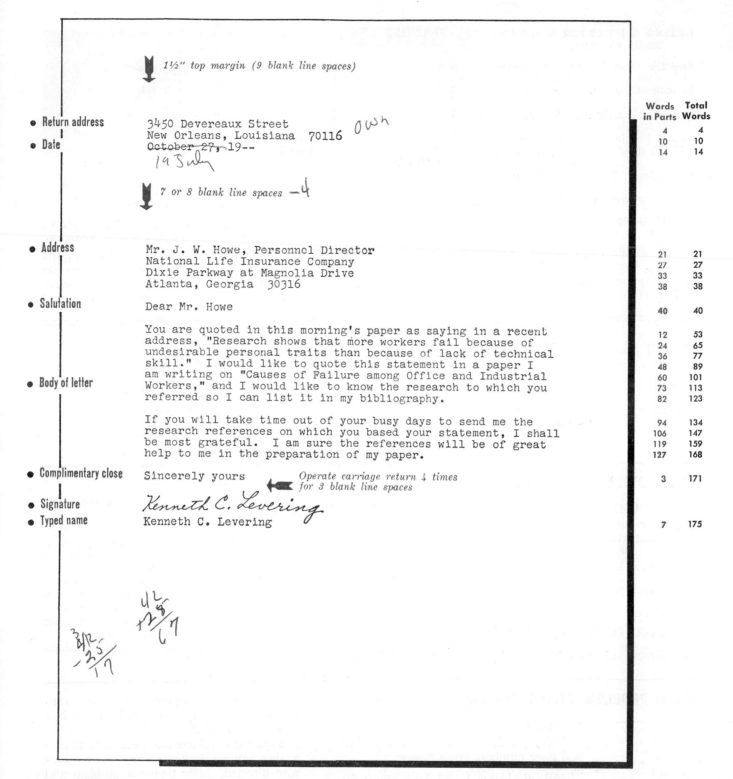

		Words in Parts	Total Words
1½" top margin (9 blank line spaces)			
Return address	3450 Devereaux Street *owh*	4	4
	New Orleans, Louisiana 70116	10	10
Date	~~October 27,~~ 19--	14	14
	19 July		
7 or 8 blank line spaces *-4*			
Address	Mr. J. W. Howe, Personnel Director	21	21
	National Life Insurance Company	27	27
	Dixie Parkway at Magnolia Drive	33	33
	Atlanta, Georgia 30316	38	38
Salutation	Dear Mr. Howe	40	40
Body of letter	You are quoted in this morning's paper as saying in a recent	12	53
	address, "Research shows that more workers fail because of	24	65
	undesirable personal traits than because of lack of technical	36	77
	skill." I would like to quote this statement in a paper I	48	89
	am writing on "Causes of Failure among Office and Industrial	60	101
	Workers," and I would like to know the research to which you	73	113
	referred so I can list it in my bibliography.	82	123
	If you will take time out of your busy days to send me the	94	134
	research references on which you based your statement, I shall	106	147
	be most grateful. I am sure the references will be of great	119	159
	help to me in the preparation of my paper.	127	168
Complimentary close	Sincerely yours *Operate carriage return 4 times for 3 blank line spaces*	3	171
Signature	*Kenneth C. Levering*		
Typed name	Kenneth C. Levering	7	175

STYLE LETTER 1 *Personal Letter in Block Style with Open Punctuation*

OPEN PUNCTUATION

Open punctuation is used in this style letter. Punctuation marks are omitted after the date, address, salutation, and complimentary close unless an abbreviation is used, in which case the period is typed as a part of the abbreviation.

FOLDING A LETTER FOR A SMALL ENVELOPE

Step 1 With the letter face up on the desk, fold from the bottom up to ½ inch of the top.

Step 2 Fold right third to left.

Step 3 Folding from left to right, fold left third to ½″ of last crease.

Step 4 Insert last creased edge first.

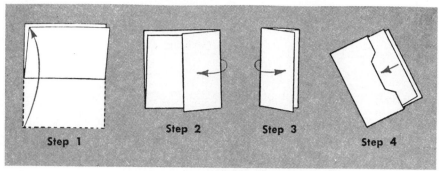

Step 1   Step 2   Step 3   Step 4

Problem 2: Letter with Changes

PROCEDURE Type the letter given as Problem 1, page 83, addressed to **Mrs. Joan Taylor, Principal | Stevens Junior High School | Clarksville, Tennessee 37040 |**. Use an appropriate salutation. Change the title of the series to OUR EXPANDING UNIVERSE. Fold and insert the letter into the envelope.

Problem 3: Postal Card

PROCEDURE Address the card to **Mr. Ralph E. Bruce, Principal | Ardmore High School | Ardmore, Oklahoma   73401 |**. Use the first paragraph of the letter of Problem 1, page 83. Use an appropriate salutation. Omit the complimentary close and reference initials.

LESSON 49 | 49A ● PREPARATORY PRACTICE *5 minutes (each line three or more times)*

Alphabetic   The Klondyck Festival may award a gold plaque to the best jazz sextet.

Figures   Please turn to page 350 and answer Questions 2, 4, 6, 7, 8, 9, and 16.

Fluency   The good writer is careful to avoid the use of long and obscure terms.
| 1 | 2 | 3 | 4 | 5 | 6 | 7 | 8 | 9 | 10 | 11 | 12 | 13 | 14 |

49B ● DRILL ON ERASING *10 minutes*

PROCEDURE Type Sentence 1 as it is shown below; then study the Guides for Erasing given at the right. Erase each error and type the correct word. Type the remaining sentences in a similar way.

1. Move the carriage to right or letf.

2. Rurn paper forward ro backward.

3. Ersae lightly. Vrush eraser particles away.

4. Avoid toiching other lettres.

5. Erase thoroughyl; retype the wrod lightly.

GUIDES FOR ERASING

1 Use a plastic shield and a typewriter (hard) eraser.

2 Lift the paper bail.

3 Turn the paper forward if the error is on the upper two thirds or backward if the error is on the lower third of the page.

4 Move the carriage to the left or right as far as you can so the eraser crumbs will not fall into the typewriter mechanism.

5 Erase lightly. Brush the eraser particles away from the typewriter mechanism.

6 Turn the paper back to writing position and type.

49C ● PROBLEM TYPING REVIEW *30 minutes*

SUPPLIES NEEDED
4 letterheads or full sheets
4 small envelopes
1 postal card

PROCEDURE

1 Make pencil notations of the problems and page numbers given below:

46B, Problems 1 and 2 ... page 80
47D, Problems 2 and 3 ... page 82
48C, Problem 1 .... page 83

Place the notation sheet beside the typewriter. You will be timed for 25 minutes.

Accuracy is most important, but work rapidly—not hurriedly—as speed of production is also needed.

2 Type each problem *once*, erasing and correcting any errors you make, unless otherwise directed. After typing a problem and before removing it from the typewriter, proofread the typing and erase and correct all errors that are correctible.

3 Address an envelope for each letter typed. Fold and insert the letter into it.

Alphabetic   W. J. Bixler amazed us by reporting so quickly on the five test items.

Figures   The 15 girls typed 203 letters, 46 reports, and 78 invoices on June 9.

Fluency   We must often make a choice between the easy wrong and the hard right.
| 1 | 2 | 3 | 4 | 5 | 6 | 7 | 8 | 9 | 10 | 11 | 12 | 13 | 14 |

HOW TO ADDRESS A SMALL ENVELOPE

Type your return address (with ZIP code) in the upper left corner of the envelope: Begin on the second line space from the top edge and 3 spaces from the left edge.

Type the first line of the address approximately 2 inches from the top of the envelope. Start 5 to 8 spaces to the left of the horizontal center of the envelope. Use the block style and omit end-of-line punctuation unless an abbreviation is used, which must be punctuated with a period.

● Type a 3-line address with double spacing; use single spacing for 4 or more lines.

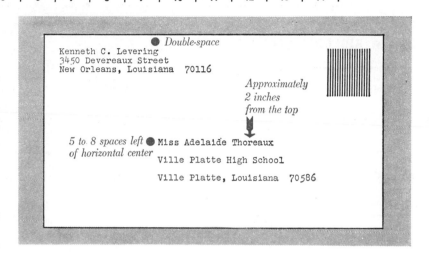

39B ● PROBLEM TYPING: Personal Letter in Block Style *25 minutes*

Full sheet, 60-space line, current date

PROCEDURE

1 Type the letter twice in a form similar to Style Letter 1, page 69. Use the same return address, but use the current date.

2 Study the information given above; then, address an envelope.

3 Type two 5-minute writings on the letter, starting with the return address.

		Words in Parts	Total Words
● Begin on Line 10	*Return address and date**│Miss Adelaide Thoreaux│Ville Platte	20	20
	High School│Ville Platte, Louisiana 70586│Dear Miss Thoreaux	32	32
	Because I remember so well the stacks of themes you always	12	45
	read so carefully and corrected so thoroughly, I have been	24	56
	hesitant to write this letter even though it is to thank you	36	68
	for all you did for me when I was in your class in English.	48	80
	There must have been times when you despaired of my learning	60	93
	anything except by rote memory, but I learned more than you	72	105
	knew. What you were as well as what you taught influenced	84	116
	me greatly. You brought a measure of greatness to a small	96	128
	classroom in a very small high school.	104	136
	My name may not make the Dean's List, but I'm getting along	116	148
	all right. Classes are often challenging and sometimes even	128	160
	exciting. I think I am doing well this first year in college.	141	173
	For that, I thank my high school teachers--and I thank you	153	185
	most of all.	155	187
	Sincerely yours│Kenneth C. Levering	7	194/224**

* *Three words (15 strokes) are counted for the current date although the date you will use may have more or fewer than 15 strokes.*

** *The first of the two figures represents the count for the letter itself; the second figure includes the count for the envelope (in this problem, the return address as well as the envelope address).*

LESSON 48 | 48A ● PREPARATORY PRACTICE *5 minutes (each line three or more times)*

Alphabetic   J. G. found sixty more volumes of the quaint book on Zen in Pawtucket.

Figures   Industrial stocks moved up 3.60; rails, up 2.47; utilities, down 5.89.

Fluency   If you wish to write well, use small words that all should understand.
   | 1 | 2 | 3 | 4 | 5 | 6 | 7 | 8 | 9 | 10 | 11 | 12 | 13 | 14 |

48B ● BUILDING SPEED AND CONTROL *10 minutes*

Full sheet,
70-space line,
double spacing,
5-space ¶ indention

PROCEDURE

1 Use 46D, page 81, and 47C, page 82, for a 5-minute writing typed on the *control level.* When you complete typing 46D, flip the page quickly and type 47C.

2 Using 47C, page 82, type a 3-minute writing on the *exploration level.*

48C ● PROBLEM TYPING: Business Letter and Postal Card *30 minutes*

Problem 1: Letter from Rough Draft

| Letterhead (or full sheet) 60-space line | ● | Modified block, blocked ¶s Mixed punctuation | ● | Address an envelope |

PROCEDURE Type the letter with the corrections indicated. After you have addressed the envelope, fold and insert the letter into the envelope (as illustrated and explained on page 84).

PROOFREADER'S MARKS: ⌐ means **move to left**   ⌐ means **move to right**   your your Your means **capitalize**

Words

December 6, 19--   *HAVE 7 BLANK LINES HERE*   3

Mrs. Mary Rafferty, *Librarian*   9
Dixon Junior High School   14
722 Wakefield St. *spell out*   19
Arlington, Virginia 22206   24
Dear Mrs. Rafferty: 28

Thank you for your letter with *an* order for *our* new serials, THE   41
MYSTERIES OF THE EARTH. I am certain you will be pleased with   54
the exciting books. As you requested, the bill *has been* sent   66
to your board of education. *← correct spacing here will be*   72

Your name does *not* appear on our list to receive *our monthly* publication   88
entitled NEW DIMENSIONS IN EDUCATION, *which is* an informative   99
discussion of education trends and problems in general and   111
of our new publications in particular. I am sending you a copy   124
of this month's issue, *as I think it will be of interest to you.*   137

If you like NEW DIMENSIONS as *much as* I hope you will, I want to add   151
your name to the mailing list to receive the publication *free of charge.*   166

Sincerely *yours,*   169
ADD SPACE
Lawrence K. Brooks   173
Sales Manager   176
177/197

LKB:ksv

39C ● TECHNIQUE PRACTICE: Response Patterns *10 minutes (each line three or more times)*

NOTE *The symbol* | *appearing in the first two explanatory paragraphs will be used in Lesson 40.*

At first your typing was almost entirely by stroke (or | letter) response. You type by this response pattern when | you see, think, and type letter by letter. |

Through direct dictation of simple words and through | repetitive practice of sentences and paragraphs,

you have | been led to type short, simple, and easy words *as word wholes* | without thinking the letters. When you see, think, and type | words as words, you are typing by *word-recognition response,* | a quicker and higher form of response than stroke response. |

Much of your typing will necessarily be by *combination response,* which is appropriate for typing copy that has some easy and some difficult combinations. The correct response patterns will evolve naturally and gradually as you use right practice procedures.

1	Stroke	The disaster afforded Edward the opportunity to display great courage.
2	Stroke	Shepman's Order #546 for 870# of 123-X @ 19¢ a pound comes to $165.30.
3	Combination	You did not use the * (asterisk) very often in typing this manuscript.
4	Word-recognition	It is fun to type with high speed; but we must type with control, too.
5	Word-recognition	This light touch is the right touch to use to build good typing skill.

| 1 | 2 | 3 | 4 | 5 | 6 | 7 | 8 | 9 | 10 | 11 | 12 | 13 | 14 |

39D ● DRILL ON TYPING OUTSIDE THE MARGINS *5 minutes (type the line three times)*

60-space line

PROCEDURE Begin 5 spaces to the left of the left margin. If the carriage locks before the sentence is completed, depress the margin release key and type on.

You will type from copy that will not have the line endings indicated.

| 1 | 2 | 3 | 4 | 5 | 6 | 7 | 8 | 9 | 10 | 11 | 12 | 13 | 14 |

LESSON 40 | 40A ● PREPARATORY PRACTICE *5 minutes (each line three or more times)*

Alphabetic — M. B. Parks organized the excellent aquatic show given for us in July.

Figure-symbol — The box is 6 5/8 by 9 1/2 feet long and weighs from 375 to 400 pounds.

Fluency — The auditor for the firm of Rodman & Mantis will make a report in May.

| 1 | 2 | 3 | 4 | 5 | 6 | 7 | 8 | 9 | 10 | 11 | 12 | 13 | 14 |

40B ● DRILL ON TYPING FROM PRINTED COPY *5 minutes*

Half sheet,
60-space line,
5-space ¶ indention,
single spacing,
1½" top margin

PROCEDURE

Type the three explanatory paragraphs of 39C Technique Practice, above. The line ending symbol (|) given with the first two paragraphs indicates the point at which you are to return the carriage. Listen for the ringing of the bell to know when to return the carriage when typing the final paragraph.

NOTE *Words printed in italics should be underlined when typed.*

40C ● TECHNIQUE PRACTICE: Response Patterns *10 minutes*

PROCEDURE **1** Type the first three lines of 39C Technique Practice, above, three times on the *control level.*

2 Type two 1-minute writings on Sentence 4 and two on Sentence 5, typing on the *exploration level.*

47C ● BUILDING CONTROL *10 minutes*

*Full sheet,
70-space line,
double spacing,
5-space ¶ indention*

PROCEDURE

1 Type a 1-minute writing on each paragraph, typing on the *control level*.

2 Type a 3-minute writing on the *control level*, trying to type at your 1-minute rate.

● All letters are used in the paragraphs.

	GWAM		
	1'	3'	

¶ 1
1.31 si
72 words

Do you realize the styles that are used most frequently in business — 14 — 5 — 54
letters are the block style and the modified block style with blocked or — 28 — 9 — 58
indented paragraphs? Since all the parts of the block style start at the — 43 — 14 — 63
left margin, some may claim that this style is the best as it is quick. — 58 — 19 — 68
A good many companies use the block style while others use variations. — 72 — 24 — 73

¶ 2
1.31 si
76 words

When you write a letter, you may wish to use the modified block — 13 — 28 — 77
style with blocked paragraphs. In this style all letter parts start at — 27 — 33 — 82
the left margin except for the date and closing lines; these lines start — 42 — 38 — 87
at the center point of the page. The modified block style with indented — 56 — 43 — 92
paragraphs is just the same except that the first line in each paragraph — 71 — 48 — 97
is indented five spaces. — 76 — 49 — 98

1' | 1 | 2 | 3 | 4 | 5 | 6 | 7 | 8 | 9 | 10 | 11 | 12 | 13 | 14 |
3' | 1 | 2 | 3 | 4 | 5 |

47D ● PROBLEM TYPING: Business Letters and Postal Card *25 minutes*

Problem 1: Letter with Line Endings Indicated

*Letterhead
(or full sheet)* ●
Current date

*Modified block,
blocked ¶s
Mixed punctuation*
●

*60-space line
Address an
envelope*

● 6 blank line spaces after the date

	Words
Miss Elizabeth N. Dahlinger	Department	11
of Secretarial Studies	Westmont Junior	19
College	Fort Lauderdale, Florida 33309		27
Dear Miss Dahlinger:	(¶1) Your letter	33
asking about the types of errors we find	42
in the	manuscripts we receive prompted	49
me to ask for a study of the	manuscripts	58
that are now being read by our editorial	66
staff.	It was found that incorrect punc-	74
tuation ranked first in the	errors in Eng-	82
lish. Misspelling ranked second.	(¶2)	89
We do not reject a manuscript because it	98
has typing errors,	but we often wonder	105
why a writer will submit material to a	113
publisher with a great many typing errors	122
and messy erasures.	(¶3) In writing for	129
publication, the thought is all important,	137
of	course; but how the thought is	144
"clothed" is also important.	Writers may	153
know good form and not use it. The ap-	160
pearance of	a manuscript affects the edi-	169

	Words
torial reader's first impression,	if not his	178
final judgment, of its value.	(¶4) Please	185
tell your students that we editors appre-	193
ciate a manu-	script that is well typed	201
and relatively free of errors in	technical	210
English.	Sincerely yours,	Everett Leigh	218
Hunter	Editor in Chief	(*Your initials*)		223/247

Problem 2: Letter with Changes

PROCEDURE Using ¶s 2 and 3 of the letter typed as Problem 1, type a letter to **Mr. Samuel Norton** | **387 Freemont Hall** | **Fairmont, West Virginia 26550** |. Have 8 blank line spaces after the date, and add an appropriate salutation. Use this final paragraph:

	Words
I urge you to take a course in typewriting	123
if you can do so	while in college.	141/154

Problem 3: Postal Card

PROCEDURE Address the card to **Miss Dorothy Bond** | **216 Taylor Hall** | **Knoxville, Tennessee 37904** |, using the first sentence of ¶ 2 and the final ¶ of the Problem 2 letter. Use an appropriate salutation; omit the complimentary close and reference initials. Use Mr. Hunter's name and title.

40D ● PROBLEM TYPING: Personal Letters in Block Style *25 minutes*

Problem 1: Letter with Line Endings Indicated

___
Full sheet, 60-space line, current date
___

PROCEDURE Type the letter in a style similar to Style Letter 1, page 69. Use your own return address. (If you do not have a street address or a box number, type the city name on the first line *without a comma* and the state and ZIP code number on the second line.) Address an envelope.

● 7 or 8 blank line spaces after current date

	Words *
Mr. Murray J. Hatcher	3478 N. Thomas	18
Boulevard	(*Nearby city, state,* ZIP	27
code)	Dear Murray	(¶1) I'm no golf	32
pro, I must confess; but I must be better	41
than	I thought because I've survived the	49
Qualifying Round for the	Men's Club	56
Championship. Next comes the big Tour-	64
nament.	(¶2) The whole Tournament	70
will be played week after next, but I	77
shall play just one match on Thursday of	86
that week. The semi-	finals follow on	93
Friday and the finals on Saturday.	(¶3)	100
Can you come for a visit with me from	108

	Words
Thursday to Monday of	Tournament	115
Week? Win or lose, after the Tournament	123
ends on	Saturday, we'll celebrate with a	131
party at our house. I hope	you can come	139
for the long weekend.	(¶4) Write or	146
telephone to say when you'll arrive——or	154
just come	on, but in time for the match	162
on Thursday afternoon.	Yours	(*Your*	171
name)		197

*Since the exact number of words for certain letter parts cannot be determined, 11 words are counted for the return address and current date; 6 words for the city, state, and ZIP code; and 3 words for the student's name.

Problem 2: Letter with Changes

PROCEDURE Type the letter of Problem 1, but address it to **Mr. Roger Hunter** | **2560 Bennington Road** | (*Nearby city, state, ZIP code*). Have 9 or 10 blank line spaces between the date and address. Add an appropriate salutation; change the first sentence of ¶3 to read "*. . . from Saturday to Monday . . .*"; omit the final paragraph. Address an envelope.

Problem 3: Letter from Corrected Copy

PROCEDURE Make pencil corrections in the letters typed as Problems 1 and 2, if corrections in typing or in form are needed; then retype one or both letters if they are not typed correctly and if time permits. When you have completed the typing, proofread the copy and circle any errors found.

LESSON 41 | 41A ● PREPARATORY PRACTICE *5 minutes (each line three or more times)*

Alphabetic   Will Frank Glick pay a quick visit to Mazie and Howard Baxter in July?

Figure-symbol Order #7894-0 (dated 3/26) must be shipped by May 15 to McKee & Thorp.

Fluency   Judge Henry Workman signed the order for the sale of the big building.
       | 1 | 2 | 3 | 4 | 5 | 6 | 7 | 8 | 9 | 10 | 11 | 12 | 13 | 14 |

41B ● BUILDING SPEED AND CONTROL *5 minutes*

PROCEDURE 1 Type two 1-minute writings on Sentence 3 of 41A Preparatory Practice, immediately above. Type on the *exploration level*. Use the stroking pattern appropriate for improving speed.
           2 Type two 1-minute writings on Sentence 1 of 41A. Type on the *control level* by stroke response to assure control over yourself and your machine.

46D ● BUILDING CONTROL *5 minutes*

Full sheet,
  70-space line
  double spacing,
  5-space ¶ indention

PROCEDURE

1 Type a 1-minute writing on the *control level*.

2 Type a 3-minute writing on the *control level*, trying to type at your 1-minute rate.

● All letters are used in the paragraphs.

		GWAM
	1'	3'

¶ 1
1.30 si
72 words

The letter is one of the most commonly used business tools. Thousands of letters are written by business firms daily. You must learn
how to write as well as how to type a good letter if you plan to enter
the business world. Most companies seek those who can write and type
well. If you excel in letter writing, you will forge ahead of your
fellow workers.

¶ 2
1.30 si
72 words

Letters must be typed neatly. A well-typed letter is clean and
well spaced. It does not have obvious erasures, strikeovers, or a zig-
zag right-hand margin. The letter should be placed on the page so that
it is pleasing to the eye. Most companies use one of the standard letter styles. You can learn about any new job quickly if you know these
styles well.

GWAM table (1' and 3'):

1'	3'	
13	4	52
27	9	57
41	13	61
55	18	66
69	23	71
72	24	72
13	28	76
27	33	81
41	38	86
56	43	91
70	47	95
72	48	96

1' | 1 | 2 | 3 | 4 | 5 | 6 | 7 | 8 | 9 | 10 | 11 | 12 | 13 | 14 |
3' | 1 | 2 | 3 | 4 | 5 |

46E ● COMPOSING AND TYPING *5 minutes*

PROCEDURE Assume you are living A.D. 3000 and know absolutely nothing about our present civilization. You find a 1-cent piece of 1963 coinage. After studying the coin, type a brief paragraph describing what the coin tells you about our civilization; then make needed corrections and retype the paragraph.

LESSON 47 | 47A ● PREPARATORY PRACTICE *5 minutes (each line three or more times)*

14
5
70

Alphabetic Dave O. Maxwell hopes to have a quick jet flight to Brazil on July 29.

Figure-symbol Won't the B & B (Bixler & Barnes) stock pay 4%, plus a $2.30 dividend?

Fluency At times, you will find it best to type at a slow, even rate of speed.

| 1 | 2 | 3 | 4 | 5 | 6 | 7 | 8 | 9 | 10 | 11 | 12 | 13 | 14 |

47B ● BUILDING SPEED *5 minutes*

Full sheet ● Double spacing
70-space line   5-space ¶ indention

PROCEDURE Type a 1- and a 3-minute writing on 46D Building Control, above, typing on the *exploration level*. Determine your *gwam*.

41C ● DRILL ON LISTENING FOR THE BELL *5 minutes*

Half sheet, single spacing, 60-space line,
5-space ¶ indention, 1½" top margin

PROCEDURE Type the drill twice. Use the full 60-space line. Your typed lines will not be the same as those in the copy. Be guided by the ringing of the bell.

Hold the hands and arms as quiet as you can as you type. Let the typing action be in the fingers. When the hands bound in the air with each stroke and the elbows move in or out, you will have a lot of waste motion that can hold you to a low level of typing skill.

41D ● PROBLEM TYPING: Themes *30 minutes*

Problem 1: Theme

PROCEDURE After typing the problem, proofread it and circle any errors found; then retype from your corrected copy.

Full sheet,
60-space line,
double spacing,
2½" top margin,
5-space ¶ indention

	Words in Para.	Total Words
↓½ 3⁴		
TOWARD · THE · SHORE		3
● Triple-space		
Big drops of rain spattered on the still waters of the	11	14
little bay, causing tiny circles of waves to spread over the	24	27
surface in quick ripples. As the cool raindrops fell more	35	38
quickly, the waves rushed to meet each other; and my small	47	50
boat began to sway and move jerkily. High above, the black	59	62
clouds were massed in the sky. The space between heaven and	71	74
earth was curtained by a sheath of rain arrows. The answer	83	86
I had sought on the still waters that earlier had mirrored the	96	99
blue sky was lost in wind and rain. I looked quickly toward	108	111
the shore line and saw Him standing there, quietly looking	121	124
toward me and the moving boat. I took up the oars and rowed	133	136
happily through mist and rain toward the shore--and Him.	144	147

| 1 | 2 | 3 | 4 | 5 | 6 | 7 | 8 | 9 | 10 | 11 | 12 |

Problem 2: Theme with Line Endings Indicated

PROCEDURE Type the problem in a form similar to Problem 1, above. As the title, type *THE SYMBOL*.

	Words
(¶) Standing where the driveway should	9
have been, I had to | look through a maze	17
of tangled vine to see the house---what |	25
was left of it. The thatched roof hung	33
down between rotting | uprights. Wild	40
trumpet vine filled the window openings,	49
the | lemon-yellow trumpets waving rhyth-	56
mically in the wind. From | behind the	64
house a mammoth cotton-silk tree spread	72
its gawky | branches, the frost-gray bark	80
a ghost tone in the lush tropic | green.	88
Arresting and depressing, this was a pic-	96
ture of decay | for which there was no	104
relief; then the flight of an oriole | car-	112
ried my eye to the tumbling wall. There	120
in an open pool | of sunlight bloomed a	128
tall red rose.	131

Problem 3: Listening for the Ringing of the Bell

PROCEDURE Using a 50-space line, type the theme of Problem 2. As your line of typing will not be the same as that indicated by the line-ending symbol (\|) given in the copy, you must listen for the ringing of the bell to warn you that you are nearing the end of your 50-space writing line. If you are typing a word when the bell rings, finish typing it; but if the carriage locks, depress the margin release key and type the remainder of the word.

LESSON 46 | 46A ● PREPARATORY PRACTICE *5 minutes* *(each line three or more times)*

Alphabetic | Paula was amazed when the jury acquitted Boyd V. Knox of manslaughter.

Figures | Use 1/2 and 1/4—not ½ and ¼—with such fractions as 3/5, 7/8, or 6/9.

Fluency | Think the words as you type, but let your fingers do the work for you.

| 1 | 2 | 3 | 4 | 5 | 6 | 7 | 8 | 9 | 10 | 11 | 12 | 13 | 14 |

46B ● PROBLEM TYPING: Business Letter in Modified Block Style *25 minutes*

Problem 1: Letter with Line Endings Indicated

| Letterhead (or full sheet) Current date | ● | Modified block, blocked ¶s Mixed punctuation | ● | 60-space line Address an envelope |

● 7 or 8 blank line spaces after the date

	Words
Dr. Ralph O. Knight │ Westminster Junior	11
High School │ St. Louis, Missouri 63105 │	19
Dear Dr. Knight: │ (¶ 1) We have just	25
published a series of six well-written	33
books on │	34

● Double-space

| OUR EXPANDING UNIVERSE │ | 39 |

● Double-space

A copy of the first volume is being sent	47
to you today. Put │ it in your library.	55
When your teachers and students get to │	63
know this interesting and authoritative	71
work, we are sure │ they will want the	78
series at the low price of $49.50. (¶ 2)	86
If you will order the series promptly, we	94
will be able to │ make shipment in time for	102
you to use the books in the next │ semes-	110
ter. Whether you order the series or not,	119
we want you │ to keep the first volume	126
because we want your students to │ know	134
OUR EXPANDING UNIVERSE. │ Sincerely	141
yours, │ Lawrence K. Brooks │ Sales Man-	148
ager │ (*Your initials*)	150
	165

Problem 2: Letter Without Line Endings Indicated

PROCEDURE Type the letter as directed for Problem 1, but have 8 blank line spaces after the date.

	Words
Mrs. Joan Taylor, Principal Stevens Jun-	11
ior High School Clarksville, Tennessee	19
37040 Dear Mrs. Taylor: (¶ 1) We have	25
a new series of books just off the press	34
entitled	35

| OUR EXPANDING UNIVERSE | 40 |

The first volume of the series is being	48
sent to you for use for ten days. We are	56
sure your teachers and students will find	65
this book so valuable they will want the	73
whole series. The special price of $49.50	82
is being made to schools that place their	90
order promptly. (¶ 2) Whether you order	97
the series or not, we want you to keep the	106
volume we are sending you, for we want	113
your students to know OUR EXPANDING	121
UNIVERSE. Sincerely yours, Lawrence K.	129
Brooks Sales Manager (*Your initials*)	133/150

Problem 3: Timed Writing on Letter

PROCEDURE Type Problem 2 as a 5-minute writing, but change the title in ¶ 1 to *THE MYSTERIES OF THE EARTH.* Add 1 to the total words typed for the letter; divide by 5 to determine *gwam.* Make pencil corrections in the letter; retype it, if time permits.

46C ● SENTENCE WRITINGS FOR CONTROL *5 minutes*

PROCEDURE Use a 70-space line. Type each sentence as two 1' writings, typing on the *control level.*

You should try to have more insight and foresight than hindsight.

A man must learn to control himself before he tries to control others.

| 1 | 2 | 3 | 4 | 5 | 6 | 7 | 8 | 9 | 10 | 11 | 12 | 13 | 14 |

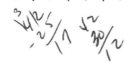
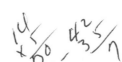

LESSON 42

42A ● PREPARATORY PRACTICE 5 minutes (each line three or more times)

Alphabetic   R. J. Buckham will fly to Quito and La Paz for V. M. Dexter in August.

Figure-symbol   Joe got 82 pencils @ 8¢ each; 36 erasers at 10¢ each; 1 punch @ $5.49.

Fluency   When you can type 40 words a minute, try to build your speed up to 50.

| 1 | 2 | 3 | 4 | 5 | 6 | 7 | 8 | 9 | 10 | 11 | 12 | 13 | 14 |

42B ● BUILDING CONTROL 5 minutes

Full sheet, 70-space line,
1½″ top margin,
5-space ¶ indention

PROCEDURE

Type Problem 1 of 41D, Problem Typing, page 73, as a 4-minute writing. Omit the title. Your typed lines will not be the same as the lines of the copy.

42C ● PROBLEM TYPING: Personal Letters in Block Style 25 minutes

Problem 1: Letter with Line Endings Indicated

Full sheet   ●   Block style   ●   Current date
60-space line   Open punctuation   Envelope

PROCEDURE Type the letter in a style similar to Style Letter 1, page 69. Use your own return address. Place the typed letter under the flap of the envelope, *address side up*, for your instructor's approval.

● 7 or 8 blank line spaces after the date

	Words
Miss Mary Lou Dixon | 800 Fourth Street,	19
S. W. | Washington, D. C. 20024 | Dear	26
Mary Lou | (¶1) If you haven't seen the	32
announcement that Mr. Thompson, our |	40
high school English teacher, has been	47
awarded the "Princeton | Prize for Dis-	55
tinguished Secondary School Teaching,"	62
let me | be the first to tell you of it. |	70
(¶2) The citation said the award was	77
given for "fruitful teaching, | devoted	84
service, and human as well as professional	93
qualities." | That fits Mr. Thompson to a	101
"T." | (¶3) How goes life in Washington?	108
Do you often see important men | from	116
other countries? Have you found a con-	123
genial group of | young friends? (¶4)	130
Don't be so miserly with your letters. I	138
am now one up on | you, so write me soon.	146
Tell me about life in the city of | the "Great	155
White Father." | Sincerely | (*Your name*)	164/188

Problem 2: Letter Without Line Endings Indicated

PROCEDURE Type the letter as directed for Problem 1, but have 8 blank lines between the date and the address. Remember to listen for the ringing of the bell.

	Words
Miss Alice Klingensmith 4100 Shore Line	19
Drive Myrtle Beach, South Carolina	26
29577 Dear Alice (¶1) My "bread and	32
butter" letter was sent by airmail yes-	40
terday and should reach your mother	47
promptly. I am sorry for the delay in	55
writing to her, but I had a terrific cold	64
that kept me in bed for almost a week	71
right after I got home. I am still snort-	80
ing, blowing, sneezing, and wheezing; but	88
I think I'll live! I know I'll never forget	97
my visit. You folks certainly know how	105
to make a guest feel welcome, and I am	113
most grateful to you. (¶2) I shall write	120
you again soon. In the meantime, my	128
thanks to all of you for a wonderful time.	136
Sincerely (*Your name*)	141/169

Problem 3: Timed Writings on a Letter

PROCEDURE Type the letter of Problem 1 as a 3- or 5-minute writing, as directed. Determine *gwam*.

42D ● DRILL ON COMPOSING AT THE TYPEWRITER 10 minutes

Half sheet, 70-space line, 1″ top margin, double spacing

PROCEDURE. Number and type *complete* sentences. Ignore typing errors, if any. When you have completed the typing, remove the paper and make pencil corrections; then retype the drill in a form you consider appropriate. *Type as you think.*

1. I am_____ (*your name*).
2. My address is_____ (*street, city, state, ZIP code*).
3. I was graduated from_____.
4. Now a student at_____.
5. Typing instructor is_____.
6. Name of typewriter I use is_____.
7. My *gwam* is_____.
8. Chief reason for taking typewriting_____.
9. Chief difficulty in building speed_____.
10. Chief difficulty in building accuracy_____.

Keystone Publishing Company

Ⓚ

● 535 WEST WASHINGTON STREET
INDIANAPOLIS, INDIANA 46203
AREA CODE ● 317 TELEPHONE 635-3710

November 12, 19--   4   4

↓ *6 or 7 blank line spaces*

line 23

Mrs. Mary Rafferty, Librarian	10	10
Dixon Junior High School	15	15
722 Wakefield Street	19	19
Arlington, Virginia 22206	24	24

- Salutation with mixed punctuation

Dear Mrs. Rafferty: 28   28

After many years of extensive research and study by eminent   12   40
scientists throughout the world, we are pleased to announce   24   52
the publication of our richly illustrated series   34   62

- Centered line in body of letter

THE MYSTERIES OF THE EARTH   39   67

This series was designed especially for junior high school   51   79
students. The text has been written in easy, concise lan-   63   91
guage so the ideas can be grasped quickly by young students.   75   103
Your students will find this series exciting and interesting.   88   116

We are sure you will want this series for your library. We   100   128
are, therefore, sending you, free of charge, a copy of the   111   140
first volume. Examine it carefully; then order the series   123   151
quickly so you will have the books for the beginning of your   135   164
next semester.   139   167

- Indented complimentary close; mixed punctuation

Sincerely yours,   3   170

Lawrence K. Brooks

Lawrence K. Brooks   7   174

- Dictator's name and title

Sales Manager   10   177

- Typist's initials   ksv   11   178

STYLE LETTER 2 *Modified Block Style with Blocked Paragraphs*

MIXED PUNCTUATION

Mixed punctuation is used in this letter. In this punctuation style, the colon is used after the salutation and the comma after the complimentary close. Marks are not required after the return address, the date, or the letter address unless an abbreviation (which must be followed by a period) is used.

When the dictator's name is typed as a part of the closing lines, it is not necessary to type his initials as a part of the reference line (with the initials of the typist), although it is permissible to do so.

LESSON 43 | **43A ● PREPARATORY PRACTICE** *5 minutes (each line three or more times)*

Alphabetic   Gladys saw the May and June prizes won at Fox School by Vera O. Quick.

Figure-symbol   Item #56-B, page 293, was billed to O'Henry & Son at $147.90 on May 8.

Fluency   Let the man who can do the best work have the first chance at the job.
| 1 | 2 | 3 | 4 | 5 | 6 | 7 | 8 | 9 | 10 | 11 | 12 | 13 | 14 |

43B ● COMPOSING AND TYPING *10 minutes*

2 full sheets,
60-space line,
5-space ¶ indention,
double spacing,
2" top margin

PROCEDURE

1 Center horizontally and type the heading **"Unu Lingvo por Mondo Celo de Experantistoj"**; then, triple-space before typing the first paragraph given below.

2 Type a second paragraph in your own words to tell some advantage you think

would come from the adoption of "One Tongue for World," which is the aim of Esperantists, as the title says.

3 Make pencil corrections on your composition; then retype it from your corrected copy.

Esperanto was created as an international language in 1877 by a Polish linguist, Dr. L. L. Zamenhof. Millions of people speak it today and can read the 30,000 books and 100 magazines and newspapers regularly published in Esperanto.

43C ● PROBLEM TYPING REVIEW *30 minutes*

4 full sheets

PROCEDURE

1 Make pencil notations of the problems and page numbers listed below. Place the notation sheet beside the typewriter.

     38D, Problem 1, page 68
     40D, Problem 1, page 72
     41D, Problem 2, page 73
     42C, Problem 1, page 74

2 Type each problem *once* only and in the order of listing. You will be timed for 25 minutes. Work rapidly but not hurriedly.

3 After typing a problem, proofread it and circle any errors you find.

LESSON 44 | **44A ● PREPARATORY PRACTICE** *5 minutes (each line three or more times)*

Alphabetic   The big jigsaw puzzle will be solved quickly by Fanny and Pam Wexford.

Figure-symbol   Mason's Check #678 is for $211.27 for Invoice #161 ($234.75 less 10%).

Fluency   When a man needs help, he generally needs more than words of sympathy.
| 1 | 2 | 3 | 4 | 5 | 6 | 7 | 8 | 9 | 10 | 11 | 12 | 13 | 14 |

44B ● BUILDING CONTROL *5 minutes*

PROCEDURE Use the first and third sentences of 43A, Preparatory Practice, above, for two 1-minute writings. Type on the *control level*, trying for errorless writings. Ignore your speed of writing at this time and pace yourself at a rate that you can maintain with ease and accuracy.

SECTION 8 | BUSINESS LETTERS
Lessons 45–50

STANDARD PROCEDURES FOR SECTION 8

GET READY TO TYPE
Clear the desk. Use full sheets; 70-space line; single spacing, unless otherwise directed.

SELF-IMPROVEMENT PRACTICE
As time permits, type the sentences of Self-Improvement Practice, page 86, three or more times. Type on the *control level*. Identify errorless lines.

LESSON 45 | **45A ● PREPARATORY PRACTICE** *5 minutes (each line three or more times)*

Alphabetic   My skill will improve quickly if I execute my job with zeal and vigor.

Figures   Dial 926-5718 or 926-5739 to obtain your copy of this 40-page booklet.

Fluency   Both speed and control will increase if you do the work well each day.
| 1 | 2 | 3 | 4 | 5 | 6 | 7 | 8 | 9 | 10 | 11 | 12 | 13 | 14 |

45B ● PARAGRAPH GUIDED WRITING *5 minutes*

PROCEDURE   Use 44D Growth Index, page 77. Type a 1-minute writing on each paragraph; then a 2-minute writing on both paragraphs. Be guided by the 15″ call. Type on the *control level*.

45C ● TECHNIQUE PRACTICE *10 minutes (each line three or more times)*

1   Capitals   Jane, Elvin, and Paul saw the "Early Morning Show" on TV Station WJIC.

2   Figure-symbol   Their T & C bill reads: "#8 thread @ $46 a gross (less 6% discount)."

3   Double letters   Will Jeff carry to Dallas the letter from the boss about his new book?

4   Left-hand   A few extra seats were set up on the vast stage as dessert was served.

5   Right-hand   Jimmy Polk pulled the oily junk from the hilly knoll as Jon looked on.
| 1 | 2 | 3 | 4 | 5 | 6 | 7 | 8 | 9 | 10 | 11 | 12 | 13 | 14 |

45D ● DRILL ON CENTERING FROM ROUGH DRAFT *5 minutes*

Half sheet, double spacing

PROCEDURE   Center the drill vertically, and center each line horizontally. For a recall of steps in horizontal centering, see page 58; for vertical centering, page 64.

ALL CAPS
The Keystone Publishing Co*mpany*
Announces
Outstanding
Publication of Two Series
THE MYSTERY OF THE EARTH
OUR UNIVERSE EXPANDING

45E ● PROBLEM TYPING: Business Letter in Modified Block Style *20 minutes*

PROCEDURE
1 Study Style Letter 2, page 79. Note the placement of the date and the closing lines. Read the brief explanation of *mixed punctuation*.
2 Use a 60-space line; modified block style with blocked paragraphs; mixed punctuation; current date, typed a double-space below the last line of the letter-

head or on Line 12 or 13 if plain paper is used.
3 Set a tabulator stop *at the center point* to indent to the position for typing the date and closing lines.
4 When the letter has been typed, make pencil corrections as needed; then retype the letter, typing on the *control level*.

Problem 1: Letter with Line Endings Indicated

Full sheet 60-space line	●	Block style Open punctuation	●	Current date Envelope

PROCEDURE Type the personal letter in a style similar to Style Letter 1, page 69. Use your own return address. Center the address given as Line 2 in the letter.

Words

● 7 or 8 blank line spaces after the date

Mr. Grant U. Robertson │ 361 Mt. Pleasant	19
Road │ Boston, Massachusetts 02115 │	26
Dear Grant │ (¶ 1) We are moving to	31
Winter Park, Florida. The address will be │	40

● Double-space

760 Via Lugano │	43

● Double-space

and the ZIP code is 32789. │ (¶ 2) Our	49
things will be moved on Wednesday of	57
next week. We plan │ to motor down in	64
time to be there when the van arrives, so	73
I │ expect to be basking in sunshine in a	81
few days. │ (¶ 3) I hope you will plan to	88
spend some time with us during your │	95
Christmas holidays. By then you'll be	103
glad to get out of the │ "frozen North,"	110
and I'll be glad to have you soak up sun-	119
shine │ with me. I already know some	126
longtime residents who have │ said they	133
will see that I meet some interesting peo-	142
ple. I │ think I can promise you a good	150
time if you will come down. │ (¶ 4) Give	156
my new address to any friends who in-	164
quire about me, and │ write soon––and	171
often, please. │ Yours │ (*Your Name*) │	181
	204

Problem 2: Theme with Line Endings Indicated

Full sheet, 60-space line, double spacing, 3″ top margin, 5-space ¶ indention	**PROCEDURE** After typing the problem, proofread it and circle any errors found; retype if time permits.

NOTE Although a 2- or 2½-inch top margin is customary, for very short, informal themes or reports a 3-inch top margin gives better placement.

Words

CAVEAT VENDITOR
3

● Triple-space

(¶ 1) *Caveat emptor*––"Let the buyer be-	12
ware"––has long been a │ basic rule of the	21
marketplace. *Caveat venditor*––"Let the │	32
seller beware"––is the basic rule that must	40
come next. │ (¶ 2) Laws and regulations	47
will require those who sell goods │ to state	56
just what it is they sell. New terms will	64
be used │ to help us know the full meaning	72
of what the sellers put on │ their labels.	81
Proof for compliance with the laws on	88
honest │ and full disclosure will rest with	97
the seller. *Caveat emptor* │ is done for;	107
caveat venditor will be prized by con-	118
sumers in the │ coming years.	123

Problem 3: Postal Cards

| 2 postal cards Current date | **PROCEDURE** Using your typed copy of the letter given as Problem 1, above, type a postal card to each of the names at the right. Omit the inside address. Type the date on Line 3 of the card; triple-space. Add an appropriate salutation. Type ¶ 1, incorporating the address given as Line 2 as part of the paragraph. Then, type ¶ 4 and the complimentary close of the letter. When addressing the card, add a personal title before the name. | Susan Townsend 1287 Commonwealth Avenue Boston, Massachusets   02135

Torrence L. Babcock 43 Ingraham Road Wellesley, Massachusets 01581 |

NOTE It is never correct to type a letter, envelope, or card addressed to an individual without the use of an appropriate personal title. When a woman's marital status is not known, use *Miss* as the personal title. (*Ms.* may also be used.)

44D ● GROWTH INDEX *5 minutes*

Full sheet   ● 70-space line
Double spacing.   5-space ¶ indention

PROCEDURE Type a 3-minute writing on the *control level*. Determine your *gwam* and the number of errors. If time permits, type a 1-minute writing on the *control level*.

● All letters are used in the paragraphs.

		G W A M	
		1'	3'

¶ 1
1.25 si
68 words

If things don't go just right, do you begin to sizzle? Do you   13   4   49
become tense if you have an exam to take? A little tension may be quite   27   9   54
good. Too much tension can tear you apart, cutting your production and   42   14   59
sending you home at night with a head ready for shrinking. It can gnaw   56   19   64
holes in your stomach and block the lifelines of your heart.   68.   24   69

¶ 2
1.25 si
68 words

You don't have to let nerves make life a tensed-up affair. You   13   27   72
don't need magic to cope with them——just common sense. You can learn   27   32   77
to relax when you work, know the difference between a healthy concern   41   36   81
for something and an unhealthy worry about it, and find the best way to   53   41   86
do what you do. It's as simple as that——but that's not simple!   68.   45   90

1' | 1 | 2 | 3 | 4 | 5 | 6 | 7 | 8 | 9 | 10 | 11 | 12 | 13 | 14 |
3' | 1 | 2 | 3 | 4 | 5 |

44E ● DRILL ON COMPOSING AT THE TYPEWRITER *5 minutes*

Half sheet,
double spacing,
60-space line,
1" top margin

PROCEDURE Quickly glance through the paragraphs of 44D, above. Center and type the heading *TENSION AND ME*, and type in your own words a summarizing paragraph of the ideas given in the two paragraphs.

Add as your second paragraph some of the things that cause your own tension and what you do or can do about them. Type as slowly as you must to think what you want to say—and as rapidly as you can when you think and type.

SELF-IMPROVEMENT PRACTICE ● *(each line three or more times)*

● All letters and figures are used in the sentences.

		Words in Line	20"	15"	12"
1	Curve your fingers and hold them lightly over the keys.	11	33	44	55
2	You should underline (or type in caps) titles of books.	11	33	44	55
3	Hold the hands and arms as quiet as possible while you type.	12	36	48	60
4	Pay Allen & Howe's Bill #390-X for $871.50 less 2% discount.	12	36	48	60
5	How you sit at the machine has a lot to do with the way you type.	13	39	52	65
6	Read the article "The Expert's Practice" or the book TYPING TIPS.	13	39	52	65
7	Build the expert typing skill that you can use often and prize always.	14	42	56	70
8	The * refers to the items given on page 123 of our Fall Bulletin #567.	14	42	56	70
9	Many of you will lend a hand to any man who needs help to do his work.	14	42	56	70
10	The * refers to 6½ dozen #20 @ 9¼¢ each and to 4 dozen #56 @ 13¢ each.	14	42	56	70

| 1 | 2 | 3 | 4 | 5 | 6 | 7 | 8 | 9 | 10 | 11 | 12 | 13 | 14 |

● CHANGING THE FABRIC TYPEWRITER RIBBON

GENERAL PROCEDURE FOR ELECTRICS AND NONELECTRICS

1 Wind the used ribbon on one spool (preferably the right spool). As you wind, observe the path of the ribbon. Note, too, how the ribbon is threaded through the ribbon-carrier mechanism.

2 *To make ribbon threading easier:*
  (a) Lock the shift key.
  (b) Move the ribbon-control indicator to typing position on the bottom portion of the ribbon.
  (c) Hold the ribbon carrier to its higher position by raising two adjacent type bars *y* and *u*— equally to locked position.

3 Lift the right spool slightly off its hub to see if both sides are the same. If not, study both sides of the spool so that you will place the new spool properly on the hub.

> NOTE Always place the black side of a two-color ribbon on top.

4 Remove the ribbon from the carrier. Then remove both spools; note how the ribbon is attached to the empty spool. Fasten the new ribbon to the empty spool in the same manner, and wind several inches of the new ribbon on it.

> NOTE On the R. C. Allen nonelectric the ribbon must be wound around a ribbon-reverse trigger inside the spool cup. Refer to the R. C. Allen instruction booklet.

5 Place both spools on their hubs, and thread the ribbon through the carrier. Make sure the ribbon is straight.

6 Finally, release the shift-lock key, drop the type bars that were used to raise the carrier mechanism to rest position, and move the ribbon-control indicator to typing position on the top portion of the ribbon.

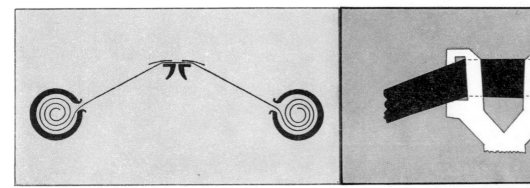

Path of the ribbon as it winds and unwinds on the two spools; on some machines, however, the ribbon feeds from the back of the spool

Ribbon threaded through the ribbon-carrier mechanism

PROCEDURE FOR OTHER TYPEWRITERS

IBM "MODEL C" ELECTRIC

Depress the electric ribbon rewind to wind all the old ribbon onto the left spool. Change ribbon by always removing the left-hand spool. Loosen and eject the metal clip from the right spool slot by bending it downward and lifting out. Pick up the left-hand spool and pull the remaining ribbon through the guides and discard. Remove the left-hand spool and place the new ribbon on the left pin. Grasp the metal clip and thread the ribbon through the guides. Place the ribbon end clip into the empty spool slot.

IBM "SELECTRIC"

Refer to the "Selectric" instructional booklet for specific directions on changing the typewriter ribbon.

REMINGTON AND SMITH-CORONA ELECTRICS

First, place the ribbon reverse lever to the right, lock the shift, and move the ribbon indicator to typing position for the bottom portion of the ribbon. Depress the electric ribbon rewind to wind the used ribbon onto the left spool. Remove the left spool and replace it with a new spool. Attach the free end of the new ribbon to the right spool. Thread the ribbon through the carrier mechanism.

ROYAL ELECTRIC AND NONELECTRIC

Lock the shift key. Lift out both used ribbon cartridges. Separate the two new cartridges and draw out 3" to 3½" of ribbon. Holding the round side of the cartridges toward you, drop the ribbon into the ribbon carrier and draw out two more inches of ribbon. Place the cartridges in the holders, being certain that the ribbon falls into the guides at the side of each cup.

UNDERWOOD ELECTRIC AND NONELECTRIC

Lock the shift key, and open the ribbon carrier by moving the two finger pieces together. Lift out both used ribbon cartridges. Separate the two new cartridges and draw out 3" to 3½" of ribbon. Holding the round side of the cartridges toward you, drop the ribbon into the ribbon carrier and draw out two more inches of ribbon. Place the cartridges in the holders, being certain that the ribbon falls into the guides at the side of each cup. The first type strike will automatically close the ribbon carrier.